Without Compromise

75 Years of Service

The Idaho State Police

District 5 Commander, Captain Eric Dayley places an Idaho State Police flag on the grave of Fontaine Cooper for Law Enforcement Memorial Day. Photo courtesy of the Idaho State Police.

Without Compromise

75 Years of Service
Idaho State Police

★

Kelly Kast

2013 ★ Ridenbaugh Press

WITHOUT COMPROMISE: 75 YEARS OF SERVICE, IDAHO STATE POLICE

For more information, contact Ridenbaugh Press, P.O. Box 834, Carlton OR 97111.

Printed and bound in the United States of America.

First edition July 2013

10 9 8 7 6 5 4 3 2 1

Library of Congress Cataloging in Publication Data

Max C. Black

Without Compromise: 75 Years of Service, Idaho State Police

Bibliography

1. Idaho Politics and Government. 2. Idaho-Law Enforcement. 3. Idaho-History.

I. Kast, Kelly. II. Title.

ISBN 978-0-945648-09-3 (softbound)

Cover design by Kristy Albrecht.

Ridenbaugh Press
P.O. Box 834, Carlton OR 97111
Phone (503) 852-0010
www.ridenbaugh.com

Contents

Introduction

Colonel Ralph W. Powell

What a privilege and honor it is to represent the Idaho State Police as we invite you to enjoy this compilation of the Idaho State Police history.

We express our heartfelt gratitude to Kelly Kast for the long hours and dedication she has put toward this project to see it through to full fruition. As we all know, sometimes "cops" can be difficult interviewees, and on occasion, Kelly had to resort to less conventional ways of extracting information from otherwise uncooperative "detainees." Job well done! We also express our appreciation to Colonel G. Jerry Russell for authorizing and supporting this effort whole heartedly, and to all of you, the Idaho State Police family both seasoned and contemporary, who participated in so many ways to prepare this chronology for generations to come.

The Idaho State Police has a rich heritage of esprit de corps, an abiding sense of professional responsibility, and an innate desire to earn the title given us long ago as, "Idaho's Finest." It has been said that he who controls the past controls the future. Indeed our history and our roots have laid a foundation of consummate accountability and untethered expectation. Our respect for our history shapes the way we view not only our present, but our future. The Idaho State Police has been built on the shoulders of those who asked: “If not me, who? If not now, when?” And because of that history, that echoing challenge now comes a new generation of Idaho State Police Troopers, Detectives, Specialists, and Civilian Employees, who enter our ranks to serve a cause higher than they themselves. These are the ones who stand ready to fight that battle against those who would do us harm; whose charge it is to champion the inalienable rights of those who can't protect themselves, and to stand tall and firm between evil and good.

From our Code of Ethics and our Conduct Expectations to our mantra of “Uncompromised Integrity,” the Idaho State Police continues to be an agency that insists on earning the trust placed in us by the public. Not everyone is willing to take this journey and make the sacrifices necessary to become an Idaho State Police Trooper. From our ranks we jettison those who cannot, or will not, achieve and maintain the high expectations and ambitious level of professionalism required to earn this title. Our commitment to these standards of personal integrity, in the end, transcends all other requirements. This is the very essence of the Idaho State Police.

To those who have gone before us, and those who now serve, I honor you for the contributions you have made and the sacrifices you have endured to make this agency what it is today. To those who will carry this proud tradition well into the future, I salute you for the positive difference you will make in our communities tomorrow, and in the years to come. You are society's proud warriors of justice.

Respectfully,

Colonel Ralph W. Powell
Director, MPA
Idaho State Police

1 ★ Prologue

The volumes of written works that chronicle the development and growth of government in Idaho are peppered with intriguing and inspiring tales. These works describe the epic journey of Idaho's pioneers and are rife with accounts of peril, resourcefulness, and courage. Those who found themselves leading Idaho after statehood was granted in 1890 were both adventurous and inventive. These were necessary traits, as it was on their shoulders to shape the future of Idaho and provide not only the foundations of its government, but the means to enforce law and bring order to its budding population.

When Congress established the Idaho Territory in 1863, the area encompassed all of present day Idaho, Montana, and much of Wyoming. In May of 1864, the territory shrank dramatically when the state of Montana was formed. By 1868, Idaho's present shape was created when Congress carved away the area that is now the southern portion of Yellowstone National Park, and the Grand Tetons, which became part of present day Wyoming.

Idaho Territory's early years were troubled times. Although Congress appeared willing to arbitrarily tinker with the boundaries of the territory, it was far less concerned with ensuring the citizens of the territory were protected from violence or lawlessness. The United States was embroiled in the Civil War, and Congress, which was responsible for providing the necessary funds to run its territories, had little time and even less money to ensure effective government in Idaho Territory. One of the first issues was that the new territory had no criminal laws.

When Lewiston businessman Lloyd Magruder was murdered by four bandits on the Nez Pierce Trail that connected Lewiston to the Virginia City mining area, Magruder's friend, Hill Beachy, tracked the murderers to California and had them returned to Idaho for trial. During the trial, officials discovered no laws existed under which the men could be tried, let alone punished. Despite the lack of laws and statutes, three of the four men were hanged.

The reason for this lack of territorial laws wasn't because those who settled the area were lawless criminals without scruple. The loophole existed because the congressional act passed to create Idaho Territory had failed to codify the laws created in other territories which served as temporary laws until local legislators could convene. The Territorial Supreme Court was forced to free two convicted murderers in 1866 upon discovering their crime was committed prior to January of 1864 when Idaho Territorial Laws came into effect. A robber named Williams was also freed when he proved no laws existed under which he could be tried.

When the discrepancy was discovered, the territorial legislators immediately went to work on enacting civil and criminal codes, and after the third legislative session met in 1865, the codes were decided upon; however, Idaho Territory's law enforcement problems were far from fixed. Territorial Secretary, Horace Gilson, stole the money provided to print the new codes and run the territorial government, and fled to Hong Kong. For three years, the print shop in San Francisco kept the printed but un-paid-for code. Meanwhile folks in Idaho Territory were left to rely on condensed, and as often as not, inaccurate newspaper reprints of the territory's laws.

By 1890, when Idaho was granted statehood, criminal codes had been established and printed versions were available to law makers. Law enforcement entities from town constable to county sheriff existed. There was still a fair amount of lawlessness in the state, but those caught committing the more violent crimes could now legally be punished by a fatal procedure many Idahoans referred to as "neck trouble." Still, even with the establishment of laws and law enforcers, from 1866 through the turn of the century, a fair amount of policing in Idaho was conducted through vigilance committees, and more often than not, vigilance committees didn't bother with trials or the American ideal of innocent until proven guilty. One of the most fascinating stories of vigilante justice in Idaho involved the Payette Vigilantes and Ada County Sheriff, David C. Updyke.

Sheriff Updyke was elected sheriff of Ada County in 1865, despite many rumors and a large amount of other compelling evidence that he often aided, abetted, and with some frequency, participated in stage robberies, murders, and other crimes. The Payette Vigilantes were aware of the sheriff's nefarious activities and determined it was high time to put an end to Updyke's wicked ways. Updyke, aware he was under suspicion by the Payette Vigilantes, decided to launch a surprise attack against them. Tipped off about the sheriff's intentions, the vigilantes launched a surprise of their own and foiled Updyke's attempt. Updyke fled to the mountains northeast of Boise with one of his friends, Jake Dixon. Two days later, the pair was discovered holed up in a cabin near Syrup Creek and both experienced "neck trouble."

Congressional inattentiveness was not the only dynamic involved in the early development of law enforcement in Idaho. Of equal importance is Idaho's unique and difficult topography. One can reasonably assume the day-to-day duties of Idaho's early law officers were not hindered by the mountain ranges that makes up the northern two-thirds of the state, or by the high desert that slashes like a grin through the south-central part of the state. But when the most crucial aspect of any law enforcement agency is considered – its availability to react quickly to threats against law and order – Idaho's topography becomes an issue of great importance indeed.

From 1890 to 1919, Idaho lawmakers grappled with a number of ideas about how and with what resources they could best ensure law and order in their fast-growing state. Prohibition enforcement, union violence, and organization of state, county, and municipal peace officers were at the top of Idaho's law enforcement agenda.

In 1919, Governor David William Davis solved part of Idaho's law enforcement problem. Governor Davis was a Republican and a fierce pro-business, small government conservative. He won the gubernatorial election and immediately set about changing Idaho's way of conducting its business, in particular, its law enforcement business. Davis established a number of governmental reforms, such as reducing the number of governmental cabinet posts from forty-six to nine, and created the Department of Law Enforcement and the Bureau of Constabulary, the foundation organization of the modern-day Idaho State Police.

In celebration of its seventy-five years of dedicated service to the citizens of Idaho, the Idaho State Police commissioned this history as a tribute to past and present employees:

"If I have seen further, it is by standing on the shoulders of Giants."
– Sir Isaac Newton

2 ★ Fighting Syndicalism, Establishing Law

In keeping people straight, principle is not as powerful as a policeman.

Abel Hermant, *Le Bourgeois* (1906)

While departments of law enforcement, or similar organizations, had been established in other states, the creation of this type of organization in Idaho presented Governor Davis with a set of unique circumstances other states had not been faced with. Chief among these circumstances is that over sixty percent of Idaho is federally owned lands. The largest portion of this federally owned area is located in the central part of the state, which makes Idaho unique as the only state nearly severed in two by lands under federal jurisdiction.

This topographic boundary, combined with the fact that southern Idaho was fast becoming an agricultural Mecca while northern Idaho's economy centered on mining and logging, caused much talk in the early 1900s of dividing Idaho into two states. Idaho's leaders considered both the northern and southern part of the state as equal and vital to the state's economy, but they understood the law enforcement needs of each region were vastly different.

When Governor Davis took office, the antics of union organizers, in particular an ideologically socialist and dangerously fanatical organization, known as the Industrial Workers of the World, or Wobblies, were making front page news across the Pacific Northwest and the nation. The Wobblies posed a serious threat to northern Idaho's industries through their active attempts to unionize mining and logging. Although most union organizers of the early 1900s were looked on suspiciously by state governments, the Wobblies were the most feared. Wobblies not only advocated pro-socialist ideology, they encouraged syndicalism, the doctrine of controlling the production and distribution of industrial wealth by means of sabotage, terrorism, and violence.

In 1917, Idaho enacted a criminal syndicalism law, which made it unlawful to advocate crime, sabotage, violence, or terrorism as a means of accomplishing industrial or political reform. While the majority of Idahoans may have supported the legislation, the majority of Idahoans were also an independent lot. It was fine to create laws to subdue socialist groups like the Wobblies, but most Idahoans didn't support creating a "police state" in order to deal with the Wobbly threat.

Shortly after its passage, Governor Davis realized the 1917 law didn't have near the muscle it needed to curb the Wobbly threat. He recommended the legislature beef-up the syndicalism law, which it did, and following a clash in Centralia, Washington between Wobblies and the American Legion, Davis ordered a major crackdown and responded to the Wobbly menace. He established the Idaho Bureau of Constabulary, for the purpose of cooperating with and assisting the governor in the performance of his constitutional duty. Governor Davis wasn't the first governor to create a state police organization, but he was among the first to ensure his officers had statewide jurisdiction to enforce *all* of Idaho's laws. This statewide authority gave the Constabulary the clout needed to dispose of the Wobbly threat and enforce a number of other laws to boot.

The outcry from Idaho labor unionists, business owners, and even farmers against establishing the Bureau of Constabulary was fierce. Newspapers across the state published letters to the editor accusing the governor of being a "little Czar," referring to the tyranny of Russia's Czar, whose irresponsible behavior sparked the Russian Revolution. One letter claimed: "In short the state will have a horde of 'state policemen' running about doing as they see fit in the enforcement of the law. This provision is absolutely vicious and in the hands of an unscrupulous Department of Law Enforcement might become a terror to the people of the state (Davis)."

Another letter weighed in with: "Even a blind man familiar with the political alliances and influences of this state can understand what will be the results of such a measure." Newspaper editorials urged Idahoans to write to their legislative representatives denouncing the establishment of the Department of Law Enforcement, and the Bureau of Constabulary. "The [Constabulary] bill is the most dangerous one to the rights and liberties of the people of Idaho ever proposed in this state, and the State Federation of Labor strongly urges that every liberty-loving citizen of the state forward immediately, a protest to the governor and to members of the legislature (Davis)."

Despite massive opposition to establishing the Department of Law Enforcement and the constabulary, legislators gave Davis the necessary votes to pass the bill into law. In the *Coeur d'Alene Journal,* an unnamed senate leader was quoted as saying: "It took courage for Governor Davis to insist on passing this bill. He knows we must face a hard financial situation, that we must change the primary law, and that the party is on trial. Still he asks us to tackle this big thing. I am going to give him my earnest support and rise or fall with the record that is made by my party and its leader."

As it turned out, the Bureau of Constabulary was established just in time to take on the Wobblies. In his biennial report to Governor Davis, the Bureau of Constabulary's first and only superintendent, Frank Breshears, reported: "At the time the legislature passed the statute creating the constabulary, the most serious problem facing the peace officers of the state was the enforcement of the syndicalism law." After a rather lengthy description of the many sins of the Wobblies, Breshears concludes: "The Bureau of Constabulary, after much labor and expense, has completed a roster containing the names and card numbers of ninety percent of the Wobbly members of the Northwest and the situation, so far as Idaho is concerned, appears now to be well in hand (Breshears)."

Among the chief complaints registered by those who opposed the creation of a constabulary, was the fear that because state policemen had the same powers as elected sheriffs, the state policemen would use their powers to usurp the authority of sheriffs. The antics of one state officer seemed to prove the opposition's point. Governor Davis received a letter from Attorney Albert H. Featherstone of Wallace, in which he accused an Idaho State Constable of being extremely dangerous.

> I saw him Thursday evening and he was drunk. He had been searching autos around town belonging to private parties, was insulting to men, used rough language in the presence of ladies, and was making himself generally obnoxious. Just before I saw him, he was sitting on the curb in the center of town holding his loaded gun. The people here are very much wrought up over the performance and it is up to you to show them that you don't stand for that kind of official, and he will certainly never bring you and your administration anything but trouble (Davis).

The letter was dated June 27, 1919. The governor's reaction was swift. The constable was fired by telegram the day the governor received the letter and by July 8, Jesse Freeman of Wallace, Idaho was appointed to the constabulary. Freeman was well respected by the people of

Wallace and helped establish an appreciation in that area for the constabulary.

Within a year of the establishment of the Bureau of Constabulary, the Wobbly threat to north Idaho was brought under control. Many of the organization's leaders were arrested, and although only a few of the known Wobbly leaders were actually accused and tried for syndicalism, the message was clear to all Wobbly members. As Breshears put it, Idaho would not, "...tolerate an uprising by a bunch of no-account 'Reds' intent on causing trouble..."

Breshears also understood the need to set the people's mind at ease concerning the "sweeping powers," of the constabulary. Breshears set the stage for cooperation among Idaho's police entities. In his report he stated:

> "It was early realized that because of the small number of men available for duty in this bureau, together with the vast amount of territory to be covered that it would be impossible to get good results without a general unified police effort. In practically every instance sheriffs and police departments have been friendly and given assistance (Breshears)." (sic)

On February 6 and 7, 1920, the first Idaho convention of peace officers was held in Boise and Breshears recommended this become at least a biennial arrangement.

Throughout his report Breshears appealed for more officers, and more duties:

> A much larger force than we now have could be used to a profitable advantage, especially on the Canadian boundary where a large international liquor traffic is carried on and to which we have not been able to give proper attention owing to the demands of the Wobbly situation (Breshears). (sic)

Breshears also recommended a law creating a Bureau of Criminal Identification be established, a finger-printing system implemented, and the enactment of an anti-theft law covering motor vehicles. He ended his report with a summary of activities, which included 284 arrests and 204 bond forfeitures.

Despite its initial successes, by 1923 the Bureau of Constabulary was under fire again. In 1922 Constabulary officers were tasked with deputizing men to patrol the railroad area around Pocatello due to a railroad strike. Fearing a return of the type of violence seen with the Wobblies, Governor Davis secured funds and sent his officers to ensure no "...irresponsible, radical, outsiders..." stirred up any trouble. Unfortunately, Chief of the State Constabulary at Pocatello, K. L. McBurney, deputized some individuals of dubious character.

McBurney's deputies were accused of arresting people on trumped-up charges and walking about, "...with guns strapped to their belts with the apparent intention of creating strife." There must have been some validity to the complaints. McBurney wrote a letter to Governor Davis on August 31, 1922, explaining why he, McBurney, stripped W. A. Howard of his, Howard's, constabulary badge.

> There is no question as to Mr. Howard's education and ability as he tells you, but from inquiries made, Howard is a periodical moonshine drinker and when a man wearing a constabulary badge under me thinks he can step out and buy whisky, have a party in a n---- shack, and display a gun and badge, he has another thought coming (Davis).

Just as there had been great opposition to the establishment of the constabulary, there was in 1922 and 1923 great opposition to its abolishment. In a letter to its members and to Governor Davis, the Idaho Congregational Conference claimed the effort to abolish the constabulary was backed by bootleggers, moonshiners, boozers, law-breakers, and Wobbly radicals.

Frederick Burbidge, the General Manager of the Federal Mining and Smelting Company, implored Governor Davis to take whatever measures were necessary to keep the constabulary active. Referring to the Wobblies, Burbidge wrote:

> The state constabulary has had in the past a steadying effect on this element. We believe the organization is still strong and active in the mining camps, holding their meetings without any attempt at concealment; and making only thinly veiled threats of trouble soon to come (Davis).

Letters with similar verbiage were also received from other law enforcement entities within Idaho and from other states.

W. H. Hiatt, the Chief of the Bureau of Constabulary, added another growing problem to the list of reasons why the constabulary should not be disbanded – narcotic drug abuse. In a letter to Governor Davis in April of 1922, Hiatt responded to a request for information he received from the Narcotic Drug Control League of New York City. The League sent a questionnaire to Governor Davis requesting information interpreting whether or not the state's crime had increased due to drug addiction, to what extent the manufacture and dispensation of narcotics were controlled by law, what provisions existed for the treatment of addicts, what steps were being taken to treat young addicts, and how many licenses were issued in the state for the manufacture of narcotic drugs.

Hiatt's four-page response was chilling. He attributed a ten percent increase in statewide crimes to drug addiction. Hiatt added there were about seventy-five addicts currently in state care for addiction, but said the care was, "…at best inadequate. I believe there are at the present time about twelve hundred drug addicts in the state. Commissioner Burrell of the Department of Public Welfare believes there are many more than this."

Hiatt added he felt narcotic drug abuse was the largest problem concerning the American people. "Today and in the future some very drastic steps will be necessary to prevent this menace from spreading over the entire country (Davis)."

These pleas did not fall on deaf ears, but Governor Davis was on his way out of office. His successor, C. C. Moore, citing the constabulary had been intended as only a temporary force to begin with, replaced the constabulary law with a law which allowed the governor to appoint a state officer and sheriffs on an "as needed" basis. On February 8, 1923, the State Bureau of Constabulary was abolished. Later, in the same legislative session however, a new statute restored to the Department of Law Enforcement the powers which had been vested in the constabulary.

Governor Moore, the first person in Idaho history to successfully run for governor after serving as lieutenant governor, was re-elected in 1924. Although the Wobbly threat was under control, Moore recognized there was still a need for state police officers to combat a variety of crimes, including citizens flouting Idaho's prohibition laws. In 1926, Theodore Goeckner was commissioned by the Idaho Department of Law Enforcement to conduct 'special jobs' in Idaho County. The following information is taken from an oral history given by Theodore Goeckner, and provided by the Goeckner family.

I was working near Cottonwood, Idaho and I had a chance to get an old motorcycle, which became the basis for my being suggested by the local management of the hotel there in Cottonwood to assist the Department of Law Enforcement. Idaho County wanted to start a highway patrol and because I was recommended, I got the job. The job led me to move back to Grangeville. I wasn't quite twenty-one when I took the job so I had to wait two weeks in order to be sworn in.

Theodore Goeckner was one of the first three state police officers commissioned by the Idaho Department of Law Enforcement. This photo was taken near Grangeville, Idaho. Photo courtesy of the Goeckner family.

Goeckner said the Department of Law Enforcement tasked him with various law enforcement jobs.

Rather than send a man up from Boise, they tasked me with taking care of some of the little jobs that came up in Idaho

County. As money is always tight from the legislature, the state wasn't ready yet to organize the state police but I was commissioned to take care of several jobs.

Goeckner said because he did not get 'messed up' financially, politically, or in any other way, when the state was ready to take a sample of the attitude of the people regarding the organizing of a state police, he was called on to conduct a statewide survey.

The first badge issued to highway patrol officers. Goeckner was badge number 74. Interestingly, the badge does not depict the Great Seal of The State of Idaho, or any of the territorial seals used prior to Idaho becoming a state. Photo courtesy of the Goeckner family.

They had to be sure they were ready to do this. The governor and legislators had made so much noise about it they sent me from one part of the state to another just to sample the attitude of the people toward organizing a state police force. (Forming a state police) would make it necessary for the state legislators to legislate so much money for paying the men on the road as well as the office force that would be needed at the state capitol.

Goeckner said he was able to bring in good reports about the attitude of people toward a state police, and the following year, state lawmakers organized a state police highway patrol.

I got my appointment and the headquarters for my job was in Twin Falls. I worked out of Twin Falls for the next two years but there was a big election coming. This was a state election which included the election of a new governor and of course it ended with a change of politics all around (Goeckner).

Goeckner was among the first three men hired to work as an Idaho State Patrolman. In 1927 Governor H.C. Baldridge, was sworn in as Idaho's fourteenth governor. Goeckner's work for the state provided the ground work Baldridge needed to carry out his mission of forming a state police organization, which included hiring patrol officers and lobbying legislators to provide his budding force with equipment, uniforms, and pay. Baldridge appointed fifteen men to the Idaho State Traffic Patrol, and within a short time, these men made an excellent name for themselves and the Department of Law Enforcement.

In 1930, Baldridge lost the gubernatorial election, to Democrat C. Ben Ross. Goeckner and his fellow patrol officers were not re-appointed. Goeckner continued his law enforcement career as a patrol officer for the City of Twin Falls, and after four years owned and operated the Twin Falls Merchant Police Service, which provided security for over one hundred Twin Falls City merchants.

Despite the change in politics at the highest level of Idaho government, however, the state was still in need of state patrol officers, and Governor Ross followed Baldridge's example, and also appointed fifteen patrol officers and named Emmitt Pfost as the Commissioner of Law Enforcement.

3 ★ Fontaine Cooper

Coming together is a beginning; keeping together is progress; working together is success.

Henry Ford

While the automobile is certainly considered a marvel of human ingenuity, and among the major advances in Twentieth Century technology, its remarkable history has a dark and bloody side. Thousands of people die every year in automobile accidents.

In the early 1920s, automobile technology was still in its infancy, but law enforcement agencies nationwide recognized in order to keep this modern marvel/menace under control, traffic laws and traffic enforcement would have to be developed. Thus, the concept of traffic patrol officers was born. Despite the fact Idaho had only 103 miles of oiled roads, and 310 miles of paved roads throughout the majority of the 1920s, the state experienced fatality crashes at an alarming rate and Idaho's law enforcement leaders went to work on ways to educate motorists, enforce traffic laws, and reduce the frequency of fatality crashes.

In the 1931-32 biennial report to the Governor, Commissioner of Law Enforcement, Emmitt Pfost, crowed over the many and varied accomplishments of the fifteen-man Idaho State Traffic Patrol.

> When the Department of Law Enforcement is mentioned, the first thing that flashes across the mind of the average citizen is a traffic officer. Few of us ever stop to think about the multitude of daily services rendered to the public by its officers and personnel. Traffic officers are always glad to aid a motorist in distress, and in case of an accident are qualified to render effective first aid (ISP).

The state was divided into fifteen patrol districts with about 300 miles of road in each district. Over the two year period, Pfost reported his patrol officers covered 808,746 miles, issued 1,956 speeding tickets, arrested 1,455 offenders, issued tickets for 76 intoxicated drivers, and collected a total of $13,238.47 in fines. Traffic officers were also responsible for systematically testing headlights and brakes and for assisting in the recovery of stolen vehicles.

Pfost had less to say about his traffic officers in the 1933-34 biennial report, except to note the state was now divided into twenty-one districts with one officer in each district. Despite having little to write about his men, Pfost was extremely busy promoting changes within the Department of Law Enforcement with the intention of bringing a new image to traffic patrol, and clarifying the duties of his patrolmen. A veteran of law enforcement since 1914, Pfost understood the need for his officers to have training. He coordinated the first training schools in the state, the first in 1932, the second in 1934.

Pfost had a great deal more to say about his patrolmen in the 1935-36 biennial report. He referred to them as Idaho State Police for the first time. Pfost's referral to his men as state police officers was likely intended to remind both Idaho's governing body and Idaho's citizens that although the primary duty of his officers was highway patrol; his officers from the inception of the state police had legislative authority to enforce all of Idaho's laws and the authority to enforce laws anywhere within the state's boundary.

> The officers of the Idaho State Police are a highly respected and efficient body of men. The activities of the officers are manifold. They range in variety from the scouting of anglers permits to the investigation of cosmetic licenses and in degree from returning lost children to the capturing of maniacs. (sic)

This is the only report in which Pfost refers to the capturing of maniacs, and although he makes no specific mention of the murder of State Patrolman Fontaine Cooper on November 25, 1935. His reference to maniacs most likely refers in part, to the capture of Douglas Van Vlack. Van Vlack gunned down Cooper, Twin Falls Deputy Sheriff Henry C. Givins, and his own ex-wife, Mildred Hook.

The chain of events leading up to the triple murder, began on February 23, 1935, in Tacoma, Washington, when Van Vlack kidnapped his ex-wife Mildred at gunpoint as she was returning home from work. The Tacoma Police alerted allied law enforcement agencies across the Pacific Northwest to be on the lookout for the couple.

Van Vlack was driving a slate-gray, 1931 Ford Model A Coupe, and at 2:00 p.m. on November 25, Patrolman Cooper and Deputy Givins spotted the vehicle on Highway 30, one-half mile east of Buhl, Idaho. The officers stopped Van Vlack and approached the car. Cooper ordered Van Vlack out of the vehicle, but Van Vlack ignored the order. As Cooper approached Van Vlack's door, Van Vlack pulled a pistol and shot Cooper through the left eye. Givins attempted to pull his pistol, but Van Vlack shot him three times. Cooper was killed instantly. Givins was hit in the throat, the left arm, and the left hand. He lived for fourteen days before succumbing to an infection in his throat wound that lead to pneumonia.

Fontaine Cooper's uniform badge and hat badge. Photo courtesy of the Cooper family.

After the shooting, Van Vlack drove away with Mildred. Twin Falls County Sheriff Edwin Prater organized a Sheriff's posse and set up roadblocks on all roads leading out of the area. Radio stations broadcast descriptions of Van Vlack and Mildred, and asked the public for assistance. At the time this was the biggest manhunt in south-central Idaho's history, but Van Vlack managed to evade authorities throughout the night.

The next morning, Van Vlack was found in a ditch about two miles north of the tiny town of Hollister. Mildred was not with him and Van Vlack claimed he had abandoned her the night before. He told Sheriff Prater she was most likely making her way back to Tacoma. Prater suspected Van Vlack was lying and on November 29, when Mildred's body was found near Berger, Sheriff Prater's hunch was confirmed. Mildred had been severely beaten and shot in the head. Her body was stuffed in a culvert and covered with brush.

Originally, Van Vlack was charged with first-degree murder in the death of Patrolman Cooper, but the charge was later dismissed and replaced with the premeditated murder of Mildred Hook. Van Vlack was found guilty and sentenced to death. The night before his execution, Van Vlack was visited by his mother and father. After his parents left, he broke away from the guard and climbed up three tiers of cells into the rafters of the prison. In the moments prior to plunging headfirst onto the concrete thirty feet below him, Van Vlack shouted: "I have a right to choose the way I die" – a choice Van Vlack certainly hadn't offered his three victims.

Patrolman Cooper was thirty-four years old. He was a twelve year veteran of law enforcement, having served with the Pocatello Police Department before his appointment to the Idaho State Police. He left behind a wife and daughter. Deputy Givins was forty-five years old and had been a Twin Falls County deputy sheriff for three years. He left behind a wife and six children. Mildred Hook was twenty-two years old.

Fontaine Cooper was the first Idaho State Police officer killed in the line of duty. He was buried in his home town of Lava Hot Springs after an elaborate funeral service that was attended by Idaho Governor C. Ben Ross, and numerous police officers from Idaho and surrounding states. Givins' funeral was held in Twin Falls and was also attended by a large number of police officers from Idaho and surrounding states. Mildred's body was returned to her family. She was entombed in a crypt at the Tacoma Mausoleum.

On September 14, 2012, seventy-seven years after Patrolman Cooper's death, his daughter, Dorothy Cooper Swainston, attended the dedication of the Idaho State Police District Four building in Jerome, Idaho as the Fontaine Cooper Building. Although she was only six years old when her father was killed, Dorothy said she still has very clear memories of him.

> Father was raised in Pocatello and he was a Pocatello City officer for several years. His father was also in law enforcement and was the first sheriff of Bannock County. I don't remember how many years my grandfather was sheriff, but I know it was several.

Dorothy said becoming a state patrolman in those days was always based on political appointment.

When father was an officer for Pocatello City, C. Ben Ross was the mayor of Pocatello. When Ross was elected governor he talked father into becoming a state police officer. Our first assignment was to Idaho Falls and we were there about six months. Father had to drive his own car because the state didn't give him one. His car number was 214 and his badge number was 14. After father got his uniform, I really don't remember seeing him in much else. He loved being a state patrolman.

In October of 1931, Dorothy said, the family moved to Twin Falls. Her father's area of coverage was from the Nevada line north to Hailey, east to American Falls, and west to Glenns Ferry.

He covered from 2,500 to 3,500 miles every month, and he kept a very detailed day book on his activities. In reading his day book I discovered he worked quite a bit with Twin Falls County Sheriff Prater and shared office space at the sheriff's office. He also did a lot of investigative work for Governor Ross. Throughout his day books he makes references to these investigations, but they must have been hush-hush because on these investigations, he didn't go into any detail.

In 1933, Patrolman Cooper received his issued car, and Dorothy recalled her, "wonderful memories" of going with her father on patrol.

Sometimes I got to ride with father. He had a Ford Coupe and I used to curl up in the window seat and ride with him. One incident I remember, we were driving down the road and we came across a boy sleeping in the middle of the road. Father hit the brakes and I must have been sleeping too because I flew out of the window seat! Father woke the boy up and told him he couldn't be sleeping on the road because it was too dangerous, so we took the boy to town and father found him a place to stay.

Dorothy said despite her many good memories of her father, she is still haunted by the memories she carries from the day of his murder, and the years following his death.

> Father and I used to joke about me giving him a kiss good-bye before he went on patrol. The morning he was killed he told me I had to come give him his kiss because he was in a hurry. I told him no, he had to come give *me* a kiss. He really was in quite a hurry and that's the first time in my memory that father left for work without me giving him a kiss. That has preyed on my mind all these years. Later that day, I went to a movie with my class. At the end of the movie they played Taps. I remember a bunch of third graders joking about Taps being played for a cop that just got killed. I don't know why, but somehow I just knew it was my father.

Patrolman Cooper's death sent a shockwave through the entire community and Dorothy said because of her young age, people shielded her from everything concerning her father's death, including his funeral.

> I wasn't allowed to go to the funeral. Governor Ross was the speaker at the funeral so his wife tended me during the service. Afterwards, I wasn't allowed to talk about it or to cry about it. Everyone kept telling me to be a big girl. My mother had a nervous breakdown and it was years before she could really function. We traveled to new homes all the time because she was running away from it. In all, I went to school in Idaho, California, Iowa, New York, and ended up graduating from high school in Logan, Utah.

Following her father's death, Dorothy said the community and the state gave financial assistance to her and her mother. Mrs. Cooper received $52 a month until Dorothy reached age twelve at which time Dorothy received $18 a month until she turned eighteen. "I was given a scholarship to attend college, but I didn't go to college because I got married. I was also given a life-time pass to the Lava Hot Springs swimming pool." Dorothy currently lives with her daughter in Kent, Washington. Prior to the dedication ceremony, Dorothy donated her father's uniform and patrol weapon to the Idaho State Police for permanent display in the District Four building.

In the wake of Patrolman Cooper's death, Pfost worked even harder to convince legislators to hire more patrol officers, and to clarify and expand the duties of the state police officer. His efforts did not come to fruition as much as he would have liked during his time as Commissioner of Law Enforcement. However, his hard work was put to good use in 1937 by the newly appointed Commissioner of Law Enforcement, J. L. Balderston.

Balderston was appointed by Governor Barzilla Clark, who served as governor from 1937 to 1939. Balderston was very specific in his 1937-38 report concerning his vision for the Idaho State Highway Patrol. He recommended the establishment of an Idaho State Police force of at least fifty trained officers with the officers placed on a merit system and subject to civil service regulations. Among the reasons Balderston gave for his recommendation was the 1938 completion of U.S. Highway 95, which at long last connected northern and southern Idaho within Idaho's boundary.

Public and officer safety concerns were also of the utmost importance to Balderston. He encouraged the continuance of the police training schools (which had been held in 1937 and 1938), modernized equipment, and created a well-balanced safety program. In a report to Governor Clark, Balderston claimed the efforts already made in these areas had, "...won the support and cooperation of the peace officers of the state as well as the general public."

Balderston added because of the extensive operations of his patrol units, it was necessary and advisable to modernize automotive equipment, purchase firearms, upgrade gas equipment, first- aid supplies and emergency ambulance service equipment, and provide fingerprint supplies, radios, and public address systems.

For the first time in a Department of Law Enforcement Biennial Report, Balderston also included graphic pictures of fatality accidents and a picture of the new patrol car, a black Chevrolet with a distinctive white stripe along the side, and a hand-painted image of the state of Idaho. The new patrol car was equipped with first-aid and ambulance facilities.

Balderston further recommended:

> The officials of the Department of State Police consist of a superintendent, inspector, three captains, three sergeants, and such

> officers and patrolmen as are needed. Further, for the purpose of highway safety and driver control and accident prevention, the Driver's License Bureau be incorporated in the Department of State Police, enabling the Superintendent to maintain a permanent operators' record file on accidents, arrests, and convictions. That the Idaho Motor Vehicle Laws be amended transferring the authority of the Commissioner of Law Enforcement to the Superintendent of the State Police (Balderston). (sic)

On February 20, 1939, Pfost and Balderston's vision became reality. Governor C. A. Bottolfsen, inaugurated as Idaho's seventeenth Governor in 1939, signed the Idaho State Police Act. Among its several provisions, this act gave the Idaho State Police the authority to enforce all of the penal and regulatory laws of the state, prevent and detect crime, apprehend criminals and maintain order, require all persons using the highways in the state to do so carefully, safely, and with the exercise of care for the persons, property, and safety of others.

The governor appointed Harry M. Rayner as Superintendent of State Police. Rayner also acted in the capacity of Commissioner of Law Enforcement, and appointed one captain and five lieutenants to the state police. The Idaho State Police was divided into five districts with one lieutenant in charge of each district.

Rayner and his men looked forward to the coming decade with enthusiasm and a sense of purpose. In a letter to Governor Balderston, Rayner wrote:

> We deeply realize the tremendous costs in money and in human lives which this crusade against the forces of crime and accidents has already exacted. We face with no small measure of trepidation the vast need for still greater funds and still more State Police in this battle for society, safety, and the very foundation of civilization itself (Rayner).

Rayner's accurate assessment of the needs of the Idaho State Police might well have been realized within a few short years if, "…the battle for society, safety, and the very foundation of civilization itself," hadn't manifested itself in the form of World War II eighteen months later.

4 ★ War and Safety

You must inspire in them, confidence in you. You are the State Police.

From the minutes of the Idaho Police Training School held October 11-27, 1938

Idahoans had good reason to look forward to the decade of the 1940s with optimism. The Great Depression was over; the state was preparing to celebrate its fiftieth birthday on July 3, 1940, with parades and other special events; and perhaps most importantly of all to the majority of Idahoans, the conflicts raging in Europe and Asia were, "…not America's problem." In short, it appeared the future for most Idahoans held more promise than it ever had.

Idaho's governing body was optimistic as well. There were plenty of issues concerning Idaho that needed to be addressed, but overall, the state was in good financial shape and its population had grown to over half a million. For those employed in Idaho law enforcement, the state's population growth meant an increased, although not unwelcome, work load. In a letter to the governor Raynor wrote:

> The Idaho State Police with the aid of all who enjoyed the distinction of bearing the name of police and sheriff have greatly increased the number of warning and arrest tickets given our motorists in the past biennium. Although our fatality death record shows an increase for 1940 over 1939, we feel that it has not been the officers who were at fault but the fault of the motorists themselves in many interests (ISP).

Rayner's eloquent argument for more officers, more funding, and additional duties was echoed by other officers of the law. In his February 16, 1940 letter to Governor Bottolfsen, Geo. W. Edgington, Prosecuting Attorney of Bonneville County, asked the governor to refrain from charging Idaho State Police Lieutenant Dwight R. Vickrey a week of vacation time for Vickrey's trip to Omaha, Nebraska with Bonneville County Sheriff Meppen.

> Sheriff Meppen enlisted the services of Lieutenant Vickery of the State Patrol to accompany him to Omaha for the purpose of returning a two-time loser charged with various felonies in this county; the loser was and is a bad egg; the trip required officers of the competent order. The sheriff's office has been sadly handicapped in regard to help, which created an emergency situation in Bonneville County. The availability of a State Police officer to assist the Sheriff was a great necessity (Bottolfsen).

On July 15, 1940, H. H. Barton, Justice of the Peace, Coeur d'Alene Precinct, sent a letter to Governor Bottolfsen urging him to authorize additional State Police officers in Kootenai County. Recounting an incident in which a car driven by an intoxicated man was "…cross-wise of the yellow line between two guard rails." Barton explained two conservation officers, returning to their duty station, barely managed to prevent any collisions of cars approaching the scene, but Barton insisted the prevention of a serious collision was simply a matter of luck. "At the present time this section of the highway witness's almost continuous violations of the traffic regulations." For this reason, Barton said he was urged to call attention to the necessity for an additional State Traffic Officer for Kootenai County.

Governor Bottolfsen did not appoint more state police officers, instead, recognizing the continuing increase in traffic accidents and fatalities across the state, Bottolfsen created a state-wide safety campaign, calling on his state officers to assist his safety ambassador. The duties of the new office were to educate both adults and school children on the possible hazards of operating vehicles, and the hazards of motor vehicles to pedestrians. On September 3, 1940, Bottolfsen sent a bulletin to all school principals across the state:

> For the first time in history, on this our fiftieth anniversary of statehood, we are glad to announce a new program of school safety education. The white sound truck from the Bureau of Safety will be used full time to help perfect and maintain this great safety program started this year in Idaho. We wish to give our full cooperation to every civic- minded organization which has given so much time and money to make possible the good record our

elementary schools have shown. Realizing the demand for help along this line is increasing very rapidly and the need for more school safety work to cover all Idaho schools, Governor Bottolfsen offers his help and asks your full cooperation (Bottolfsen).

An unidentified patrol officer stands next to the state safety vehicle used by "Safety" Davis. Photo courtesy of the Idaho State Police.

Schools were asked to contact their local state police officer in order to set up an itinerary and give G. H. "Safety" Davis, the governor's newly appointed Ambassador of Safety, an opportunity to share his message. State police officers accompanied "Safety" Davis to schools throughout the state and assisted in giving safety talks and organizing students to serve as officers in student-led school safety patrols.

State police officers were also tasked with returning to the schools regularly to check on the functions of the student-led safety patrols. From September through December of 1940, "Safety" Davis presented his program to over 25,000 school children. The number of students who participated in the student-led safety patrols varied by the size of the school, and no information is available to indicate, state-wide, how many students participated as safety officers.

The American Automobile Association sponsored the student-led safety patrols nationwide. The main function of the patrols was to protect the pupils against street hazards. Most of the patrol members were stationed at intersections. They stood at the curb and cautioned schoolmates to cross in an orderly manner when there was a safe lull in vehicle traffic. In 1940, the work of safety patrols was recognized nation-wide when fifty-six senators and thirty-five governors sent letters to the American Automobile Association commending the work of the School Safety Patrols.

Idaho was among the states to recognize both the excellent training Idaho State Patrolmen gave to the student-led safety patrols, and the individual heroism of the school patrolmen. On February 19, 1940, Governor Bottolfsen received information from Idaho State Patrolman, Harry Clark that student patrol officer, H. Pelton of Ahsahka, Idaho, had saved the life of an eight-year-old girl who darted in front of traffic.

The young school patrolman saw the girl enter the roadway in front of an on-coming car, and raced to grab her out of harm's way before she was struck. Governor Bottolfsen sent a letter to the school district, thanking Pelton for his quick action and commending him for saving the girl from critical, and possibly fatal injury.

> Will you please express to this student patrol officer my commendation for his act and assure him that such attention to duty and realization of his responsibilities will contribute greatly to the program we are attempting to carry out in improving safe roadway conditions (Bottolfsen).

In the 1939-40 Biennial Report, Rayner reported many school children wrote letters to the governor expressing their favorable opinion of the new safety campaign and requesting membership in the Idaho State School Safety League. Each student who requested to join the League received a membership card and their letters were placed on file in the Bureau of Safety office. "We feel this program is playing a very important part in the safety campaign which has become a national challenge," Rayner wrote.

Governor Bottolfsen's safety campaign didn't stop with school-aged children. He also used his Idaho State Patrol Officers, billboard signs along highways, and "Safety" Davis to help spread the safety message to all Idaho motorists. One speech by "Safety" Davis in particular drove home the point that operators of motor vehicles were required to master specialized tasks never before used in the course of human history. In the speech, "old Dobbin" is slang for horse.

> When old Dobbin furnished horse power for highway transportation, horse sense supplemented driver's judgment, to place a double safeguard on the traffic that used the roads. With old Dobbin seldom seen on the roads anymore, his successor, the motor vehicle, performs faithfully the demands of its master, regardless of how wise or how foolish they may be. In former days, the horse's instinct of self-preservation prevented some of the accidents which driving failures many now cause. Few persons ever saw two horses collide head-on. How different was this from the condition now, when a powerful machine may be guided head-on into another vehicle, into a train, or over a cliff without any attempt to resist. This is not a plea for the return of the horse and buggy days, it is not intended to be a reminiscence of the good old days, or an outburst of remorse over its passing. This is intended merely to show the great responsibility of the driver as well as the great hazard in modern transportation (Bottolfsen).

Because safety enhancements to vehicles, such as seatbelts and airbags, were as yet unheard of, and the few ambulance services in existence were generally limited to urban areas, Idaho citizens were very supportive of the governor's safety campaign. People understood their chances of surviving critical injury in a crash depended on the first-aid savvy of other motorists who stopped to assist, or the patrol officers who responded to the scene. Governor Bottolfsen received several letters from citizens commending the safety campaign, and in one, the governor was asked to send commendation to a truck driver who saved the lives of two men involved in a fatality crash.

Idaho State Patrolman Sam Webb investigated the crash. In his report, Webb states Consolidated Freightways driver Francis Weeks noticed wheel tracks, nearly obliterated by falling snow, going off the shoulder of the road near Kellogg. Parking his truck, Weeks followed the tracks on foot and noticed a car on its top in about four feet of water. Weeks waded into the icy water and rescued two men trapped in the front seat of the car. Both men were weak from exhaustion and hypothermia. Unfortunately, Weeks was unable to save a woman and her six-year-old son who were in the rear seat of the car. Weeks drove both men to the Kellogg hospital and reported the accident location.

Another of the Governor's top law enforcement priorities in 1940 was stopping the theft of livestock which had become somewhat of an epidemic, especially in the southern part of the state. The inauguration of a brand inspection and livestock anti-theft program was under the direction of O. J. Shaw as State Brand Inspector. A road check plan was started where a uniformed state patrolman checked stock trucks on highways throughout the state. From April 1 through November 9, 1940, patrol officers checked 1,600 vehicles and instigated "numerous" investigations on stolen stock. The actual number of stock rustlers arrested is lost to history.

By the end of 1940, war was raging in Europe, Asia, and Africa. Americans were still hopeful of avoiding involvement in these conflagrations, but it was clear to America's leaders, the United States would eventually be drawn into the conflicts. In August of 1940, a Federal-State Conference on Law Enforcement Problems of National Defense was held in Washington.

D.C. Hubert Gallagher, Secretary of the Joint Conference Committee, sent a letter to Governor Bottolfsen explaining that the committee had revised drafts of proposed law-enforcement acts. These drafts included a sabotage prevention act, a state explosives act, a state act for the protection of public property, an act to provide for a state guard, and an act providing for fresh pursuit by military forces.

> A special committee of the National Conference of Commissioners on Uniform State Laws ably assisted the committee in the technical work of preparing the bills for introduction into the legislatures. Copies of the bills will also be sent to the Attorneys General, to Commissions and Committees on Interstate Cooperation, and to representatives of the Interstate Commission on Crime for inclusion in their legislative programs for the coming year (Bottolfsen).

Governors were asked to act on the recommendations which were sent to them by the Federal-State conference on Law Enforcement Problems of National Defense.

Governor Bottolfsen understood if the United States was drawn into war, the Idaho State Police in particular would play a pivotal role in protecting Idaho citizens from all manner of sabotage, espionage, and sedition, the last being an issue Idaho had already dealt with in the late 1910s-'20s.

Governor Bottolfsen was a Republican, and lost his campaign for re-election in the 1940 gubernatorial race. In January, 1941, Democrat Chase A. Clark was sworn in as Idaho's eighteenth governor. Although the change in Idaho's governing political party most likely had little effect on the majority of Idaho's business enterprises, for the Idaho State Police, the change of leadership from one political party to another literally meant every state patrolman lost his job. For the Idaho State Police, the task of preparing state-wide security protocol should the United States enter into the war, along with the task of determining how best to continue the day-to-day operations, now fell to an entirely new group of state officers.

Prior to 1947, Idaho State Patrol officers wore a mish-mash of uniforms. Often the style resembled the uniforms worn by officers in WWII. Some officers wore cowboy style hats, others wore the police visor-style cap. In 1947 state patrolmen were issued new cars and uniforms. The patrol officer in this photo is not identified. Photo courtesy of the Idaho State Police.

Governor Clark appointed J. L. Balderston again to serve as Commissioner of Law Enforcement and placed the Safety and Publicity Bureau under Balderston's leadership. The Idaho State Police continued promoting safety programs across the state and conducting all manner of law enforcement duties, but on December 7, 1941 the Japanese attack on Pearl Harbor changed everything.

The duties of the Idaho State Police suddenly increased and became far more complex. Along with the regular duties that were part of the Idaho State Police mandate, state patrolmen assisted in the convoying of troops, investigating reports of sabotage and espionage, investigating the character of applicants for the military and various war industries, and training recruits, auxiliary deputies, and guards employed throughout the state.

Despite the outbreak of war, state patrolmen were able to attend the state's Police Training School, and six other schools conducted by the Federal Bureau of Investigation. The Idaho State Patrolmen also attended military training conducted by the U.S. Army. Balderston reported in the 1941-1942 Biennial Report to the Governor, this training was, "...very helpful and necessary to cope with present day conditions inasmuch as it provides the police with first-hand knowledge of modern police problems necessary by reason of war conditions."

Balderston further commented on the usefulness of the state's newspapers and radio broadcasters in assisting the Idaho State Police with its efforts to promote safety. During the 1941-42 time period Balderston was proud to report traffic fatalities in Idaho reached the lowest point in the state's history, adding that Idaho ranked among the six leading states, with a more than forty percent decrease in fatality accidents.

For Idahoans, as for all Americans, the war that had until 1941 been oceans away from America's shores, was by the end of February 1942 affecting the lives of everyone. In February 1942, newspapers across the nation reported British forces in Malaya had been cutting down rubber trees in retreat toward Singapore; thus, newspapers warned, rubber shortages were inevitable. The February 5, 1942 *Gooding County Leader* reported:

> Tire recapping is frozen. Essential vehicles such as those used in law enforcement, and school buses are eligible for tires but these vehicles cannot be used for excursions, sports, etc. The new rubber conserving speed-limit of thirty-five miles-per-hour is being enforced throughout the state (Leader).

Rationing of rubber, gasoline, and metal meant fewer people driving, which contributed to a further decrease in fatality accidents nationwide. However, there were plenty of other issues law enforcement officers were tasked with. J. L. DeWitt, a Lieutenant General in the U. S. Army, made it clear the responsibility for the protection of property and some of Idaho's vital installations would fall first to Idaho law enforcement and deputized citizens, and not the military, "...unless or until all means of protection by the owner, operator, local or state governments, have been exhausted or have been found insufficient to meet the emergency."

The Idaho State Police did its best to prepare for and to meet the many new demands of war; unfortunately, because of budgetary shortfalls faced by the state in 1942 and 1943 and because many state patrolmen enlisted in the armed forces, the number of state patrolmen available to complete the many tasks now assigned to them, was reduced from forty-two patrolmen, to ten.

Governor Clark determined the best way to ensure a continued level of excellence within state law-enforcement, was to deputize private citizens as special-deputy law enforcement officers under the command of the Department of Law Enforcement. These deputies were to, "... assist in the preservation of the order and enforcement of laws incidental to the preservation of the peace, protection of property, and the promotion of the welfare of the people of the state of Idaho during this extraordinary emergency."

Of particular concern to Governor Clark were repeated reports of coordinated sabotage, and the possible reaction of "enemy aliens," in connection with the evacuation of Japanese internees from the coastal states to the Minidoka Internment Camp, near Jerome. Lieutenant General DeWitt directed all military forces to take every precaution against sabotage and requested Governor Clark direct his state patrolmen to exercise the same precautions. The number of sabotage investigations conducted by the Idaho State Police is unknown, as is the outcome of any of those investigations, because DeWitt demanded all investigations be kept strictly confidential and given absolutely no publicity.

Governor Clark lost his bid for a second term in office in the 1942 gubernatorial election, to his predecessor Governor Bottolfsen. Bottolfsen appointed Chas E. Spoor as Commissioner of Law Enforcement, and once again, the Idaho State Police found itself with a new group of state patrolmen, albeit far fewer in number than Bottolfsen had during his first term. In the 1943-44 Biennial Report, Spoor recognized although his officers were still called upon to convoy troops, investigate espionage and sabotage, and to investigate the character of military applicants, the function of highway patrol was also a top priority.

Spoor reported fatalities for the first eighteen months of the biennium were again the lowest of any in the state's history, with only 100 fatalities as compared with 256 in 1941-42. Rationing of gasoline and rubber was cited as a contributing factor to the decrease in fatality accidents, as was the restriction of new car production. Another contributing factor in the reduction of fatality accidents was vehicle checkpoints conducted by the Idaho State Police. Patrol officers checked vehicles for properly working brakes and headlights.

Bottolfsen tasked his state patrolmen with finding ways to reduce the number of train-vehicle accidents which had been on the rise since 1942, despite a 1942 law which required all vehicles to come to a full stop at railroad crossings. “Railroads are the backbone of the nation’s security,” he stated. One accident in particular that prompted the governor to include railroad safety education into the safety talks given by his state patrolmen and other safety officers, was the death of five migrant workers in a car-train collision near Gooding, Idaho on November 2, 1944.

The see-saw of Republican-Democrat leadership in Idaho continued with the 1945 election of Democrat Charles C. Gossett, who served as governor for ten months before accepting an appointment to the U.S. Senate. Gossett’s Lieutenant Governor, Arnold Williams, served as governor until 1947, when Republican C.A. Robins won the election. Gossett named Boise G. Riggs as Commissioner of Law Enforcement. The Idaho State Police was still only ten officers strong, but many returning war veterans hoped to receive an appointment from Gossett to the Idaho State Police.

Such an appointment was not based on an officer’s experience nearly as much as it was on a prospective officer’s political affiliation. Gossett received numerous letters from returning servicemen who had received endorsements from their local Democratic Committees or other Democratic Party members. Sometimes, the letters were written by the parents of the returning servicemen, hopeful of calling in a favor.

One such letter was written by Virgil L. McEwen, who reminded the governor of his (McEwen’s) support during the election; he hoped his son would receive an appointment to the Idaho State Police.

> My son, Norman R. McEwen, is a discharged soldier and has been endorsed by the Kootenai County Democratic Committee. I endorsed the Democratic Party at the last election and you wrote me if you could be of any assistance to let you know. I remain a good Democrat (Gossett).

Unfortunately for returning servicemen, as well as other citizens who hoped to find employment in the ranks of state law enforcement, there were no jobs available within the Idaho State Police ranks. By the time the Department of Law Enforcement was given the opportunity to hire more patrol officers, the Democrats were out of office and the Republican Party was again in control.

With thousands of servicemen returning to Idaho at the end of the war, the end of rubber, gasoline, and metal rationing, and an increase in car production and sales, it soon became apparent to Idaho's law-enforcement officials that the decrease in automobile fatalities witnessed from 1942 through the early months of 1945, was over. Governor Gossett received a letter from M. D. Riner, a real estate and insurance agent from Caldwell, Idaho, begging for more enforcement of traffic laws on Idaho's highways. Riner refers to the governor as "Charlie," throughout the letter.

> I have heard several times criticism against the law enforcement department. It appears we are so shorthanded in this department that a State Highway Patrolman is never available and, Charlie, I think it is money well spent to triple this force, regardless of cost, and give them authority to step on this deal as it is not only going to avoid the serious property damage but it is going to help wonderfully to eliminate these bodily injury deaths (Gossett).

Riner specifically complained about the Gayway Dance Hall which was generally hopping on Saturday nights, and sold not only beer but the "hard sauce." Riner states:

> I am telling the world when these youngsters leave that place it is not safe to be on the highways. I had a sheriff admit to me Thursday morning the place is not being patrolled at all. Now I am sure, Charlie that the better class of people in the State of Idaho and especially the fathers and mothers of these youngsters would be grateful to you for any move that you should take in eliminating this traffic situation (Gossett). (sic)

Gossett's response to the letter commiserated with Riner on the fact that Idaho roadways were becoming less safe, but admitted the work of law-enforcement was hampered because of a limited number of patrolmen. "However, acting upon your suggestion, I will call this matter to the attention of Mr. Boise Riggs, Commissioner of Law Enforcement, and see that a patrol is placed in the neighborhood of the Gayway."

By the end of 1946, Gossett was able to add a few more officers to the Idaho State Police, increasing its number to twenty-one patrol officers. Gossett resigned November 17,1945, and was replaced by Arnold Williams; Williams then appointed Gossett to the Senate. Both were defeated at the polls in 1946. The same year, a State Constitutional Amendment meant Idaho governors, beginning with C.A. Robins, would serve a four year term. Governor Robins made a number of changes in Idaho government, including an increase in state transportation efforts.

Robins appointed R. C. Lewis as Commissioner of Law Enforcement, and a Superintendent of the State Police was created. Alton. P. Bunderson was appointed to this position. Another change in the Idaho State Police was the creation of six districts, which still exist. District One was headquartered in Coeur d' Alene, District Two in Lewiston, District Three in Boise, District Four in Twin Falls, District Five in Pocatello, and District Six in Idaho Falls. District Four headquarters was moved to Jerome in 2004.

From 1945 to 1948, Idaho State Police Patrolmen were paid $200 a month. The Superintendent was paid $250, and the Commissioner of Law Enforcement was paid $300.

Lewis reported in the 1947-48 Biennial Report the State Police had increased from twenty-two officers to forty, adding the Idaho State Police would soon be getting, "...communication ability across the state."

> In 1948 the State of Idaho submitted to the Federal Communications Commission a plan whereby all cities, counties, and the state would pay one-third the cost of purchasing and installing FM radio fix stations which would operate on the 42.54 m.c. and be licensed under the State of Idaho. The Idaho State Police and other law-enforcement agencies will, by June 1, 1949, have complete coverage for police communication in the state (Lewis).

State Police Officers continued to assist in safety talks to students and civic organizations, and the Idaho State Police continued its sponsorship of the Junior Patrol. State Patrolman Jack McGinnis of Coeur d' Alene supervised twelve Junior Patrol members between fifteen and eighteen years of age.

> The group was organized six years ago in the school, and just recently received complete uniforms. The uniforms include gray

> blouses and trousers, with red pockets, shoulder tabs, and cuffs, while their billed caps are also gray. Neckties and boots are black. Each member has a chrome whistle, cap, and shirt badge. The patrol was organized for the purpose of having immediately available some trained help in the event of emergencies. They have been called out many times to help in searching for lost persons, looking for bodies of drowning victims, or to direct traffic (Lewis).

As Superintendant of the Idaho State Police, Bunderson lobbied hard for the recruitment of more state officers, and received authority to hire an additional officer to each district. Corporal Cyril B. (C. B.) Roberts, retired, ISP 404, remembered the first interview he had with Superintendent Bunderson. "I was living in Montpelier and Bunderson came down to meet with the Republican Committee. I knew him and he told me he had an opening in the Idaho State Police and asked if I was interested."

Out of a job and eager for work, Roberts agreed to travel to Boise for an interview. He had no law enforcement experience and had never thought about law enforcement as a career. "Before I went to Boise, I had to meet with the Republican Committee and get their endorsement. Getting into the Idaho State Police back then was very political. You really had to know someone to get hired."

With his endorsement in hand, Roberts said he traveled to Boise for an oral exam with Bunderson.

> After the interview he asked when I could start. I told him the next Monday. He said there was an opening in Idaho Falls and gave me a week to get my stuff out of Montpelier and up to Idaho Falls. I went back to Boise a week later, picked up my car, my uniform, and my equipment. I had never been to Idaho Falls before so I arrived in an unfamiliar area as a brand new patrolman. When I arrived there was only one other officer in town and it was up to him to show me the ropes. His name was Bob Lewis. He hadn't been on for very long either.

Roberts recalled the road system in Idaho then was completely different than today: "There weren't any Interstate highways and most of the roads we patrolled weren't even paved. The area we covered was from Fort Hall to the Montana border and from Arco to the Wyoming border; a lot of area for two of us."

Roberts hadn't been on the force very long when he had his first major incident. "We got notified by Montana Highway Patrol to be on the lookout for a car that had been involved in a shooting. Two deputies, I don't remember from which Montana county, had been shot at and the suspect was headed for Idaho."

Roberts said Patrolman Lewis, and Lieutenant Dunn, the District Six Commander, were out of town so he was on his own. "I headed toward Salmon watching for the car. Two Montana officers were attempting to follow the car south. I got up to Salmon and still hadn't seen the car, so I decided to go slowly toward the Montana line." Roberts recalled it was a little past noon when he passed a "rough" road going off the highway. "I just had a feeling I should take that road, and low and behold I didn't get very far down the road and there was the car we were searching for." Roberts requested his position be given to the Montana officers and went to check out the car.

> I noticed it was unoccupied and I figured the suspect was probably trying to escape into the forested area on foot. I started looking around and out of the corner of my eye I caught a flash. I just had a hunch it was a gun barrel. I dropped to the ground and he shot the spotlight right off my car. If I hadn't dropped he would have had me. The suspect was behind a large boulder partway up a hillside. He couldn't leave the shelter of the rock without exposing himself so I just moved back a ways and waited for the Montana boys to show up. I figured the suspect would put up a fight but he didn't. I stayed at the base of the hill, while the two Montana officers made their way up to the boulder without the suspect seeing them. We had him and he knew it, so he just surrendered.

Another of Bunderson's recruits, District Four Patrolman Karl Robert (Jack) Lewis was not as fortunate as Roberts in escaping injury when a "deranged" motorist stabbed him multiple times with a pocket knife after Lewis issued the motorist a warning for having a defective signal arm on his truck. An April 10, 1948 *Twin Falls Times News* article reported Robert McKissick, thirty-four, of Twin Falls, was shot and killed by Patrolman Lewis, after McKissick attacked Lewis. "McKissick was shot in the abdomen and right arm in the fight," the article states. "Lewis was taken home with knife wounds in his left side, cheek, and right hand and thumb."

Lieutenant A.E. Perkins investigated the incident, which occurred at about 10 a.m., near "Deadman's Curve" on U.S. Highway 30 between Buhl and Filer. Perkins reported McKissick attacked Lewis as Lewis was getting back into his patrol car. Lewis and McKissick fought on the ground for several minutes until Lewis freed the gun from his holster and shot McKissick twice. Perkins said it was revealed by McKissick's parents that their son had been in a mental hospital in California. Another of their sons was arrested in 1947 and sent to a mental hospital, and at the time of his brother's arrest, Robert McKissick was alleged to have become enraged and threatened police. Lewis was cleared of blame at an inquest. A ten-man jury found Lewis was acting in the line of duty and in self-defense in the shooting.

Out of control motorists were another threat faced by state officers in the late 1940s. Patrolman Clark Hand and Patrolman Carl Muir escaped serious injury when the patrol car they were traveling in was forced off the highway three miles west of Lava Hot Springs by a speeding car that skidded sideways on a turn. Hand was driving and was forced to swerve his car onto the shoulder of the road, which gave way, thus causing him to roll. The patrol car flipped onto its top in a borrow pit fifteen feet below the highway. Muir suffered severe gashes on his right knee, and his head, and also received a sprained neck. Hand said the car that ran them off the road was going an estimated sixty miles-per-hour. The driver of the speeding car was not apprehended.

Roberts said despite the series of close calls experienced by him and his fellow officers, "Working as a state patrolman was a fun and interesting job," and added the conditions for patrolmen were dramatically improved with the introduction of new uniforms and cars.

"When I joined the Idaho State Police, we had a real mish-mash of cars and uniforms. Getting new cars and uniforms gave us a sense of uniformity which was important to us," Roberts said. "I guess it was about October or November of 1947 when we all got our cars and uniforms." Roberts said there were both a summer and a winter uniform, and both uniforms presented a "sharp" appearance. The summer uniform was "…different than the typical policeman blue."

The uniform consisted of a light-brown shirt and gray-gabardine pants with an Eisenhower battle jacket. Troopers wore gray western hats and wine colored ties that matched the wine colored striping on the pants and cuff trim. The winter uniforms consisted of light-blue pants, navy-blue shirts with light-blue ties, and blue visor-style hats. But it was the memories of the first fleet of uniform cars that really made Roberts' eyes sparkle. By July 1, 1947, each patrol officer had a spanking-new black Chevrolet two-door patrol car with block letters painted on each side forming the legend, "State Police." Both doors had an outline of the Idaho map with the wording, "State of Idaho Department of Law Enforcement" printed in the inside, and most impressive of all, two white lines which ran diagonally from the front of the hood back along each side of the vehicle. "They were really something," Roberts said.

Bunderson's push for uniformity in patrol uniforms and patrol vehicles was an integral part of his overall plan for tasking his patrolmen with reducing the sharply increasing incidents of serious injury and fatality crashes on Idaho highways. Bunderson was determined to educate Idaho drivers on the deadly consequences of dangerous driving habits through education efforts and, if their driving offense was serious enough, through the pocket book. On September 11, 1947, the *Salmon Recorder-Herald* reported Louis Jakich entered a plea of guilty to the charge of operating a motor vehicle while under the influence of intoxicating liquor. He was fined $100.

While Bunderson's desire to educate motorists and reduce traffic fatalities was supported by the majority of Idaho's law-makers and citizens, the tactic of using safety traffic lanes, which all vehicles were required to pull into for inspection by the Idaho State Police, and which Bunderson had begun upon being appointed as superintendant, became increasingly unpopular as the decade drew to a close.

"A road block, in which minions of the law rise up to halt all the sundry travelers, is a grievous thing from the standpoint of any wayfarer," wrote a citizen, who wished to remain anonymous, to the governor. Joining the fray, newspapers throughout the state began reporting on protests from city chambers of commerce, city councils, civic groups, and individual citizens.

The Mayor of Caldwell, R.H. McNeill, went so far as to issue an order for state police officers to discontinue the safety lanes conducted on Caldwell streets. McNeill was found in contempt of court when he barged into court during a hearing of a motorist cited for an alleged traffic violation in the lane. McNeill was not fined or incarcerated for the contempt charge, although the judge in the case did give him a "lecture." For Bunderson, it was apparent the traffic lanes were extremely unpopular, and despite how useful they might be in reducing traffic incidents, they were discontinued for a few months while the Idaho State Police revamped its traffic lane policy to make it more "motorist friendly."

State Patrolmen were now seen manning "Courtesy Traffic Lanes." Although officers did not ticket motorists, (They were given five days in which to correct the deficiency), all motorists were required to stop at the courtesy lanes. Patrolmen reported a huge percentage of the cars going through these lanes had something wrong, usually with their brakes, horns, windshield wipers, or lights. Many of the vehicles were operated by drivers with expired driver's licenses. The courtesy lanes were vastly more popular than the traffic lanes. Troopers Bob McCall and D. F. Kelly are credited with the idea of courtesy lanes.

McCall was also well known in the Emmett area for devising roadside signs. Among his more popular signs was the caricature of a police officer blowing a whistle, with his left arm extended palm out. The sign carried the caption "Children should be seen not hurt," and was placed near several area schools.

Bunderson and his men were once again on favorable terms with the majority of Idaho's law officers and law makers. He continued his push for more and better equipment, increased training, and still more officers to patrol Idaho's expanding road system. Many of his requests would be addressed in the 1950 legislative session, but the decade of the 1940s had one last punch to deliver to the woefully understaffed Idaho State Police—the winter of 1948-49.

5 ★ Natural Disaster

An Idaho State Police Officer is always *on duty no matter what, no matter when, no matter where.*

Idaho State Police Trooper Jack Lewis, 1949

"Considerable hardship and suffering is being encountered in our county, snow conditions have made it impossible for our rural families to obtain necessary supplies. Situation critical" (Robins).

M. D. Hart, Chairman of the Board of Commissioners of Bonner County, sent this urgent telegram to Governor Robins on February 9, 1949. His telegram was one of many received by the governor from every county in the state. Vern Eames of American Falls sent a rush telegram begging for assistance on February 17, 1949.

> We need state equipment to clear highways of snow immediately. Human lives and thousands of livestock are in severe distress. All state, county, and city roads are blocked with snow (Robins).

The forces of nature had declared war on Idaho and, in truth, the entire Pacific Northwest. For nearly four months, Idaho was slammed with record setting snow storms, wind storms, and temperatures that day-after-day dropped below minus twenty-five degrees. "We are in desperate need," wired the Gooding County Commissioners to Governor Robins. "Roads snowed in, food scarce in many areas, and fuel limited. Help needed now."

Inundated with requests for relief from Idaho's county leaders, Robins sent an urgent message to Washington D.C.

> Situation serious. We need moneys allotted to Idaho for heavy snow removal equipment. Situation serious (Robins). (sic).

The winter of 1948-49 was the worst winter in Idaho's history. Blizzards dumped record levels of snow and temperatures for many days were well below sub-zero. C. B. Roberts said: "State patrolmen were supposed to wear only state authorized uniforms, but most of us wore our own coats because the state police didn't issue winter coats until 1950. I don't know about everyone else, but I was out of uniform the entire winter. It was either that or freeze to death." Photo courtesy of the Idaho State Police.

Robins reminded the nation's leaders, Idaho's farming and livestock raising operations were a critical part of the nation's security, and within hours, Robins received a reply from U.S. Senator Glen H. Taylor:

> President Truman has instructed the Federal Works Agency and the Bureau of Land Management to give full aid, even beyond the funds appropriated if necessary, to assist Idaho in this emergency. The administration has appropriated $1,300,000 for assistance to stricken areas of the west (Robins).

With funds secured to assist his fellow Idahoans, Robins declared all of Idaho was under a state of emergency.

> It is felt proper to declare a state of emergency in the state of Idaho because of the blocking of roads and highways, the isolation of large numbers of stock from food and the stranding of motorists. The declaration of such a state of emergency will permit the American Red Cross and similar agencies to participate with state and federal agencies in such relief as may be possible (Robins). (sic)

Robins sent messages to his various department heads, instructing them to do whatever they could to help those in distress. The majority of Robin's directives involving assistance issues went to the Idaho State Police. "…determine what is needed. You are authorized to hire for snow removal and clearing of highways." In a speech to legislators, Robins declared every county in Idaho was in a "…severe state of emergency."

For C. B. Roberts the ability to hire help wherever he could came as a huge relief. "That winter was the worst in Idaho's history," he said. "It was a time when the organizational strength of the Idaho State Police and individual commitment of every state patrolman was tested. I think news writers of the day called it the Great Winter, but to me it was just miserable, sometimes terrifying, and very cold."

Roberts recalled the winter started in early November 1948 and didn't let up until the end of March, 1949. Extreme winter conditions brought traffic to a standstill in many Idaho towns stranding motorists, some of them many miles from any sort of assistance.

> There were many, many nights we were called out in the middle of blizzards to try to locate stranded motorists. Until the governor gave us permission to hire whoever we could with tractors big enough to clear the roads, we basically had two rotary plows to cover the area from Burley to the Utah border to Idaho Falls, and it simply wasn't enough. It was a terrible time because we were supposed to help the people and we wanted to help the people, but we couldn't always do it.

Roberts said the difficulty of assisting motorists and others in need increased significantly with every storm that slammed into the state.

> There were times I was on duty for sixteen or eighteen hours, sometimes twenty hours for several days in a row. I know every

other state patrolman was working the same hours. It was difficult on all of us, but we all felt it was our duty to help as many people as we could and we were very proud of that.

Roberts said only those who went through that winter can truly understand its destructiveness.

Just to give you an idea of how deep the snow drifts were, I saw many pictures of people walking over the top of telephone poles. Granted, telephone poles then were shorter than modern telephone poles, but we're still talking about fifteen to twenty or more feet of snow.

Roberts added that in areas with a lot of wind, some of the snow drifts were over thirty feet. "The snow was so deep when the roads were finally dug out, the snow on either side of the road made it seem like every road was a long, dark tunnel."

Roberts does not recall if an official death toll for the Great Winter was ever determined, but he does recall two incidents that have stayed with him over the years.

I remember getting a call about a missing motorist up by Dubois. It was a young man who was on his way to Idaho Falls. I don't recall the man's name, but we looked and looked for him. Sadly, we didn't find him. When spring came it was discovered he had driven off the road in a bad storm and been covered by a snowdrift. He was still frozen when they found him.

Roberts' other memory involved an accident in which he was involved.

I was out in a blizzard after hearing about a group of cars that were stranded on a road coming into Idaho Falls. I was driving in the direction I was told the cars were stranded, and it was snowing so hard I couldn't see very far in front of me. Well, I didn't know a local farmer had hooked a V-shaped blade on the front of his tractor and was clearing the road for the cars. He was driving

> toward me and we couldn't see each other at all. I realized I was really in a predicament, when my car was caught up by the V-shaped blade and neatly deposited on its side on top of a huge drift. I wasn't hurt, and after me and some assistants tipped my car back on its wheels I was able to do a sort of slide-drive, off the snowdrift. I felt true terror when, for those first few seconds, all I could see was a huge wall of snow bearing down on me.

In a letter to the governor dated March 16, 1949, Grover W. Jensen of Bonneville County provided a glimpse of the effects of the winter and the appreciation for the governor's storm relief efforts:

> I wish to express the appreciation of Bonneville County for the splendid help you gave in obtaining the emergency fund of $375,000 for opening the highways in this section of the state. Without that help, the county would have lost at least a million dollars because of the inability to transport the products, especially potatoes, in an orderly manner to the markets. Over nine hundred miles of our farm and market roads were completely blocked and impassable a good portion of the time (Robins).

As winter conditions lessened with the coming of spring, Roberts said he and his fellow patrolmen were relieved to finally be able to return to their usual six-day-a-week, ten-to- twelve-hour per-day shifts, with the primary role of enforcing traffic laws and investigating traffic accidents. "It was also that spring (1949) we were issued summer uniforms," Roberts said. "The colors were a light tan shirt, light tan trousers, and an "Ike" jacket. We wore wine colored ties and a light-brown western hat." Until this time, state patrolmen wore police-style caps. "We had to buy the new uniform, but the blue winter uniform was still issued on an as-needed basis."

Jack Tucker, ISP 418, and Dean Bennett, ISP 438, were assigned to District Three. In a weekly report to Bunderson, both gave information on what Roberts called, "…a typical kind of shift." Tucker reported he had stopped several cars at an intersection for running the stop sign at the intersection. None of the drivers were happy about receiving a ticket for their, "…lead footedness," and Tucker reported he responded to all of the complaints he received by educating the offenders about the dangers of ignoring traffic control devices. "It is my hope that punishing them with a ticket and a fine will save their life or the life of another motorist." Bennett's report included an incident with a reckless driver. "These drivers always have excuses," Bennett said. "But they have to be educated that this behavior is often deadly."

This typical time for state patrolmen didn't last very long before another catastrophe consumed both the state's limited funds, and the time of its state officers. The Great Winter was over, but the spring thaw had just begun and several counties were to feel the effects of the copious amounts of water unleashed by the thaw.

The governor was once again presented with numerous requests for immediate assistance. Across the state, roads were washed out, low-lying lands were swamped and rural families and livestock were in need of immediate relief. Salmon resident and attorney Frederick Snook wired the Governor on May 17, 1949, to request assistance, "...with respect to the emergency flood condition now threatening a part of the City of Salmon." Gooding County Commissioners also wired a request for emergency funds as the Army Corps of Engineers warned of imminent flooding in the city as spring run-off hit its peak. Hardest hit of all Idaho counties, though, was Boundary County.

On June 18, the governor issued a proclamation declaring a state of insurrection in Boundary County and declaring martial law because the Kootenai River, "...is flooding, and there is imminent danger that it will rage uncontrolled over valuable farm lands and other properties thereby endangering the safety of life and property." The Idaho State Police was sent in force to assist with patrolling traffic and providing security against looting.

Despite the hardships suffered by the state, and the consequent increase in duties for the Idaho State Police, Superintendent A. P. Bunderson was pleased to report the many accomplishments of his patrolmen in the 1950-1952 Biennial Report to the governor. He began his report by announcing Idaho State Police personnel were no longer selected based on political affiliation, but on a state police merit system, whereby retention and promotion was now based on the personal record of each patrolman. For the first time in its history, the Idaho State Police would no longer change its patrolmen with every gubernatorial election.

From July 1, 1950, to July 1, 1951, the state police had a force of forty state patrolmen. On July 1, 1951, the force was reduced by fifteen men, leaving twenty-five men to patrol the traffic on Idaho highways. The reason for the decrease in patrol officers was the creation and staffing of the Idaho State Police Ports of Entry program. The program was approved by the 1949 Idaho State Legislature, and was in full operation by December 31, 1951. The program consisted of five fixed ports, and three roving ports. The five fixed ports were located at McCammon, Idaho Falls, Heutter, Hollister, and Strevell. The roving stations were located in Boise, Pocatello-Idaho Falls, and Lewiston.

State police officers set up a roving port of entry. Photo courtesy of the Idaho State Police.

"The fixed stations are manned by a force of twenty uniformed officers, and are operated around-the-clock seven-days a week," Bunderson said. The purpose of the ports was to protect Idaho highways and bridges by enforcing load restrictions and keeping uniform the lawful weight and size of the vehicles and loads. "In addition to this, during this biennium, the Ports of Entry collected $288,404.12 in revenue for the State of Idaho."

Bunderson was particularly pleased with the benefits the ports offered to the motoring public.

> The stations provide rest stops for tourists and truckers, with an information service consisting of travel information, and job information for transient workers under an agreement with the Employment Security Agency. The stations have soft drink

machines and coffee for the convenience of the motorists and truckers, who are encouraged to stop and become acquainted with the officers, their duties, and the traffic laws as part of the Idaho State Police Relations program (Bunderson).

Following the creation of the Ports of Entry, the Legislature, passed the Motor Carrier Act. Bunderson said the Motor Carrier Act was a complete revision of the registrations of the old truck law. Bunderson sent his five state police lieutenants for a one-week extensive training on the law, and familiarization of the department's policy, so they could in turn pass the information on to all state police personnel, county assessors, and truck operators in their respective districts. Bunderson said training on the new law took several man days, but added it was the most effective way to educate those affected by the new law.

The crowning achievement for Bunderson and for the Idaho State Police was the completion and installation of "…one of the most outstanding police communication radio systems in the west," a feat made even more remarkable by the state's unique and extremely rugged topography. The communication system consisted of thirty-seven fixed stations, thirty-seven mobile units, fourteen "handie talkies," and an aircraft radio for emergency needs where vehicles couldn't reach. "We are anticipating the increase of more base stations to cover the areas which now are isolated. The system has been adapted into the Civilian Defense Program and can be used to utmost capacity in disasters and emergencies of nearly every type," Bunderson said.

Prior to the installation of the communication system, the Idaho State Police and other law enforcement agencies in the state, often relied on passing motorists and local radio stations to assist in relaying information to patrol officers. This was often a monumental task as Bunderson pointed out in providing this information to the governor:

> In the State of Idaho we have 4,511 miles of highway under state control, which gives each officer 282 miles of highway to patrol. We have 39,421 miles of rural highways, which leaves each officer 2,464 miles of rural highway to patrol. Some of the officers in their respective territories have as many as four counties in their territory to patrol. The dedicated patrol of these roads, I believe, has resulted in increased safety on all Idaho roadways (Bunderson).

In 1951, the Idaho State Police and county and city law enforcement officers across the state and the nation also started seeing an increase in another "evil" that still today strains the resources of every law enforcement organization in America; the resurgence of drug use and the negative and enduring effects of drug addiction. Throughout the Great Depression and World War II., drug use and addiction statistics dropped dramatically, but in the midst of one of America's most prosperous decades, young people in particular discovered marijuana and its social use grew exponentially with the resurgence of America's prosperity.

The identification of the marijuana plant and the typical symptoms or behaviors of an individual under the influence of marijuana were now topping the agenda in various law enforcement schools and seminars conducted for Idaho's law enforcement officers. The biggest fear of law enforcement officials at the time was the increased use of marijuana would lead to higher crime rates, and that marijuana users would have an increased willingness to experiment with more potent and addictive drugs.

In May of 1951, Governor Len Jordan appointed Mahlin S. Hansen to a newly created position within the Department of Law Enforcement, to handle the educational angle in teaching young people about the negative effects of drug use. "If everybody learns to recognize the marijuana plant and report its discovery, its growth can be stamped out in Idaho," Hansen said, adding the next step in combating an increase in marijuana or other drug use, was to educate people on its harmful potential, and put "teeth" into the enforcement of narcotic laws.

Bunderson recognized the marijuana threat, but with only twenty-five patrol officers under his command, stated his first priority was continuing the aggressive safety campaign aimed at the motoring public. Bunderson was always on the alert for ways to make the public more aware of the need for safety and along with increased enforcement campaigns; he began the Gold Star Safety program to recognize drivers who had operated motor vehicles for many accident-free and arrest-free years.

In discussing the program, Bunderson stated, "Of course, safety like virtue is its own reward, but a well-deserved pat on the back is seldom, if ever, misunderstood." Bunderson added the program was specifically designed to give a little hard-earned recognition to deserving drivers. Drivers who earned a Gold Star Award received a safety emblem to place on the windshield of their car. The emblem was blue and gold on the front, the exact duplicate of the Idaho State Police badge, and had a short safety pledge on the reverse side on which the driver, through his signature, promised to continue to drive, "...with utmost courtesy and due regard for the safety of others."

Governor Jordan was among the first in the state to receive a Gold Star Award and said he felt the honor would encourage good driving. "It is quite apparent," he said:

> If we are ever going to stop the useless slaughter on our highways, we are going to have to enlist the active support and cooperation of our good drivers, as well as correcting the bad driving habits of our poor ones. This program is one of the finest means of filling that much-needed service that has ever come to my attention.

It was Bunderson's hope the Gold Star Award campaign would especially encourage young people to pay closer attention to the merits of safe driving.

Bunderson may have wanted the main focus of his officers on traffic safety, but in May of 1951, extreme flood conditions in Boundary County once again took the majority of his men off the road, and once again stretched the resources of the Idaho State Police. "This flood condition necessitated our state police force to spend 159 man days in patrolling the flood area and also setting up a communications system adequate for our operations."

A fixed radio control center was set up in the Boundary County Sheriff's Office and was manned twenty-four hours a day by the state police. The dikes in Bonners Ferry were also patrolled by state police personnel, along with observers, including some members of the Idaho Legislature, twenty-four hours a day. Bunderson reported all state cars had two-way radios, and handie talkies were used in airplane and boat equipment to ensure complete coverage of the disaster. "According to some of the reports from reliable sources in north Idaho, this department has been informed through the state police operations, several thousands of dollars worth of crops were saved, plus the security of life and limb and property."

Bunderson ended his report with a recap of the Idaho State Police involvement in ending a riot at the Idaho State Penitentiary on May 24, 1952. The riot started at about 10:45 a.m., and state patrolmen were called to the penitentiary to assist. "A radio call immediately went out to all available state police officers, and officers responded from as far away as Twin Falls. We had fifteen men within minutes that were fully equipped with rifles and gas to handle whatever condition existed, along with radio communications to cover the complete situation,"

The riot was instigated after four convicts were placed in solitary confinement for being ringleaders in several cases of "rules infractions." About 300 prisoners participated in the five-hour riot and destroyed the prison's recreation room, laundry room, shoe shop, automobile license tag factory, and they also looted the commissary. Prisoners created makeshift weapons from tools stolen from the license tag factory and used items from the laundry to set fire to a cell house under construction.

The rioting prisoners claimed prison guard brutality and solitary confinement sentences without justification, as their reason for the riot. Prison Warden Lou Clapp, after three attempts to talk the prisoners into ending the riot, ordered a tear-gas attack at 2:55 p.m. Bunderson reported the gas attack was very effective in ending the riot.

> The convicts yielded to the request of the warden and returned back to their cells and were locked up. All other law enforcement agencies were dismissed at the penitentiary and the state police personnel stood by until later in the evening in case of re-occurrence (Bunderson).

In 1951, legislation was enacted to require all Idaho citizens take an examination prior to receiving a license. By 1953, the system was completely centralized and enabled the Department of Law Enforcement's Motor Vehicle Bureau to maintain files on individual drivers. These files included all citations for moving traffic violations against the driver and became an invaluable tool for the Idaho State Police as well as city and county law enforcement agencies. The centralized records enabled the state to begin the Driver Improvement Program, which allowed city, county, and state officers, through evaluation of moving traffic violations, to determine the ability of the citizen to continue driving.

Conferences between Motor Vehicle Bureau officers, and repeat offenders whose driving violations indicated they were a hazard to the driving public were held, and as a result, some drivers were placed on probation while others lost their driving privileges completely. For the Idaho State Police, the centralization of these records meant a faster turn-around time on driver's checks, and Bunderson was quick to praise the governor and state legislators for their "...progressive attitude in making safety of the motoring public a top priority for the state."

Bunderson and other Department of Law Enforcement leaders recognized when starting a new division, or incorporating a new law, numerous obstacles must be overcome which only time and experience can correct:

> From January 1, 1951, to June 30, 1952, 5,234 cases involving approximately 10,750 persons have been processed through the Accident Records Division, and 849 suspensions of driver's licenses have been issued for non-compliance. Service of the Orders of Suspension was made by the sheriffs of the county in which the individual resides. This method of service has proven very unsatisfactory. In order that effective enforcement of the suspensions of driver's license be realized a more satisfactory method of service will be necessary (Bunderson).

No reason was given why the method of serving the notices was unsatisfactory, but Bunderson made it clear he and his state patrolmen were determined to enforce any and all safety measures allowed by law to curb the escalating incidents of serious injury and fatality accidents occurring across the state. Bunderson believed one of the most effective ways to prepare his officers for the many and varied tasks they faced was to ensure they had frequent and adequate training for themselves, as well as opportunities for state officers to train city and county law enforcement personnel. Bunderson felt cohesive training opportunities allowed all law enforcement officers to, "…coordinate the thinking of different branches of enforcement agencies."

In February and March of 1954, the Idaho State Police conducted five schools throughout the state for all phases of law enforcement. Bunderson reported to the governor:

> The schools consisted of courses in note taking, report writing, personal appearance, care of equipment, use and care of firearms, court conduct, courtesy and police personality, public speaking, scientific aid to accident investigations, laws of arrest, proper radio procedure, first aid, and search and seizure laws. A certificate of attendance signed by myself as the Superintendent of the Idaho State Police, and by Governor Jordan, was issued to each officer at the completion of the school. There were 386

certificates issued to attendees from city, county, state, and federal agencies (Bunderson).

In addition to the Idaho State Police sponsored schools, Bunderson was able to send two of his patrol officers to a two week traffic school in Denver, Colorado. The school was conducted by the Colorado Highway Patrol. In 1935, Colorado developed the Colorado State Highway Courtesy Patrol as a division of the Colorado Department of Highways. At this time, police training academies in Idaho were few and far between, and Idaho did not have a centralized training program for patrol officers. The mandate of the Colorado State Highway Courtesy Patrol echoed the ideals The Idaho State Police reinforced in its patrol officers—namely courteous but strict traffic law enforcement, and safety education.

Bunderson added: "The Idaho State Police also had four of its members graduate from the first Police Training Academy held at the Idaho State College in Pocatello."

The years of 1953 and 1954 were extremely busy times for the Idaho State Police. Several new laws to improve safety on Idaho's roadways were introduced to the Idaho Legislature. In January of 1954, legislators approved the removal of the old prima facie speed limit (prima facie speed limit is a default speed limit that applies when no other specific speed limit is posted), and instituted the sixty mile-per-hour day-time speed limit and fifty-five mile-per-hour night-time speed limit on all U.S. and state highways.

The Idaho State Police purchased six radar sets to aid in controlling the speeding motorists. These were dubbed "electronic cops," by the news media, and the Idaho State Police launched publicity ads across the state warning motorists to, "Take your foot off the gas, driver, or a State Police radar gadget'll get you!"

Other safety campaigns were launched, including leaflets given to drivers at the Idaho Ports-of-Entry and other locations. The leaflet was titled: "1954 Watchwords of the Highways…SLOW DOWN and LIVE!" The leaflet was part of a nationwide campaign to reminded motorists: "To safeguard the lives of everybody, this state must deal severely with any driver afflicted with the 'In a Hurry' complex. So…abide by the watchwords and remember if you are fatigued, stop and rest. If you are drinking, don't drive."

In June of 1954, the Idaho State Police once again found itself temporarily out of the highway safety business and back on the front lines of a natural disaster when Boundary County was, as it had been in 1950 and 1951, besieged by massive flooding. "This flood necessitated our state police force to spend 170 man days in patrolling the flood area and also setting up a communications system adequate for our operations," Bunderson said. "Again, the fixed radio control center was set up in the Boundary County Sheriff's Office and was manned twenty-four hours a day by the Idaho State Police. All cars had three-way radio. We also used handie talkies in airplanes and boat equipment so that all of the operations were completely covered by the Idaho State Police communication system."

Bunderson was quick to tout the advantages of a state-wide communication system and used its success in, "…helping to maintain order," during flood disasters, to promote continued improvements upgrades to the communication system.

Kenneth Hastings, Ruth Sekinger, and William Owens were captured after the murder of Boise grocer Bert McCurry. Hastings and Owens were sentenced to death, which was commuted later to life without parole. Sekinger was sentenced to fourteen years in prison for her part in the hold-up. Photo courtesy of the Idaho State Police.

He received an unexpected boon for his claims that Idaho needed such a system, when it proved its value on October 23, 1954, during a fifty-six hour manhunt for Idaho State Prison escapee Kenneth Raymond Hastings. Hastings along with another man, William Owens, had been convicted of killing Bert McCurry after a September 1, 1951, Boise hold-up at McCurry's store. After his conviction on first degree murder, Hastings was originally sentenced to death, but prior to his escape, his sentence was commuted to life.

In his report following the manhunt, Bunderson stated Associate Warden Frank O'Neil had taken Hastings to the dentist in Boise and was returning him to the penitentiary when Hastings lunged at the guard with a knife Hastings had concealed on his person earlier by taping it to his wrist. O'Neil had not felt the need for an additional guard that day, because Hastings was sporting a broken leg. O'Neil was taken by surprise, suffering severe slashes and gouges on his forearms and hands.

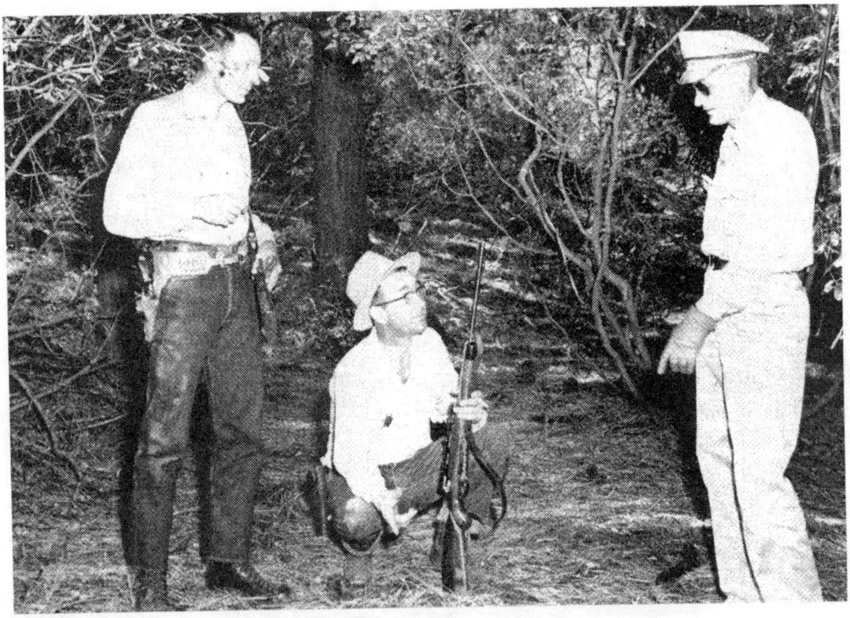

C. W. Roark, Idaho State Police, Cal Weaver, Ada County Sheriff's Office, and Lloyd Johnson, Idaho State Police, examine the spot where Hasting's left the stolen pick-up. Photo courtesy of the Idaho State Police.

Boise businessman Harold Howell, who was following behind the prison car when the attack occurred, recognized the vehicle as a prison car and when he saw numbers stenciled on the back of Hasting's shirt, realized Hasting's was attempting an escape. Howell was traveling with his business partner's wife and two children in the company truck, but as O'Neil's vehicle came to a stop, he also stopped in hopes of assisting the guard with subduing the prisoner.

Howell was unarmed and while searching for a weapon to assist O'Neil in warding off the attack, Hasting's jumped from the prison car and took Howell's pickup. Fortunately, the woman riding with Howell had exited the pickup with one of her children and Howell was able to pull the other child from the vehicle as Hastings sped away. The Idaho State Police, Boise City Police, and Ada County Sheriff's Office were notified of the escape and "Operation Brushrat," was under way. O'Neil, although seriously injured and loosing blood, drove the prison car in pursuit of Hastings until the Idaho State Police and allied agencies were in place to continue the pursuit.

Information about the escape, and a call for assistance was broadcast using the state police communication system. Within a short time, eighteen roadblocks were set up and manned by local officers and state patrolman from as far away as Twin Falls. With roadblocks in place, Bunderson was able to direct the search for Hastings: "It's a foregone conclusion," Bunderson told the men manning the roadblocks, "that although Hastings is sporting a broken leg, he will get rid of the cast on his leg at the earliest opportunity in order to be more mobile."

Bunderson's prediction was correct. Hasting's later admitted he removed his cast, "…as soon as I feasibly could," but added his leg was very weak. Hastings had made his escape into the rugged area along Daggett and Robie Creek in the Boise foothills, he was not able to drive the stolen pickup much further than Kearney Lake before he was forced to attempt an escape on foot. Hastings made it less than a mile before the pain in his leg forced him to stop. In the meantime, officers discovered the pickup, which Hastings had concealed under brush and pine boughs off an old logging trail, and decided the quickest way to find Hastings if he was still in the area, was to use a bloodhound.

D. A. New, a retired police officer living in Placerville, had a tracking dog and State Patrolman Dean Bennett was sent to pick up New and his dog, Rube. Hastings, who had found a hiding place on the hillside near where the truck was discovered, realized the dog would find him within minutes. He later told officers he decided to surrender because, "…it would be healthier to be taken down by an officer rather than by a dog."

During an interview with KIDO TV, Warden Clapp and Bunderson both agreed that while no one department could have brought "Operation Brushrat" to its successful conclusion, the ability to coordinate the manhunt through the Idaho State Police communication system made it possible for, "…all branches of law enforcement to work together as a team."

With his men returned to their regular duties following the manhunt, Bunderson went back to work lobbying for an increase in the number of patrolmen in the Idaho State Police. Bunderson cited the July 1954 National Safety Council fact sheet, which was sent to Governor Jordan and the Idaho State Legislators urging them to consider increasing the Idaho State Police force. "The force should be expanded to 122 uniformed traffic patrolmen," said National Safety Council Field Director Paul F. Hill of Chicago.

> The people of Idaho paid $18,810,000 for traffic mishaps and carelessness last year. Idahoans paid more for their traffic fatalities, injuries, and property damage than did 35 other states nationally, and more than the state of Utah, Washington, Oregon, California, and Colorado in the western states group.

Hill commended the Idaho State Police for taking steps to prepare a highway-needs study, for improvement in its central driver record program, and for its increase in traffic enforcement and safety activities.

Bunderson reported that in 1954, the Idaho State Police investigated 2,877 traffic accidents, and statewide, 242 people lost their lives on Idaho's highways. Unfortunately, despite these numbers and Bunderson's note to the governor that, "…this tally makes 1954 Idaho's deadliest year to date in terms of traffic accidents," he did not get the recommended 122 officers. Governor Jordan authorized an additional five men to become patrol officers, and those men were selected from port-of-entry personnel.

Unfortunately, the Idaho State Police, and the rest of Idaho, soon learned as deadly as 1954 was, the worst was yet to come.

6 ★ Death Toll

I know of no great men except those who have rendered great service to the human race. Voltaire

"A lot of people don't make it in law enforcement because they can't deal with fatality crashes. Personally I understand that because I think investigating fatality crashes are the worst part of being a police officer," C. B. Roberts said. "I trained a lot of new officers and lost a few of them because they couldn't handle fatal crashes." Roberts remembered one incident where his recruit lasted only two days as a state patrol officer.

> I was training a new officer in about June of 1955. I don't recall his name but he was about twenty-two years old or so when he started with the State Police. We got called out on a crash by Shelley and it was a bad one. There were two people in the car and it was later estimated the driver was going about ninety miles-per-hour when he hit a guard rail. The guard rail ended up going through the car and basically cut the driver in two. One of his legs was torn off and thrown out in a field. I told the recruit to go get the man's leg and bring it back over by the car. I thought it was odd when he didn't answer, but I was checking the passenger to see if he was alive. He wasn't. When I stood up, I could still see the driver's leg out in the field so I went around the car to find out why my recruit hadn't done what I told him and there he was, passed out cold. When he came around he quit right on the spot.

Roberts said he didn't blame the recruit for quitting. "There was a time or two I responded to bad crashes and really wondered why am I doing this? But, you just remind yourself you have a job to do and you do it. Every officer I worked with did the best they could to reduce fatality wrecks."

Bunderson was just as passionate as his patrol officers in his desire to reduce traffic fatalities, and after eight years as Superintendent of the

Idaho State Police, Bunderson resigned to take a position with the National Safety Council, where he would have the opportunity to use his vast knowledge of traffic safety issues to lobby for improvements in Idaho.

Governor Jordan also fought hard to get more patrol officers, citing the recommendation by the National Safety Council and the ever increasing number of fatalities on Idaho's roads. His efforts paid off to a small degree when legislators authorized another five patrol officers in 1955. These men were also selected from the ports-of-entry.

In January of 1955, Robert Smylie was inaugurated Idaho's twenty-fourth Governor and appointed A.E. Perkins as Bunderson's successor as Superintendent of the Idaho State Police in June of 1955. Smylie and Perkins both pledged their support of increased traffic safety measures and immediately began advocating for more patrol officers.

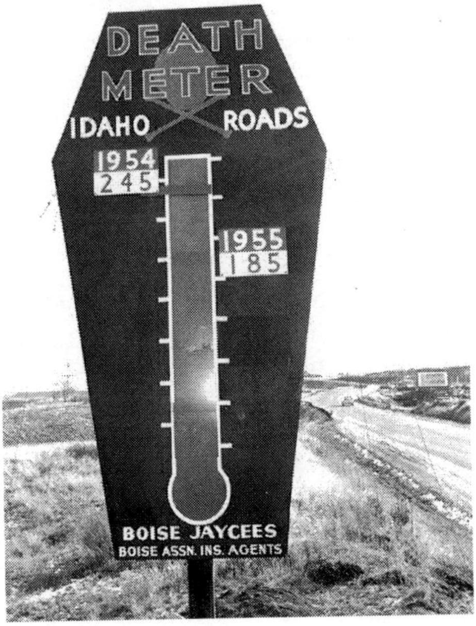

Signs such as this one were placed on Idaho's roadways in hopes motorists would pay closer attention to safe driving habits. Photo courtesy of the Idaho State Police

Governor Smylie went so far as to declare war on highway deaths in Idaho. He had little trouble convincing the legislature to authorize an additional sixteen men for the state police. These men were selected from 310 applications and were given two weeks of training. The Idaho State Police now had forty-four men to fight on the front lines of Governor Smylie's war. "We must find a way to stop the carnage on our highways," Governor Smylie declared. "Idaho currently leads the nation in the reduction of highway fatalities, but we are still losing far too many people on our roadways."

While Governor Smylie, Superintendent Perkins, and others in law enforcement tried to figure out ways to educate motorists about safe driving habits through enforcement campaigns and safety talks, the National Safety Council recognized poor driving habits weren't the only cause of traffic fatalities. Vehicles available for purchase in the 1950s were designed more to embody the free-spirited and prosperous attitude of post-war American consumers, "cool" was the catch phrase of the day and aggressive driving was culturally acceptable. Those who concerned themselves with safety were considered, "squares."

By 1955, nearly every American family owned a car, and for the first time since the invention of the automobile, people could choose color and paint schemes to fit their individual personalities. Tampa turquoise, tango red, fantasy yellow, and pink—every shade of pink—were among the favorite color choices. From the snooty lines of the Kaiser Manhattan to the dreamy sleekness of the Chevrolet Corvette, Americans also had a large number of car styles available to fit their personal wishes. However, these vehicles were not designed nor were they advertised to the American public based on their safety features, which meant the frequent incidents of fatal crashes nationwide, would not abate anytime soon.

With traffic safety still topping its agenda, the Idaho State Police underwent several other important changes in 1955 including the enactment of a state police merit system law. This law provided that officers were selected on ability and promoted on personal and efficiency ratings. For the first time in the history of the Idaho State Police, a dismissed officer could request a hearing and get it. With the advent of the merit system law, many officers started thinking of a career with the Idaho State Police. Perkins also put in effect uniform changes which had been planned and approved by Bunderson. The light-brown summer uniforms became the permanent port-of-entry uniforms, and the blue winter uniform, topped off with a western style grey Stetson hat, became the uniform of patrol officers.

The Idaho State Police was reorganized as a separate division of the Department of Law Enforcement, with the administration, management, and control of state police operations vested in the superintendent, a position now appointed by the governor. The changes were welcomed by Perkins and his patrol officers, as it allowed them more latitude to carry out Governor Smylie's mandate of reducing highway traffic deaths through aggressive safety campaigns and enforcement patrols.

As it had for the previous four years, however, the Idaho State Police would respond to a natural disaster in the form of floods, this time in the Weiser-Emmett district. This flood would consume twenty-eight man-days of patrol time. “This flood was caused by unusually heavy May rains in the area,” Perkins said, adding:

> State police officers worked with the Army National Guard and the civilian defense authorities during this operation. Our communication system was extensively used in this operation and once again proved its immense value to the state police and the citizens. The system can be used to utmost capacity in disasters and emergencies of nearly every type (Perkins).

Sergeant Walter Cox, circa 1950, investigates a fatal crash near Coeur d' Alene. Photo courtesy of Jim Fehling.

Throughout the remainder of 1955, the Idaho State Police increased its efforts to reduce highway fatalities, and worked diligently with other Idaho law enforcement agencies on patrol activities, safety talks, and other measures aimed at reducing automobile deaths. With a final tally of 186 deaths, 1955 proved to be the best year to date for Idahoans and the Idaho State Police. In a report to Governor Smylie, ISP District Three Lieutenant R.B. McCall stated:

> August 5 brought to a close the 'Slow Down and Live' campaign inaugurated by you just prior to Memorial Day 1955 in conjunction with governors from forty-seven other states. The ninety days encompassed by these dates showed ninety-one deaths in 1954. In 1955 during the same period only sixty-one lives were lost on the highways of the state. On the basis of this, the 'Slow Down and Live' campaign can be pronounced a huge success in the state of Idaho (Smylie).

The Idaho State Police would not encounter the same success in 1956. Despite stepped-up efforts by all Idaho law enforcement officers, 247 people lost their lives on Idaho highways. In a letter to Perkins, Governor Smylie referred to 1956 as a "black and bloody page in our history." Perkins sent a message to his men to step-up their radar speed enforcement and place more emphasis on hazardous moving traffic violations.

Although yet another flood in Bonners Ferry consumed 102 man-days of state police patrol time, the efforts of the Idaho State Police and other law enforcement officers resulted in 1957 ending with 205 vehicular caused fatalities. This was the last year to date Idaho had this low a number of fatalities.

Unfortunately, the Idaho State Police was still significantly undermanned according to the National Safety Council, so Idaho leaders began looking for other ways to keep Idahoans safe. One solution which was created specifically to reduce the number of Idaho State Police patrol hours lost in responding to Idaho's natural disasters came from a plan proposed by the Idaho Department of the American Legion. Although World War II was now ten years in the past, the very real threat of nuclear war was on the minds of most of America's leaders as the Soviet Union grew ever more aggressive in its stance against the United States and the NATO allies. The Idaho Department of the American Legion proposed a plan for setting up a volunteer auxiliary state police force, as an adjunct of the Idaho State Police and as an integral part of the Idaho State Civil Defense Auxiliary Police Force.

"The advent of modern weapons and rise of aggressive communist forces has imposed a serious threat to the security of our nation," wrote Hawley Atkinson, State Department Commander, Idaho American

Legion, to Governor Smylie. "This has established requirements for a strong, well-organized and informed civilian population in our country, prepared and ready in the event of a sudden major war. The occurrences and threat of natural disasters has also demonstrated such a need."

Atkinson said among the ways to train this force, the most effective would be through programs in the promotion of highway safety, and under the supervision of the Idaho State Police.

> The safeguarding and protection of the lives and interests of our people in peacetime, as well as war-time, is the concept of the Idaho Disaster Relief and Civil Defense plans. The Idaho Department of the American Legion therefore desires to initiate, enter, and aggressively pursue through its membership, a vigorous, effective highway safety program as a civil defense measure, as well as a public service (Smylie).

Perkins supported the proposal and in a letter to his patrol officers stated:

> We probably will never be able to provide regularly employed state police officers in Idaho, in sufficient numbers to curb the many needless accidents. Hence, there is a great need for a qualified volunteer auxiliary police force. An auxiliary police force of this nature will be of immeasurable value in case of a major disaster or national catastrophe for civil defense purposes.

The training of the American Legion volunteers was carried out under the supervision of commissioned state police officers. Once the training was complete, the Idaho State Police furnished each man with commission cards, badges, and part of their uniforms and equipment through matching funds from the Idaho Civil Defense. In a report to Governor Smylie, in 1958, Perkins said, "These men have proved most helpful in their own communities for such activities as helping with floods, and searching for lost persons, planes, etc."

With the creation of the auxiliary police, Perkins and his officers were able to once again focus their patrol activities and continue to search for improvements to the state police radio communication system. In an article published in the October 1957 Federal Bureau of Investigations Law Enforcement Bulletin, the Idaho State Police radio communication network was recognized as one of the most unique and outstanding systems in the west.

> The authorized federally assigned mobile-base frequency of the Idaho State Police radio is 42.54 megacycles. Other assigned higher frequencies are used to control the mountaintop remote relay station network, and to relay messages through repeater facilities installed at the mountaintop base stations. Idaho police officers operating in the rugged and frequently inaccessible territory, a vast area of nearly fifty-four million acres, need the vital assistance of such a network in order to give the public an adequate law enforcement program, increased police efficiency in every part of the state, and a practicable civil defense warning system (Perkins).

Perkins said the backbone of the radio system was a chain of remote control FM repeater and base stations, which are strategically located on seven mountain peaks situated throughout the state. Four of these operated on 250-watt power, the remaining three on 60-watt power. All seven were controlled by the Idaho State Police headquarters office in Boise, or by one of the six fixed ports-of entry stations located in each of the far corners of the state. The Idaho State Police radio system was also recognized as a key cross-monitoring link between west coast and mid-west law enforcement agencies.

> Interstate cross-monitoring is a fast, efficient weapon in the hands of law enforcement agencies pursuing a criminal suspect. In one such case, the Idaho State Police radio effectively aided the recovery of a reported stolen car when the subject was arrested and turned over to an FBI agent within thirty-three minutes from the time a call was received at Boise headquarters from Oregon State Police. The subject was stopped at a roadblock by two Idaho State Police patrol cars, which were dispatched upon our being alerted of the situation (Perkins). (sic)

Perkins added despite the twenty-seven fixed stations strategically located throughout the state, sixty-six mobile units, and fourteen handie-talkies and aircraft radios for emergency needs, the system still became so crowded, the sheriff's and city police units in the southern part of the state were forced to go on different frequencies.

In an attempt to find a solution to this issue, Perkins positioned monitoring stations in Idaho's larger cities, where the officer on duty had control over both frequencies. "We have also made three more installations, one at East Butte near Atomic City, one at the King Hill Port-of-Entry at King Hill, and one at Mica in the Coeur d' Alene area." Installation of auxiliary power plants to the most inaccessible mountaintop stations remedied the problem of power failure interruptions, and an electronic combination of available primary and alternate circuits operated by fixed port-of-entry stations through local control and mountaintop repeater facilities, guarded the systems against complete communication failure.

Don Ikenberry with his 1961 Plymouth patrol car. Photo courtesy of Don Ikenberry.

Sergeant Don Ikenberry, retired, ISP 474, recalls, however, the much lauded communication system was not nearly as perfect as Superintendent Perkins claimed it to be. "Sometimes our communications system worked great and other times it was complete hit and miss. There were a lot of times I didn't check out on a stop because I couldn't establish contact." Ikenberry said the communication system wasn't the only problem faced by patrolmen.

Back then, all of the driver's license checks were hand-searched. Depending on how many patrolmen were working, these checks could take upwards of an hour to come back. Warrant checks were also hand-searched and sometimes a return on these could take three or four days! A lot of the time we got the FBI to run our checks because they were a little faster.

Throughout 1956, Perkins continued to lobby for more patrol officers and in July of 1957, the legislature authorized an additional ten men and one personnel training lieutenant. These men were selected from the ports-of-entry ranks and given two weeks of extensive basic training and two weeks of in-service training with a seasoned patrolman. This brought the strength of the Idaho State Police to fifty-five patrolmen.

Colonel Ed Strickfaden, retired, ISP 507, said the majority of state patrol officers were selected from ports-of-entry personnel. "There may have been a few exceptions, but back then you went to the port-of-entry for generally three to five years before being promoted to patrol," he said. "A lot of the men served at the fixed ports for a year or more, and then on roving ports for a year or more, because it was a great training ground."

Ikenberry added ports-of-entry personnel and state patrolmen were rarely given a choice of where they were stationed once hired. "You went where there was a need. Perkins was adamant about that."

With a compliment of fifty-five officers, many of them new to patrol, Perkins saw the need for more "in-house" training, and sent three of his lieutenants to Los Angeles for a two-week training course conducted by the University of California and the Northwestern Traffic Institute of Evanston, Illinois. "When these lieutenants returned, we conducted five two-day training schools for all state police personnel and for federal, county, and city officers who were able to attend. This training was beneficial in preparing [patrol officers] for duty."

Ikenberry said while any training was welcomed by patrol officers, working a crash scene, and more importantly figuring out what was necessary to help the victims involved, in reality, "...required a great deal of luck, and a good understanding of Civil War medicine!"

We didn't have the array of life-saving equipment that's available to officers today. Often times, getting a trapped person out of a car meant hooking a rope or chain to the vehicle and pulling it apart with trucks. We also didn't always have ambulance service. The state police did have some advanced first-aid cars, but mostly we did whatever we could at the scene and then sometimes a passer-by or another officer would take the wounded to the hospital while we investigated the crash.

Ikenberry said investigating a crash was more a matter of "…good old common sense…" than technical knowledge. Ikenberry recalled one incident in which his unconventional method of investigation resulted in a family getting a financial settlement following the death of their son:

> I was sent to Montpelier as a resident officer, and it wasn't very long after I got there a young boy riding his bicycle was hit by a car. The guy driving the car was a federal bird biologist and he couldn't stop in time to keep from hitting the boy. The deputy sheriff scooped the kid up off the road, and took him to the hospital and I stayed to investigate the accident. During my investigation I noticed the skid marks left by the car looked pretty darn long. It didn't seem to me those skid marks would be that long unless the driver of the car was going pretty fast. For a couple of days, I used my patrol car to test skid mark lengths at different speeds. By doing that, I was able to estimate the car was going about 110 miles an hour when it hit the boy. Unfortunately, the boy died, but because of my skid-mark tests the family got a monetary settlement.

By June of 1957, the massive state-wide enforcement and safety campaign headed by Perkins and his patrolmen was showing signs of its success. In a letter to Governor Smylie, Ned Dearborn, President of the National Safety Council stated: "Idaho is to be congratulated for the outstanding traffic safety record it is making in 1957. As of June 15, Idaho has had sixty-six deaths as compared with ninety-three at this same time last year."

Perkins and his patrolmen were further commended for the creation of two traffic safety films sponsored by the state police through voluntary contributions. The two films were titled *Teenage Violators* and *Killers on the Highway.* The films were shown to over 200,000 people, mostly in schools and at civic organization meetings. Perkins said the films were not only a major part of the state police educational program, but since a uniformed officer was present at every film showing; citizens had an opportunity to meet patrol officers and ask questions about Idaho's traffic law. Once again, Idaho and law enforcement entities across the state had reason to celebrate success in the form of reduced traffic fatalities, 1957 ended with 205 deaths on Idaho's roadways.

In 1957, the state police added to its services by creating an identification section. By the end of the year, the identification section collected over 4,000 finger print cards from various police agencies throughout the state, and had logged over 6,000 names in a master file. With the creation of the identification section, the Idaho State Police was now able to send out monthly bulletins to allied law enforcement agencies in Idaho and surrounding states, with information on wanted subjects, stolen property reports, and other law enforcement concerns. By the end of 1958, with the institution of this program, the Idaho State Police recovered $254,000 in stolen property.

In a report to Governor Smylie, Perkins said the skill of his officers was enhanced even more, by their attendance in March and April of each year to in-service training. "These schools are conducted at each of the state police districts. In 1958, we had an attendance of 425 officers." The schools consisted of several areas of instruction, including note taking, testifying in court, appearance and care of equipment, and proper radio procedure. "We also sent four officers to the Law Enforcement Training Academy at the Idaho State College in Pocatello," he said. "This school is sponsored by the Idaho Peace Officers Association and the Idaho Municipal League. We have found these schools to be very beneficial to officers of all grades as they coordinate the actions of the various branches of enforcement agencies."

Perkins took the opportunity in the same report, to expound on the many accomplishments of the ports-of-entry personnel:

> During the seven years the ports-of-entry have been in existence, they've brought about $2 million a year into the state in the way of licenses and fees of one kind or another. There is also the matter of saving untold millions of dollars in road repairs during this time, and the matter of good will that has been built up for the state with tourists and commercial truckers. Ports-of-entry personnel serve as tourists guides giving information on destinations, weather concerns, and road conditions, and offer their service in hundreds of minor-service ways, such as checking oil or tire pressure. Of major importance, the ports-of-entry serve as excellent training schools for future state policemen. In fact, the more you think of the ports-of-entry and the folks who work there, the more you wonder how did the state get along without them? (Perkins)

Perkins was further proud to report each of the ports were manned on a twenty-four hour basis and the officer in charge served as both a cashier and bookkeeper. "He handles thirteen different bank accounts," he added, "and I am pleased to report of the thousands and thousands of dollars that have gone through our ports, we are only $14 off in our books."

Proud as he was of the ports and their personnel, Perkins was aware the program didn't always have the support of Idaho's legislative or judicial branches. In a book of stories compiled by Patrolman Frank York, retired, ISP 482, an incident from 1960 reported on a 'childish stomper':

> The north Idaho port car was required to patrol Benewah County near St. Maries, Idaho. The judge in St. Maries was a logger who had the habit of only requiring court costs on overweight violations. When the officers set up to weigh south of St. Maries they would set up so that the trucks had to come to the mill during the time of patrol. They caught [name omitted] or some of his trucks on a regular basis. He had received three citations with a three-day period. He became so enraged he tore off his red hat and jumped up and down like a child. (sic)

Legislators were under increasing pressure from both the trucking and farming operations who felt the roving ports specifically targeted, "their" operations and port-of-entry officers were "…in the thought process of issuing far more tickets than warnings, when warnings would suffice…".

Perkins made it clear to legislators and judges he wasn't going to make any drastic changes in how the ports-of-entry or the roving ports were operated. In a report to the governor, Perkins reported from 1956 to 1958, "The truck count through our ports-of-entry has increased twenty-two percent. Many of these trucks were found to be overweight or operating with faulty or unsafe equipment." Perkins said he and Department of Law Enforcement Commissioner Earle Koehler established very high standards for the hiring of the men who served in the port. To ensure legislators in particular got the message concerning the importance of the ports-of-entry, Perkins added:

> When you see one of those big truck and trailer jobs going through Idaho headed for Spokane with oranges from Florida, you can be sure that somebody in the capital building is figuratively ringing up $24 on the cash register. And when that truck loaded with fish, goes back through on its way home, another $24 goes into the states till. (sic)

As 1958 came to a close for the Idaho State Police, Perkins reported the reduction in highway fatalities was once again at the top of the agenda for him and his patrol officers. With 270 lives lost, 1958 proved to be far worse than "bloody" 1956. Perkins and Koehler used this increase in fatalities as part of their lobbying campaign for more patrol officers and in 1959, the legislature authorized an additional fifteen men. All fifteen were selected and promoted from the port-of-entry ranks, and given two weeks extensive basic training and three weeks in-service training with a seasoned officer.

Because part of the increase in fatality numbers was attributed to an increase in vehicle-train collisions, the Idaho State Police helped in the production of another traffic safety film. This film was sponsored by the Union Pacific Railroad, and titled: *Last Clear Chance.* "At the present time we have four copies of the film, which has been shown throughout the state," Perkins wrote to the governor. "To date, we have shown the film to approximately 24,000 students and adults in schools and through civic organizations."

The Idaho State Police identification section continued to grow, and by the end of 1959, contained 17,000 finger print cards and 50,000 names in a master file. The information from the file was used to send out monthly bulletins to all police agencies in the state, as well as agencies from neighboring states, and several subjects wanted on warrant arrests were successfully captured based on the information contained in these files.

In the 1958 Biennial Report to the governor, Commissioner Koehler stated the American Legion Auxiliary Police force was also, "...proving its worth. These men are selected from their own communities by the legion commander, a state police officer, and the adjutant in the Boise office," Koehler said. "These men have proved very helpful in their communities for activities ranging from motor patrol to search and rescue operations. They are a very valuable addition to our education and patrol efforts." Koehler added in the two year period, his patrol officers had clocked over 263,000 hours of patrol time, investigated 10,521 accidents, and out of 28,463 arrests, only thirty-four cases had resulted in acquittals.

With the addition of fifteen men to his patrol force, Perkins now had seventy-one officers to command. The port-of-entry program also grew to include six fixed ports, a port was added at Lewiston, and nine roving ports manned by forty-five officers. Perkins reported 1959 in terms of highway deaths was "slightly better" than 1958, with a total of 223 fatalities. By all accounts, Perkins was pleased with his men, the support the Idaho State Police received from the governor and legislators, and the overall direction in which the state police was moving.

In August of 1959, as it had throughout the decade, the Idaho State Police communication system would once again play a pivotal role in a natural disaster. This time the disaster would be in another state, but close enough to Idaho to have, as C. B. Roberts put it, "…a heck of an impact across the northwest."

7 ✭ Solidifying Roles and Rules

An Idaho State Police Officer's badge of office is a symbol of public faith and trust.

Idaho State Police Operations Manual 1961

Damage caused by the Hebgen earthquake in Yellowstone National Park. The earthquake caused widespread damage to roadways in the area, and triggered landslides and rock fall in many areas. Photo courtesy of the Idaho State Police.

On August 17, 1959, at 11:37 p.m., a 7.5 magnitude earthquake struck Yellowstone National Park in southern Montana. The earthquake dislodged an entire mountainside that in a split second became an enormous landslide thundering into Madison Canyon at speeds over 100 miles per hour. The landslide and the hurricane force winds it triggered, toppled and crushed trees, camp trailers, cars, and people. The massive quake also caused giant waves of water to sweep over Hebgen Dam and roar down the canyon, quickly engulfing campers trapped between the landslide and dam.

Survivors told harrowing accounts of the terror they experienced, and how they escaped the disaster. In an August 21, 1959 *Bozeman Daily Chronicle* article, Gerald L. McFarland, a news editor from Salem, Oregon shared his account:

> The side roads downstream were blocked by slides so we started upstream, hoping to find high ground. We expected to meet a wall of water at any time. The road was strewn with boulders about the size of a watermelon. We had to stop every ten feet and clear the road. Approximately one-half mile upstream, we did see a wall of water coming. We thought the dam had surely broken and this was it. The water was just beginning to creep over the side road when we found higher ground. We later learned that the water escaped over the top of the dam like a tidal wave (Bozeman).

As McFarland and other survivors later learned, the earthquake dropped the north shore of Hebgen Lake nineteen feet, and caused several large sections of Highway 287 to fall into the lake. The massive landslide caused by the forty-five-second main earthquake deposited dirt, rock, and debris nearly 300 feet high across the canyon and effectively dammed the Madison River. This created Quake Lake, which today is about 190 feet deep, and six miles long.

> The aftershocks continued all night. We counted about twenty-five of them. After each tremor, hundreds of slides would start. There were boulders the size of an automobile crashing around us. This was a horrifying sound. The biggest slide down the canyon covered the highway for about a half mile. It was just unbelievable to see. The people camped near the biggest slide immediately became engulfed in the rocks and flooding waters from the river (Bozeman).

At least twenty-eight people died in the earthquake, and many of them remain buried under the landslide.

"When the earthquake hit, the majority of us [patrol officers in District 6], figured there would be a lot of damage in Idaho," recalled C. B. Roberts. "We were surprised and grateful to learn the earthquake caused only a little damage to roads and such."

Roberts said he and his fellow patrol officers were immediately dispatched to the Henry's Lake area where SH87 and US20 intersect. "We set up a road block there to keep people from going into the quake area, and also to stop and check cars coming out of the area." Roberts said the reason for stopping cars coming out of the area was to create a list to be sent to the Red Cross, who had received thousands of requests from across the nation of families who feared their loved ones may have been caught in the earthquake.

> Montana was having a difficult time establishing communication around the quake area because the quake knocked out power in a pretty large area. I don't know how many organizations used Idaho's communication system, but I know it was used pretty extensively, with messages going into Boise and then out again to wherever they needed to go. Montana Highway Patrol sent ten cars down to the quake, but they couldn't get in because of the damage to the roads. Because I knew of a couple of logging roads that went into the area from the Idaho side, I led a few Montana Highway Patrolmen in. It was a terrible scene. You could see where the whole side of the mountain came down and there was stuff thrown all over the place. We saw houses and cars floating in the water.

Roberts said when a request came from Montana for volunteers to help search for quake victims, Idaho State Police officers, as well as officers from several other Idaho cities and counties joined in the effort. "We came across one casualty and were kind of surprised we didn't see more, but we found out later the majority of the people killed were under the landslide."

Roberts added that although HAM radio operators were used extensively for several days after the earthquake to send and receive messages to volunteers working in the slide area, the Idaho State Police communication system, "...was instrumental in coordinating the initial response of volunteers and the work we did during the time we manned our roadblocks."

He recalled the Idaho State Police spent about four days on roadblocks in the area and checked several hundred cars. "It was a good feeling when we came across a name that was on the Red Cross list as a possible casualty, and were able to report the person alive and well."

The earthquake in Montana solidified the role of the Idaho State Police as "first responders" to any natural disaster or other major incidents that impacted Idaho. Still, getting authorization to hire more officers to tackle the increasing need for a well trained, well equipped state police force was as difficult a process for Perkins as it had ever been.

The original shoulder patch of the Idaho State Police.

Among the reasons some legislators balked at increasing the manpower of the state police, was because throughout the 1950s, the nation underwent a massive trend toward urbanization. It was assumed if Idaho experienced the same trend, police units within these urbanized areas would pick up more of the financial tab and provide more of the man-power need for law enforcement. However, Idaho did not experience the population explosion of its larger cities that was witnessed by many of its neighboring states, until the 1960s; even then, urbanization in Idaho was relatively sluggish. Between the years of 1960 and 1970, Idaho's population increased from 667,191 to 712,656, or by 6.8 percent. It wasn't until 1970 over fifty percent of Idaho's population lived in urban areas of the state.

Despite this demographic change, however, nearly eighty-seven percent of motor vehicle fatalities in Idaho still occurred in rural areas. Governor Smylie, legislators, and the leadership of the Idaho State Police recognized if the Idaho State Police was going to continue its successful education and enforcement campaigns, it would need more officers. In 1960, 384,647 Idahoans registered their vehicles, and the state issued over 389,000 driver's licenses. These numbers were a large part of the formula used to determine the manpower needs of the Idaho State Police, and in July of 1961, legislators authorized the addition of twenty-nine officers.

Nineteen men were hired to the port-of-entry program and were the first to graduate from the newly-created State Police Academy. The ten men advanced to patrol duties were selected from port-of-entry personnel.

Lieutenant Harold Barnes, retired, ISP 445, was among the nineteen men hired to the port-of-entry program, and was sent to King Hill, Idaho. "There were six officers at the King Hill Port and all but one of them was promoted to patrol," Barnes said. "The ports were considered an excellent training ground for new officers, and everyone hired by the state police during that time started out in the ports."

Barnes said if an officer was lucky, he would be promoted to a patrol car within two years. However, it was common for many officers to serve two years in a fixed port, and then two more years in a roving port. "I spent five years at the King Hill Port before going to a roving port where I spent two more years. That was pretty common."

Barnes said the training officers received through the ports-of-entry system was, "invaluable," adding, "In those days things were completely different for officers because we just did not have the technology available today. For example, the state police communication system wasn't always as good as it was portrayed to be."

> We had the wind-up radios back then, so it always took a little time to wind it up enough to talk. Sometimes to get a return on a vehicle, we had to wait several hours for it to come back to us. I remember one night me and another officer were on our way to teach a first-aid class when we spotted a car weaving all over the highway. We stopped the car but we didn't have anything to hold the driver on. When the return on the car finally came back, we realized it was stolen out of California. If we'd had the communication then that we have today, we would have arrested the driver then.

Corporal Cole Watkins, retired, ISP 480, was also hired in 1961 and was sent to Strevell Port-of-Entry south of Malta, Idaho. "There were five officers at Strevell when I started there and the nearest phone was twenty-six miles away," Watkins said. "We handled all of the dispatch and Radio traffic between Idaho and Box Elder County, Utah. We did have some interesting communication problems, but I think for the most part Idaho's communication system was top grade."

Upgrading and perfecting the communication system wasn't the only item on Perkins' agenda for creating, "…an efficient, up-to-date organization." He also wanted his men to take an active part in determining the growth and management of the Idaho State Police. In May of 1961, Governor Smylie signed Executive Order 3-1961, which put into effect the Idaho State Police Operations Manual. The manual was prepared by J. R. and Eileen MacDonald, in conjunction with Idaho State Police administrators and officers.

In a letter to all employees of the Idaho State Police, Governor Smylie praised current employees, and paid tribute to the past works of state police officers. But the main objective of the letter was to remind state officers the manual created was based almost entirely on their suggestions and ideas. Smylie wrote:

> In a collective sense, this is your operation manual. As a member of the Idaho State Police system, you may proudly regard it as a tribute to the years of specialized training and experience which each of you has had in protective law enforcement. The contents reflect countless suggestions and ideas generously contributed by you as a result of that training and experience. The manual is intended for your guidance and assistance in achieving and maintaining those objectives. I trust you will make liberal use of it with that intention constantly in mind. The manual is not a compilation of static rules and regulations. Its loose-leaf form will make it easy to discard promptly, all obsolete material and to insert replacements or additions as functional and statutory changes or organizational growth occur (Smylie).

The manual contained sections ranging from recruitment ideas and regulations, to civil defense, supply regulations, and special orders. Included in the manual were the height and weight requirements of prospective police officers, as well as a list of the physical fitness tests officer recruits were required to pass before any other employment examinations could be given.

> The minimum and maximum age of the applicants shall be minimum, twenty-three years of age, maximum, thirty-five years of age. Applicants must have a high school education or approved equivalent. Applicants must be a citizen of the United States and a resident of the State of Idaho for a minimum of the past twelve months. Applicants must be a minimum of 5'10" tall and have a minimum weight of 165 pounds. Each applicant must pass the physical fitness test with a minimum score of seventy percent.

The physical fitness test required recruit officers to jump a vertical distance of four feet within three tries; complete ten dip and push-ups using a parallel bar; carry a man or other object with a weight equal to, or greater than, his own weight, up and down ten steps; run an 880-yard dash in under three minutes and ten seconds, swim 100 yards; and stand on one side of a pommel horse, or suitable substitute, and grasping the pommels, vault either left or right over the horse, keeping the body over the pommels.

The manual was administered by a three-man merit board. Board members were appointed by the governor, and according to the order,

> No member of the board may be holder of an elective office at county, state or federal level, or an officer in any political organization during his service on the merit board. Also, not more than two board members shall at any time belong to the same political party.

Other changes brought about by the enactment of the manual, were the creation of two new positions, a captain-operations officer, with the duty of ensuring efficient operation of the Idaho State Police, and a sergeant port-of-entry coordinator, with the responsibility of ensuring uniform enforcement of the state's motor vehicle laws and coordinating the operations of the fixed and roving ports. Perkins said the establishment of these new positions, "...channeled many problems and related responsibilities into specialized hands for the accomplishment of state police objectives."

Perkins was considered a tough-as-nails, no-nonsense leader and was highly respected by his port-of-entry and patrol officers especially for his desire to ensure his men were well trained. In a letter to Governor Smylie, District Five Lieutenant Al Nogo praised Perkins for Perkins' determination in ensuring his men had the most up-to-date training possible.

Department of Law Enforcement Commissioner E. R. Hopper also recognized Perkins' leadership and emphasis on the importance of training during an evaluation of the Idaho State Police training program in 1961. "The training program was evaluated by the International Association of Chiefs of Police section of the National Safety Council," Hopper reported to Governor Smylie. "The evaluators found the Idaho State Police had a very strong training program."

Perkins, while always quick to recognize the hard work of his patrol officers, seized every opportunity to extol the contributions of the Criminal Identification Division and the American Legion Auxiliary Police as well. In the 1960-1962 Biennial Report to the governor, Perkins praised the twenty-two auxiliary units placed in communities around the state for contribution of over 10,000 man hours. "These men have proved most helpful in their own communities for such activities as motor patrol, directing traffic, helping with floods, and searching for lost persons."

Concerning the Criminal Investigation Division, Perkins had even more to say. "This division has the responsibility of filing fingerprints and other information involved in criminal violation." Perkins said an average of 300 criminal fingerprints and 300 rap sheets were received every month from allied law enforcement agencies. "All criminal information is filed and made available to any peace officer or agency in the state. Current wanted files on wanted persons are maintained, and a bimonthly criminal bulletin is published. Since 1958 a total of 1,650 wanted persons have been posted and circulated."

Perkins said files were maintained on all known professional criminals operating in Idaho as well as other northwest states.

> This information is disseminated by periodic bulletins. Because of our reciprocity agreements with bordering states, we have a fluid exchange of criminal information including information on persons who have served time in state penitentiaries (Perkins).

By 1961, the investigations division had over 18,000 fingerprint cards, 18,000 rap sheets, and 50,000 name and alias-name cards on file. The effectiveness of these files was proven in June of 1962, when based on information received and disseminated by the Criminal Investigation

Division two Tucson, Arizona men were arrested and turned over to the FBI for transporting a stolen vehicle across state lines. The two nineteen year-olds were arrested by Patrolman Larry Plott, Twin Falls City Officer Harold Jensen, and Twin Falls County Deputy Sheriff Clarence Yingst. The two men were riding a blue Triumph motorcycle that had been reported stolen from Tucson on June 7.

Perkins said the section also maintained a photo laboratory for preparing crime scene and vehicle accident photos. The accident photos were often used by patrol officers for officer training purposes, and for school safety talks. The Idaho State Police had accumulated twenty-three years of experience in making Idaho roads safer, and Perkins was quick to remind his men although many of the photographs were, "...often horrific by nature, they make the kind of impression necessary to remind motorists of the importance of motor vehicle safety."

With the 1962 completion of US12, a cross-state, twisting route that parallels the Clearwater and Lochsa rivers in northern Idaho, motor vehicle fatality rates were once again increased sharply. The route became a major conduit for lumber and grain shipping, and a favorite drive for tourists. It wasn't long before the mix of commercial and tourist traffic began resulting in catastrophic accidents. Governor Smylie ordered the Idaho State Police to increase its enforcement along US12, and "...step up its program for educating motorists and ensuring safety to those traveling Idaho's newest highway."

For the leadership of the Idaho State Police, enforcing Governor Smylie's order was not open to debate, despite the fact it was hardly practical. The leadership of Idaho was not inclined to authorize the significantly more patrol officers the Idaho State Police would need to patrol US12, and the state police was already taxed to the limit fulfilling its other obligations.

In a report to Governor Smylie, Perkins and Hopper pointed out the state police spent an average of 670 hours per month in assisting other state departments.

"For example, an average of forty-five hours each month is spent making contacts for the Idaho Public Utilities Commission," Perkins stated. "Brand inspections average thirty-seven hours a month, the Department of Aeronautics requires an average of forty-five state police hours a month, while forty hours a month is spent on search and rescue missions. We also average fifteen hours a month on road checks for the Idaho Fish and Game."

The undeniable need for more state police officers was reinforced on March 3, 1962, when the Idaho State Police lost Corporal Benjamin T.

Newman. Newman, who was in effect working a double shift because of a deadly snowstorm, suffered a fatal heart attack after assisting in pushing a motorist's car out of a large snow drift.

C. B. Roberts was a colleague and close friend of Corporal Newman's. "He was a cop's, cop, a man's man, and a friend of anyone in need," Roberts said.

Newman had worked several hours helping motorists on State Highway 33, between Newdale and Tetonia, Idaho during a severe winter storm. After assisting with a stalled bus full of children, Newman was able to get a couple of hours of rest before being called out again as the storm worsened.

> He came across a stranded couple and helped them get out of a snow drift. As he was returning to his patrol vehicle, the motorist he had helped said he slumped against the front of the patrol car, and complained of massive chest pains. He coached the motorist on how to use the radio to call dispatch, and then he asked the guy to drive him to the hospital.

Newman left behind a wife and four sons. Over 1,000 people attended his funeral, including numerous police officers and state patrolmen from Idaho, Montana, and Wyoming.

On March 15, 1962, the Idaho State Police found itself facing the loss of another seasoned officer through as Perkin's described it, "... an extremely embarrassing situation for the state and the Idaho State Police." Marvin Olsen, the McCammon Port-of-Entry Supervisor, stole $6,036 and left town with his wife, four small children, and the family dog. Olsen had been employed with the Idaho State Police for seven years. A multi-state search ended with Olsen's arrest near Redding, California. Olsen pleaded guilty to the embezzlement charge for the $6,036, but Assistant Attorney General William Defenbach uncovered evidence that during his service at the McCammon port, Olsen had embezzled over $15,000. Defenbach successfully prosecuted Olsen on the charge.

With accidents again on the rise, Perkins requested fifteen more men be added to the ranks of the Idaho State Police in 1963, his request was denied. In a letter to Governor Smylie, Perkins said his request was not, "overblown," adding, "The truth is, if I didn't need fifteen more officers, I wouldn't be asking for them." The denial for more officers didn't stop Perkins or his patrolmen from finding new and innovative ways to enforce traffic laws. In 1962, the Idaho State Police began using mock patrol cars. The mock cars were painted black with the distinctive white vertical stripes, and included a fake officer, sometimes made of wood or cardboard and painted to look like a patrolman. The fake officer was propped in the driver's seat. The American Legion Auxiliary Police increased from twenty-two units to twenty-four, which provided further assistance to state officers.

In 1963, the Criminal Investigation Division also expanded its services by adding a "modis operandi" file. These files compiled specific details of various types of crimes, which enabled law enforcement to pinpoint the identification of perpetrators known to commit a certain crime. "Representatives of the bureau keep abreast of current wanted persons and the identification of professional criminals by attending crime conferences in Idaho and bordering states," Hopper stated in a yearly report to Governor Smylie.

Hopper added that files kept by the investigation division had grown to include criminal histories, criminal fingerprints, mug shots, sex offenders, narcotic offenders, burglars, car thieves, professional criminal offenders, and wanted persons. "The division upon request aids local law enforcement agencies with criminal investigations throughout the state, and conducts polygraphs, narcotic investigations, and photography services when requested."

In 1963 the state also began a forensic services unit, which added yet another enforcement tool to state patrolmen. The unit was assigned to the Division of Laboratories in the Department of Health. The Idaho State Police now had access to an analytical unit for the analysis of blood and breath alcohol levels.

Perkins continued to expand the state police training program, and in late 1963 gave his training officer the additional duty of, "...designing a selective enforcement program by initiating the necessary forms, plans, and controls on which such a program could be based, and of supervising the program." Selective enforcement was a concept designed to target the most egregious drivers, as opposed to every driver committing a traffic infraction. "It's impractical and cost prohibitive to ticket every driver we spot committing an infraction," Perkins said. "By training our officers in selective enforcement, we are seeking aggressive drivers such as those following too closely behind other vehicles and those who drive with excessive speed." Perkins made it clear selective enforcement was not intended to, "...ignore anyone who may be breaking the law," but was instead intended to give his patrol officers latitude in using their own judgment.

Perkins added although there was no recruit training academy held in 1963, training was given in each of the districts emphasizing pursuit and defensive driving. An additional course was taught in crowd and riot control. The need for this training was credited by Hopper and Perkins following the "…troubles encountered during the Diamond Cup races in Coeur d' Alene."

The Diamond Cup races had been held in Coeur d' Alene since 1958, and were a popular event that brought several thousand spectators to the area. From 1961 through 1963, the event garnered an unfortunate reputation for unruly behavior and rioting. In 1963, what some consider the worst year, the two-day Diamond Cup races were held the last weekend of July. On the evening of the first night of the race, a crowd gathered on Sherman Street and police were caught unprepared by the boisterous crowd. Several arrests were made and the police were forced to use fire hoses and tear gas to bring the crowd under control.

Corporal Harvey Riffle, retired, ISP 503, said the Idaho State Police assisted the city during the races mostly with screening traffic and traffic patrol. "The crowd could get pretty unruly at times," Riffle recalled. "We were set up on outlying streets where we could screen cars coming into the area. I remember a couple of instances where I told groups they could not enter the area because they were pretty obviously looking for trouble." Riffle said every year there were several individuals arrested for drunkenness, disorderly conduct, disturbing the peace, and other offenses, but most of the trouble was on Sherman Street and was handled by the Coeur d' Alene Police Department.

Sergeant Harold Lee, retired, ISP 403, said the Diamond Cup races were, "…a huge headache for the Coeur d' Alene Police Department and assisting law enforcement agencies."

> One year Lieutenant McGinnis and I were assigned to patrolling Sherman Street on foot. The Idaho State Police had purchased helmets from Fairchild Air Force Base. The helmets were painted white and they really stood out. We had people throwing rocks and bricks and anything else they could think of at us. One time someone threw a rock, more like a boulder, at us and it hit the brick wall we were standing by with enough force to break off part of the wall. If we hadn't been wearing the helmets, I know we would have been badly hurt or even killed.

Lee said a huge part of the problem was the traffic pattern in Coeur d' Alene wasn't designed for the massive influx of traffic, and severely overtaxed the capabilities of local law enforcement.

> I know of a couple of law enforcement officers who were seriously injured, but there were a lot of other people injured too. The police department was trying to break up a free-for-all between Third and Fifth streets—I don't recall what year it was—and they fired a tear-gas grenade. The grenade ricocheted off the curb and hit a fellow in the groin. He was very seriously injured.

Despite its rough beginning in 1962, by the end of the year the Idaho State Police had plenty of good news to report. Its enforcement campaign on US12 had curbed the number of fatality accidents, patrol officers across the state logged hundreds of hours in safety presentations, and state police pistol shooting teams were making an excellent name for themselves. Retired Idaho P.O.S.T. Director, Larry Plott served as a state patrol officer from 1960 to 1969, and was a member of the District 4 shooting team.

> There were a lot of good shooters in the state police but District 4 definitely had the dominant team. We participated in shoots all over the state and in other states. Many of us were instructed by Lieutenant M. J. Bays, he was the best shooter in the state. One of the reasons the District 4 team practiced as hard as we did, was because all of us wanted to beat him. Bays was also an excellent leader. He took excellent care of his men and always gave us the support we needed to be successful.

In 1962, a team composed of eight shooters representing the Idaho State Police from Districts One, Two, Three, and Four, won the State Outdoor Championship pistol shoot in Idaho City. In 1963, the District 4 team continued to dominate, taking first place in several meets. One contest in which District 4 took first place team honors and several individual honors, was the National Reactor Testing Station Invitational Combat Pistol Match held at the reactor site near Idaho Falls. The team earned 2,235 points out of a possible 2,400. The members of the team were Larry Plott, James Gerke, Robert Brown, Marvin Snyder, and John Brewer.

Over 100 law enforcement officers from throughout the state participated in the tournament, which required contestants to shoot .38 or larger caliber revolvers under simulated combat conditions, and prove their marksmanship using both the right and left hands from different shooting positions. "The purpose of many of these meets was to help increase the marksmanship of all Idaho law enforcement officers," Plott said.

As 1963 drew to a close, Perkins continued to lobby for more training and more officers. In the area of reducing traffic deaths, the Idaho State Police and allied law enforcement were able to report sixty-five fewer automobile fatalities in 1963 than in 1962. Unfortunately, with 207 fatalities reported on Idaho's roadways, 1963 would mark the last year for over four decades the death toll on Idaho's roads would be so low.

8 ★ Training and Tactics

You must never be fearful about what you are doing, when it's right.
Rosa Parks

Harvey Riffle joined the Idaho State Police in 1959.

I left the Navy in 1955 and thought about going to college, but I didn't have any money. When I was told the Idaho State Police was hiring, it just rang a bell with me. I'd seen state officers around and they were always an organized, professional group, which is a reflection of good training, and a reflection of an organization with good values. When I was hired and went through training, I felt like I had graduated into an organization where the badge meant we knew how to do our job, but more importantly, it meant we understood humility and service.

Across the state, the professional reputation of the state police was jealously guarded. Riffle said because officers worked alone the majority of the time, they had to rely not only on their wits, but the belief that the majority of Idaho's citizens had a high regard for state police officers.

I don't know that most people really *liked* us, but they did have a high level of respect for our professional integrity. We spent the majority of our time working alone. There might be other patrolmen on duty, but because our patrol districts covered such a large area, one of us might be on the extreme north end of the district, while the other one was on the southern border of the district.

Riffle said patrolmen received excellent training on how to approach different situations and what wasn't covered in training was often learned from more experienced officers.

> We learned very quickly to use our mouths instead of our badges when dealing with the public. There were times when we had to be quite firm but most people believed we were also fair. I learned early on that if I treated people with respect, they generally treated me with respect.

Unfortunately, as many patrol officers discovered, the youth in the 1960s didn't always have the same respect for authority as the previous generation. By 1964, the Vietnam War had escalated and while there were a large number of the 'Baby Boomer' generation who felt serving in Vietnam was their patriotic duty, there were just as many young Americans who found themselves faced with a series of unpopular choices – join the military voluntarily, be drafted into military service, or dodge the draft.

Corporal Jack Brumbaugh, retired, ISP 431, recalls there were a few hippie communes in northern Idaho, and occasionally state troopers would be called in to assist in arresting a draft dodger. "We never really had any problems, but you never knew what you were walking into. Sometimes it was tense."

Larry Plott recalled an arrest he made of a draft dodger sought by the FBI. Following a six-week search, the fugitive, Thomas Weisser, was located in the Triumph Mine commune near Hailey. Weisser had been staying with his wife at the settlement of around forty 'hippies' who rented buildings at an old mine site owned by the Triumph Mine Company. Plott said Weisser was unarmed and didn't resist arrest.

Although there were no major cases of anti-war protests or rioting in Idaho throughout the 1960s, state police and other law enforcement agencies had plenty of reasons to amp-up their training in riot control. Along with the anti-war movement that was sweeping the nation, more and more youth were aggressively voicing their opinion on race relations by forming civil-rights organizations. The status quo of American culture was under attack. America's youth made it clear they were willing and able to challenge ideals they didn't agree with.

Brumbaugh said it was during the 1960s, that monikers to describe law enforcement officers – most of them in a derogatory way – became popular. Pigs, State Bull, Smokey, Fuzzies, Bacon, Bear, and The Fuzz, were among the more popular slang words used. A favorite saying among younger people was, "I smell bacon," when a law enforcement officer approached them.

> We never had major rioting in Idaho that I recall. We certainly had a few incidents with small groups, but nothing that escalated into the riots like many other areas of the country experienced. Idaho's colleges had different organizations that were involved in anti-war or civil-rights protests, but none of these protests ever got out of hand.

Despite the 'tinderbox' attitude many law enforcement officers across the nation experienced in their respective communities, the majority of Idaho's state patrolmen indicated their intention was to make their career with the Idaho State Police. Brumbaugh said he made the decision to become a state patrolman when he was twelve years old. "I had been roller skating and I was hitch-hiking my way home when a state patrolman picked me up. He gave me a ride home and that's when I got the bug. I knew what I wanted to do."

When Brumbaugh was old enough to test for the state police, and was subsequently hired, he recalls it didn't bother him at all that it would cost him, "...a twenty-five percent cut in pay from the job I had. Being a state patrolman was what I wanted."

The Idaho Legislature in 1964 gave career-minded state police officers another reason to look forward to retirement with a sense of security. Legislators enacted a new retirement law that added to the social security program already in effect.

Unfortunately, the boon of a retirement law didn't change the fact automobile fatalities were once again rising dramatically and every state patrol officer was on the "...bloody front lines," in Smylie's war on death.

In an effort to curb speeders and aggressive drivers, Idaho State Police Lieutenant Ervin Dunn invented a new device in 1965 to assist patrol officers. Lieutenant Dunn's invention was a speed board, which was used in conjunction with a stop watch and two fixed points on a highway. An officer could set up in an area with a pre-measured distance, position himself off of the highway, and clock the speed of cars as they traveled through the measured distance.

Harold Lee said the device was so accurate there was never an issue of the results obtained from the device being accepted in court.

> It was an excellent system, and absolutely accurate. The only complaint I could make about it is you had to have two patrol units. While one patrol unit operated the device, the other patrol unit acted as the chase car.

Information obtained from the Idaho State Police archives showed: "All an officer had to do was match the time with the distance, and the speed would be shown on the board. It was so accurate Dunn received a copyright on the system." However, before Dunn could market his invention, a new device called VASCAR (Visual Average Speed Computer and Readout) was made available through federal means.

VASCAR was a small on board computer that could be placed under the seat of a patrol car and with the aid of a photo-electric eye, could calculate time and distance automatically with the aid of two switches on the gear shift lever. VASCAR was installed in several patrol units, and was hailed as the replacement for the radar. But, not long after VASCAR was in use, Kustom Signals came out with the first moving radar, the MR-7, and VASCAR became a secondary method of clocking speeds.

Governor Smylie was replaced by Governor Don L. Samuelson in 1967, and the Idaho State Police underwent a number of changes. The merit system was abolished and state police officers went under the new State Personnel Commission, which was enacted by the legislature for all state departments. Warner Mills was appointed as Commissioner of the Department of Law Enforcement, A. E. Perkins retired as Superintendent of the Idaho State Police, and Clark Hand was appointed to replace Perkins as superintendent. However the most significant change for the Idaho State Police was the abolishment of its twelve roving ports of entry.

"When the roving ports were abolished those men were transferred to patrol duty," recalled Jack Brumbaugh. "The roving ports were an excellent training grounds for officers, and they provided a great service to Idaho, so it was a surprise." In the 1968 Biennial Report to Governor Samuelson, Mills stated:

> The twenty-four men assigned to the roving ports have been transferred to patrol duty, which increased the number of patrol

officers to eighty-nine. In December of 1967, twelve additional men were hired which made a total of 101 patrol officers. Authorization was also given to hire office personnel in each of the district offices to relieve the headquarters and patrolmen of much paper work, as well as acting as receptionists. The present strength of the Idaho State Police is 116 uniformed officers and twenty-four civilians (Mills).

Although the primary function of the state police remained traffic control, accident prevention and investigation, and ensuring proper licensing and registration of vehicles on Idaho's highways, Mills reminded Governor Samuelson the state police also had the duty of preventing and detecting crimes, enforcing all state penal and regulatory law, and providing support services to other law enforcement agencies in the state.

Because of the increasing demand for support services by other law enforcement agencies, Mills started a new Aid and Assist program in 1966. He assigned two officers who were trained and equipped for service calls, "...commonly handled by city police or county deputies..." to the program. Mills added, "Due to the volume of requests, this program was increased by an additional two officers, shortly after it was implemented."

During the second half of the 1960s decade, the United States was polarized by the Vietnam War. More and more anti-war and civil-rights protest movements were being held, and law enforcement agencies across the nation were often caught unprepared when these protests disintegrated into violent riots. Although Idaho had not experienced the rioting conditions other states, such as California, Michigan, and Illinois had seen, the potential for rioting was on the minds of every leader in Idaho law enforcement.

In 1967, the Idaho State Police Training Division, in conjunction with the Federal Bureau of Investigation, trained 224 men of the newly-formed Idaho Cooperative Riot Control Group. The men were trained to serve as part of a highly mobile crowd and riot control group, which was set up by city, county, and state police agencies, to meet any riot emergency, at any location in the state.

Seventy-two Idaho State Police officers were on the team. Although several hippie communes existed in Idaho, no major rioting ever occurred in the state and the riot control group was never used for this purpose. Brumbaugh recalls one commune near St. Maries had formed around 1967. "The people there really didn't cause any trouble, and because we have fairly harsh winters here, the commune only lasted a couple of years before those folks had enough."

In a letter to Governor Samuelson and other legislators, Commissioner Mills reported the investigations division, however, was continuing specialization of its services because of the possibility of increased threats from anti-government and other violent groups:

> The division functions as a centralized records center, where law enforcement agencies may pool information on known criminals and share this information when necessary. The investigation division is a service unit for all law enforcement agencies in the state. A monthly bulletin is published and mailed to all Idaho law enforcement agencies, as well as law enforcement in bordering states (Samuelson).

Mills said the four members of the investigation division kept abreast of, "...the modern trends in identification techniques by attending various crime conferences and identification school." Unfortunately, with over 35,000 criminal records to maintain, the investigation division was woefully understaffed. Mills recognized a need for more investigators, but legislators did not authorize additional positions.

Despite being plagued by manpower shortages, Larry Plott said the Idaho State Police managed to accomplish its mission:

> Our leadership was innovative and progressive. Clark Hand was one of the finest leaders I've ever worked for. He was very smart and he looked for ways to improve our capabilities. When he was the District 4 commander, he devised a road block system using grid coordinates, that was just extremely efficient and easy to implement. His system was instrumental in helping the Idaho State Police and local law enforcement catch a lot of criminals. It was a very sophisticated system.

As the newly appointed superintendent of the state police, another of Hand's innovative ideas was the use of unmarked cars for patrol purposes. Hand recognized motorists tended to become, "...excellent drivers, until out of site of a patrol unit."

Captain Willis Brownlee, retired, ISP 504, said the unmarked cars were effective in curbing aggressive drivers and speeders. "I had a gold 1969 Plymouth, and I think I put about 90,000 miles on that car. Using unmarked vehicles was an excellent strategy and it worked very well."

The unmarked patrol vehicles were not popular with many Idahoans. Letters to Governor Samuelson and letters to newspaper editors claimed the state police would use unmarked cars to, "…hide themselves from citizens so patrol officers could get away with enforcing laws in a manner they saw fit, instead of in the manner intended by law."

Samuelson however, believed using unmarked patrol units was an excellent way to combat Idaho's increasing fatality rate. Samuelson said objections against the use of unmarked cars, "…was just a lot of monkey business. There have been unmarked cars used in highway patrol in Colorado for years, as well as in Oregon and Washington, and there have been no incidents reported in any of these states, of patrol officers using unmarked cars to behave in a manner inconsistent with the law."

Allegations were also made that unmarked cars were sometimes used to force women driving alone off of the roadway. Samuelson responded these allegations were, "…a lot of hooey," adding:

> These cars are a safety device, the officers will be in uniform and there is no reason why there should be any problem. The Idaho State Police has controls in place to keep unauthorized persons from using similar cars. I don't think there's anything sneaky in using unmarked cars. People who are obeying the law have nothing to fear, it's just the guys who are trying to get by with something, that are going to get it (Samuelson).

Samuelson said Idaho's traffic laws were unfortunately, "…written in blood…" citing Idaho's top ranking among states with large numbers of highway fatalities, with 1,105 people killed from 1965 to 1969.

Governor Samuelson and state legislators recognized increasing highway fatalities weren't the only law enforcement concerns faced by the Idaho State Police. In August of 1968, Samuelson created a fourteen-member commission charged with developing a comprehensive statewide plan for crime control. Department of Law Enforcement Commissioner Mills, and Superintendent Hand, were among those appointed to the commission, and were tasked with providing information on, "crime trends and hot spots," throughout the state. In his executive order, Samuelson stated:

> The duty of the commission is to identify the growing incidence of crime and the threat it poses to the peace, security, and general welfare of the state and its citizens. It is apparent that planning and coordination between the state and local units of government is needed in all areas to effectively control crime. This unit will develop a comprehensive statewide plan for the improvement of law enforcement throughout the state; define, develop, and correlate programs and projects for the state and units of general local government; and establish priorities for crime prevention (Samuelson).

Among the first priorities of the commission was to solve the problem of getting information on known criminals, wanted persons, stolen vehicles, and stolen weapons or property to law enforcement across the state. In February of 1968, this problem was addressed when major Idaho law enforcement agencies were tied into the Federal Bureau of Investigations National Crime Information Center.

The first agencies to tie into the system were the Idaho State Police headquarters in Boise, and the Twin Falls County Sheriff's Office. A teletype was used by both agencies to receive information, which was then sent to other law enforcement officials throughout the state.

> The Idaho State Police has been designated as the Idaho terminal unit. It will be in operation twenty-four hours per day, seven days a week, under the direction of Owen Starr, chief radio and teletype dispatcher, and Sergeant Richard Burns, officer in charge of the Idaho State Police criminal identification system. Several tests were conducted on the system, and a reply was received within seconds after requests were sent (ISP).

The increased speed in disseminating information assisted local law enforcement agencies and the Idaho State Police to quickly coordinate various operations. In September of 1969, the *Idaho Statesman* reported three suspects were captured within a short radius of the crime scene, when Parma Police Officer John Combs was murdered by gunfire. The unique operation known as "Boise Patrol" was put into effect less than half an hour after Combs was shot. Boise Patrol was a cooperative unit that initiated all police officers in the area to be at the disposal of the police agency in need of help. The *Idaho Statesman* reported:

> Roadblocks were set up around the Parma-Notus Sand Hollow area by roving patrols answering the call. When a widow and her two daughters saw a man outside their door and notified police, enough officers arrived within minutes to surround the farm house and buildings.

Combs was struck by a shotgun blast as he approached the suspect vehicle. The suspects also shot and wounded a civilian riding with Combs before stealing Comb's patrol vehicle. Two of the suspects were arrested a short time later when they overturned the patrol car. The third suspect was apprehended the next day.

Commissioner Mills and Superintendent Hand, while recognizing the efforts and successes of Idaho's varied law enforcement agencies, also realized by the end of 1969 that if the Idaho State Police was going to continue to be effective in traffic control as well as other forms of crime prevention, it would need more officers. In cooperation with the National Safety Commission, the Idaho State Police released a study that showed, "...the Idaho State Police force is grossly inadequate in relation to traffic safety and law enforcement requirements." The report was sent to Governor Samuelson and showed:

> There are 54,798 miles of highways in Idaho with approximately 5,000 miles listed as rural state highways. This presents a prime responsibility to the state police. The length of an officer's patrol on Class One highways should not exceed thirty miles in any one direction; not more than sixty miles in any direction on Class Two highways; and not more than ninety miles on Class Three highways. With the present state trooper strength of only 101 men, there is one officer for each 6,936 Idaho residents and each trooper is responsible for roughly 4,644 vehicles, not counting trailers and motorcycles (ISP).

(This report is among the first that refers to state police officers as 'Troopers' instead of state patrolmen).

County law enforcement agencies were forced to turn more and more of their traffic responsibilities over to the state police because of their own manpower shortages. The report ended with the dire prediction that as the state's population, and popularity as a tourist attraction, grew the need for more state officers would become, "…an absolute necessity for the safety of Idaho's citizens."

In another report to Governor Samuelson, Commissioner Mills and Superintendent Hand announced the Department of Law Enforcement would continue to consolidate like functions for better management and efficiency. One such consolidation was the Criminal Investigation Division and the newly formed Investigative Division, into one division known as the Special Services Division of the Idaho State Police. "A need for this consolidation was necessary, as it made it possible to take advantage of federal monies available from the Law Enforcement Assistance Administration," Mills said.

In the 1968 Biennial Report to Governor Samuelson, Mills said the Idaho State Police was continuing to produce, "best effort" in every area of its enforcement, adding the VASCAR speed control devices and other radar units were assisting the state police in targeting, "…flagrant violators of state speed laws." However, Mills said the state police would have to significantly increase its patrol officer numbers to effect, "… complete coverage of areas where accident prevention is most needed."

Mills also pointed out the newly instituted forty hour work week for patrol officers, meant less coverage. In December of 1969, Idaho's sheriffs were forced to put more deputies on traffic patrol, which left many county departments without officers to conduct other crime investigations. In a report to Governor Samuelson following the Idaho Sheriff's Association meeting in Burley in December of 1969, Mills stated:

> Superintendent Hand told the sheriffs that troopers are working fewer hours under the forty-hour plan than before, but it's the lack of wages and salaries money in our budget that's hurting us. Our budget was adopted before the legislature approved the forty-hour work week. Because there isn't any money to pay overtime accumulated by our troopers, we have to give compensatory time for their extra hours.

In 1969, the Idaho State Police had 127 uniformed officers and twenty-one civilians, which was still far shy of the numbers recommended by the National Safety Council nearly ten years before.

In October of the same year, another massive change was put into effect. The port-of-entry system was removed from the Idaho State Police and designated as a separate and distinct unit of the Department of Law Enforcement. The complete removal of the ports-of-entry and the roving ports, took away one of the state police's most valuable training tools.

The state police continued to hold training sessions for its officers, but as Mills pointed out the training was conducted using experienced officers from other agencies, and "…our qualified field personnel from the patrol units." Mills said the training program was good but still not what it needed to be.

> Eight hour schools have been held in each of the six state police districts on search and seizure, rules of evidence, police-community relations, and police-human relations. Two management courses were held for supervisors with ten officers attending, and seventeen officers have graduated from the Peace Officer Standards and Training Academy at Idaho State University in Pocatello. Courses on case preparation and courtroom demeanor were conducted in Twin Falls.

Lieutenant Ervin Dunn, the ISP training officer said the average state patrol officer should spend at least thirty hours each year in classrooms, "…where basic and advanced police associated subjects are offered." Unfortunately such training was not always available due to funding or other issues. Dunn said the training situation desperately needed to be addressed because the state police could not afford to put "first-class rookies" in patrol cars.

> Our policy is to start additional training as soon as a man joins the Idaho State Police. Our program calls for mandatory attendance in classes that cover basic police procedures and we insist that our personnel take advantage of the special courses offered. Monthly training sessions are currently held in each district that covers accident investigation, collection and preservation of evidence, interrogation, photography, and apprehension of violators (Dunn).

Dunn said the training of state troopers on the pursuit of fleeing motorists, a problem the state police was facing more and more often, was among the necessary training elements the state was lacking in. Dunn said the best case scenario for the safety of Idaho's motorists, was to ensure the state police received the training it needed.

With the FBI teletype connecting Idaho's law enforcement to the national crime reporting center, the Criminal Investigation Division was processing a massive volume of information. Mills reported the unit processed 21,595 teletype messages of a criminal nature, 8,251 rap sheets, 4,186 fingerprint cards, and 1,849 wanted bulletins, in addition to receiving 1,345 letters requesting criminal information. Over 1,337 background investigations were conducted for prosecuting attorneys, law enforcement agencies, and various courts. Over 890 documents were sent to various departments, which contained past arrest histories, fingerprint cards, handwriting samples, and mug shots; and 37,226 pieces of information on various crimes were analyzed.

One bright spot for the Idaho State Police was the continued success of its shooting teams; as the 1960s drew to a close these teams, in particular the District 4 team, continued to dominate in competitions. The District 2 pistol team took first place at the Lewis and Clark Peace Officers Association shoot in Orofino in August of 1969, and the District 4 team won an opportunity to compete in national competition in September of 1969. The District 4 team was sent to Jackson, Mississippi. The members of the team were Larry Plott, James Finch, Robert Brown, and John Brewer.

The team received congratulations from Governor Samuelson for its seventh place finish out of twenty-nine entries at the national match. The team was also congratulated for finishing second out of fifteen entries representing state police and highway patrol units. Brown took first in the sharpshooter division and won two other matches. Brewer won second in an individual match.

In the summer of 1967, the Seventh National Boy Scouts Jamboree was held at Farragut State Park, the same area that had been a major US Naval Training Center during WWII. In 1969, the Worlds Boy Scout Jamboree was also held at Farragut, and Larry Plott was among the state police officers assigned to provide security for the thousands of Boy Scout members attending the jamboree. As the top pistol shooter in Idaho, Plott was assigned to guard the money. In an unidentified news article, it was noted Plott, "...provided protection at the jamboree bank and protected scout officials as they carried out their financial business and money exchange."

Superintendent Hand was justifiably proud of his troopers, and called them, "…among the highest caliber of law enforcement officers in the nation." In a letter to Commissioner Mills, Hand said his men were, "… tried and tested."

Throughout the 1970s, the Idaho State Police would be tried and tested in more ways than it had ever been in its entire history.

9 ★ Over 300

In any moment of decision, the best thing you can do is the right thing.

The worst thing you can do is nothing.

Theodore Roosevelt

Shortly before his death in 1935, Idaho State Patrolman Fontaine Cooper gave a safety presentation to Buhl High School students. The presentation focused on the ability of young drivers to achieve the necessary skills for driving better than their parents. Cooper warned, however, that younger drivers, "…have a tendency to show off. If the young driver would combine a greater sense of responsibility with his natural qualifications, he would be the best driver." Cooper further warned students that the recipe for death in a motor vehicle accident almost always included the ingredients of speed and inattentiveness. "In rare cases mechanical failure is the cause of an accident," he said. "But almost always the accident is caused by driver failure."

Idahoans can perhaps describe the decade of the 1970s as the Over 300 Decade. Every year from 1969 to 1974 and from 1977 to 1981, over 300 people died in motor vehicle accidents on Idaho's roadways. In 1975 and 1976, the number of deaths decreased to a still staggering 284 in 1975 and 283 in 1976. Some state police officers described this decade as the, "…70s bloodbath."

The Idaho Traffic Safety Commission sent a report to Idaho Legislators in January of 1970, stating:

> The Gem State is unquestionably one of the most dangerous states in the union to travel by motor vehicle. Idaho ranks forty-eight among the fifty states for number of state policemen for each billion miles of travel, and is low among the eleven western states in most categories relating to police manpower needs. Idaho has sixteen troopers to each 100,000 citizens. Idaho needs at minimum

seventy-seven more troopers. This dire need is evidenced by our appalling traffic death toll (ISP).

In March of 1970, the reality of Idaho's rising number of traffic deaths hit home when the Idaho State Police lost its third officer. Sergeant Walter Cox was killed when his patrol vehicle was struck by a train at a crossing in the state of Washington on Northern Idaho Road. Sergeant Cox was on routine patrol at the time, and it has never been determined why Sergeant Cox failed to see the approaching train. Harold Lee, was a close friend of Cox's:

Walt called me at home the morning he was killed, because he wanted to meet up with me at the Huetter Port-of-Entry. I was patrolling at the state-line, and as I walked into the Washington State Police office, the telephone rang. I could tell by the way the person taking the call was talking that an Idaho State Police car had been involved in an accident. I just knew it was Walt.

Lee said Cox followed the same patrol routine nearly every day, which started near the state line. Cox would then patrol through the Rathdrum area on his way to Huetter.

I was among the first officers to arrive at the scene of his crash. I grabbed his hand and he was just muttering. He stopped muttering for a minute when I told him it was me. I hope that meant he knew I was there and he wasn't alone. We'll never know why he didn't see the train, but personally I think he fell asleep. He was taken to Spokane Valley Hospital Early Trauma Center, but there wasn't anything they could do.

Many who knew Cox remembered him as a, "...good friend and excellent police officer."

Lee recalls an incident that he feels sums up the kindness of Cox's character:

He was patrolling north of Coeur d' Alene on Highway 95 by the cemetery, when he noticed a cookie box by the side of the

> road. He went over to the cookie box to remove it, and discovered a newborn boy inside of it. He rushed the baby to the hospital and later he and his wife adopted the boy. He was also an excellent husband. His first wife had a terrible illness and he took great care of her. When she died I remember he really took it hard.

By 1970, the Idaho State Police had developed into a top-notch, highly-trained law enforcement agency. Its leadership did not squander the over forty years of experience the organization had garnered in every area from traffic enforcement and crash reduction, to solving major crimes. Unfortunately, much like the 1940s when serving as a state patrol officer depended more on political affiliation than ability, the Idaho State Police once again found itself at the mercy of political intrigues. This time, however, the pressure wasn't coming from a political party, but from other Idaho law enforcement agencies.

In particular, some of the state's forty-four county sheriffs felt the Idaho State Police needed to focus its attention on traffic patrol, and leave other crimes to the elected law enforcement of each county. With the alarming increase in traffic fatalities, and the fact Idaho from 1960 to 1970 had added over 14,000 miles of roads, there was little question the primary role of the Idaho State Trooper was traffic control. However, as retired Director of Law Enforcement and Superintendent of Idaho State Police, Colonel Ed Strickfaden pointed out, "...the citizens of Idaho weren't served if the authority of the Idaho State Police ended at the borrow pit."

> From the establishment of the Bureau of Constabulary to now, the Idaho legislature defines the state police as an organization with full authority to enforce any law in Idaho. It was never the intent of the legislature to keep the Idaho State Police as strictly highway patrol.

In truth, the role of the Idaho State Police could never have been strictly traffic patrol for the simple reason Idaho's historically low numbers of police officers wouldn't allow it. Corporal Delon Jones, retired, ISP 522, said as a Burley/Rupert resident officer, "...I helped local law enforcement with all kinds of calls."

We had to work very closely together. When I started as a resident officer, the Cassia County Sheriff's Office only had two deputies, as did the Minidoka County Sheriff's Office. These were both excellent organizations and more than a few times they were my back-up or I was their back-up. My primary role was traffic enforcement, and the first year I worked (in the Burley/Rupert) area, I investigated seventeen fatality crashes. I also helped the local agencies with domestic disturbance calls, robberies, etc.

Corporal Jim Fehling, retired, ISP 502, said he also had an excellent working relationship with local law enforcement officers. "We got along well because we needed each other. The sheriff's departments (in the District One area) didn't have a lot of deputies and Idaho State Police didn't have a lot of troopers. We backed each other up and that's the kind of relationship law enforcement has to have in order to be effective."

On May 2, 1972, law enforcement entities in northern Idaho were forced to put aside whatever bad feelings they may have had for allied agencies, when one of the worst mining disasters in American history, and the worst disaster in Idaho's history struck at the Sunshine Mine eight miles southeast of Kellogg in Shoshone County.

The disaster started at about 11:30 a.m. on May 2, when a fire broke out in the mine. Eighty-one men escaped the fire on May 2, and on May 9, two more survivors were rescued, but this good news was over shadowed by the devastating information that ninety-one miners died in the mine from smoke inhalation or carbon monoxide poisoning. Fehling said the horror of the event reverberated across the United States, but for people living in Idaho's northern counties, the disaster was, "mind blowing."

Among the duties of the Idaho State Police was to escort the vehicles carrying the victims from the site. The men who perished were brought up a shaft away from where the families were so that the families wouldn't have to witness that. It was a very difficult situation because so many had perished. It took a long time to recover everyone. I felt a lot of pride for the people of the area because they really banded together.

Willis Brownlee said the disaster was a devastating blow to the area and traumatized most of the region for many years.

> We were also tasked with helping manage the public and the press. This was a tragic, tragic situation and law enforcement was tasked with ensuring the families had privacy and protection. We patrolled the area and set up a command center. We also tried to keep spectators out so the recovery people could focus on their job. For a long time, the entire community was in a terrible mourning condition and in the years following the disaster we did have an increased amount of enforcement problems in that area.

Despite the bickering about the "role" of the Idaho State Police, Superintendent Hand and Commissioner Mills continued to lobby for more troopers, citing the increased road mileage as presenting, "... additional traffic supervision problems." Hand pointed out that, "Each new mile of interstate highway is the equivalent of two miles of regular highway. Accidents are more severe due to the higher speeds of 70 miles-per-hour on the freeways."

The Idaho State Police was also, as Jack Brumbaugh put it, "... suffering some growing-pains as it went through numerous changes in the late 1960s and early 1970s."

One of those changes was unanimously disliked by every state trooper; the drastic color-scheme change of their patrol vehicles. Affectionately dubbed "skunks," the first Idaho State Police cars to bear the distinctive black and white paint job, was the 1947 Chevrolet. Until the late 1960s, every Idaho State Police patrol vehicle, with the exception of a very few undercover vehicles, was black with two white stripes extending from the point of the hood, back and down over the front fenders to the front of the rear wheels. Don Ikenberry said:

> Our black and whites were very distinctive. They really stood out and everyone recognized them as a state police patrol car. We changed to the blue and white cars, which had a blue bubble on top of them. They were awful. In the 1960s, the Idaho State Police bid for all of its cars at one time. Mileage didn't matter, so the change over from black and white to blue and white was pretty quick. Most of us didn't like the blue and whites at all.

Brumbaugh says another change the majority of troopers didn't like, occurred with the election of Governor Cecil Andrus.

> When Andrus took office in 1971, he appointed John Bender as Commissioner of Law Enforcement. Shortly after Bender was appointed, he had his title changed from Commissioner to Director. Up to this point, the Idaho State Police Superintendent was on even-par with the Commissioner of Law Enforcement. Bender had it changed so the Idaho State Police Superintendent was under the Director of Law Enforcement. That's when Colonel Hand left and it was a devastating blow to the Idaho State Police.

Brumbaugh was not the only Idaho State Police officer to believe that Bender, a former sheriff, harbored a dislike of the Idaho State Police and forced changes on the Idaho State Police in hopes of diminishing the organization.

Major Glen Schwartz, retired, ISP 567, said Bender made no effort to disguise his dislike of the Idaho State Police. "He's the one we can thank for a lot of the issues ISP had with some of Idaho's sheriffs. He tried very hard during his time as the director to turn us into a strictly traffic patrol unit."

Harold Lee said Bender's attitude was "very political" and Bender made it clear he supported many of the ideas put forth by some of Idaho's sheriffs concerning the role of the Idaho State Police.

> The Idaho Sheriff's Association wanted to put the Idaho State Police in the role of traffic enforcement only, partly because of what happened in Oregon. The Oregon State Police during that time had basically become the main investigative agency in the state of Oregon. The sheriff's association argued we were "highway patrol officers." We are in fact Idaho State Police officers. We often backed-up our local law enforcement agencies just as they often backed us up. We could do that because we had state-wide law enforcement authority.

The attitude of many troopers that Bender was intent on turning the Idaho State Police into a highway patrol unit only, seemed to be proven by the Idaho State Police Mission Statement Bender released shortly after his appointment as Director of Law Enforcement:

> The mission of the Idaho State Police is to reduce death and injuries on the highway, promote the orderly flow of traffic, and provide information and assistance to the motoring public. As a trooper with the Idaho State Police, one will have the opportunity to serve his fellow man saving lives, and a feeling of pride serving his state in an organization dedicated to service (Bender).

Bender's perceived dislike of the Idaho State Police, didn't stop Superintendent Hand or the 129 men under his command from continuing to deliver exceptional service to the citizens of Idaho or allied law enforcement agencies. Shortly after the August 1971 prison riot, in which the Idaho State Police took a lead enforcement role, Hand was quick to call his officers, "… unparalleled in their commitment to service and to law and order."

A heat wave is blamed for starting the fourth riot of the Idaho Penitentiary. The riot lasted over three hours, and two prisoners were stabbed but not killed. A fire was started that destroyed the social services building and the hospital pharmacy was looted. The only casualty of the riot was a prisoner who was killed four days after the riot. The prisoner was killed in the multi-purpose room by fellow prisoners who claimed he had been, "too friendly with the guards."

Whatever the issues between Idaho State Police Troopers and their leadership at Boise may have been in the early 1970s, there was no question the state police had the support of Governor Andrus, who often referred to the Idaho State Police as, "Idaho's premier law enforcement organization."

Andrus actively supported an increase in the number of state troopers, and promoted the addition of new programs within the state police such as the creation of a motorcycle unit, and the creation of the federally funded Alcohol Safety Action Program (ASAP), both of which began in June of 1972. The 1972 legislature also authorized an additional ten troopers, twenty communication officers, and one assistant training officer. The strength of the Idaho State Police increased from 129 commissioned officers in 1971 to 195 in 1972.

Despite this addition of officers, and the subsequent increased traffic patrol of state troopers, 1972 would prove to be the second deadliest year in Idaho's history in terms of traffic fatalities with a shocking 348 people killed on Idaho's highways. The worst year in Idaho's history was 1973, when the death toll increased by one to 349.

In May of 1972, the Idaho State Police underwent a major reorganization. The restructuring reduced the number of captains and increased the number of field sergeants. The purpose of the reorganization was to decentralize administrative functions and provide more uniformity among the six districts. This uniformity was essential to incorporating the newly formed motorcycle unit and ASAP program into the state police.

Superintendent Hand was instrumental in forming the motorcycle unit, which was dispersed in districts where heavier mountain road traffic showed a need for patrol officers to be able to get to a crash scene when roads were blocked.

> Last summer we jobbed out the area around Idaho City and McCall to one of the Boise escort services. The cycle patrols were courtesy patrols and consisted mostly of off-duty Boise officers. They were paid by the hour by Idaho State Police, and were primarily used in areas where roads were blocked by traffic jams or accidents (Hand).

Heavier traffic flow in "…Idaho's peculiar mountains" was cited as the main reason for using motorcycles. The Department of Law Enforcement planned to spend $18,000 on motorcycles equipped with radios to patrol roads that were particularly narrow or known to have difficult traffic flow because of heavy traffic. Hand said the state police used bikes, "…way back when we were just starting," but phased motorcycles out in favor of patrol cars. After trying several models of motorcycle, the Idaho State Police purchased five 1971 Harley Davidson motorcycles, and four troopers were sent to the California Highway Patrol academy in Sacramento for motorcycle training.

Willis Brownlee was one of the troopers sent to this training.

> I was sent to an elite school in California to learn motorcycle patrol. The school was held in Sacramento and was a two week course. At one time there were three of us in the Coeur d' Alene area. The motorcycle patrol wasn't always as effective as we could have been. Part of the reason for this was because the (leadership in Boise) didn't understand how best to deploy us. It was an interesting concept, but most of us in the motorcycle unit were frustrated because we were not able to do what we felt (a motorcycle unit) should do.

Willis Brownlee was among the first troopers hired to the Idaho State Police motorcycles program. Photo courtesy of the Idaho State Police.

Corporal Don Hiatt, retired, ISP 407, was also sent to train with the California Highway Patrol. He said the motorcycle program was a great idea, but logistically it created a lot of headaches.

> The number one problem with the motorcycles for me was that there was no Harley Davidson dealer in Coeur d' Alene. If I needed service on my vehicle, I had to go to Spokane. Another problem was that we had to have at least two troopers on duty. If I arrested a DUI, I had to have a trooper available to transport the person to the jail. In the Coeur d' Alene area the season for riding was also quite short, only three to four months. The positive side of the motorcycle unit was we could get to areas quickly when

> traffic was backed up by an accident or other problem, and in traffic patrol, people weren't expecting us.

The ASAP program had a great deal more success and was considered a huge boost in the Idaho State Police's constant quest for more patrol officers. The ASAP program cost the state about $182,000 which was the twenty-five percent fund required by the $1.2 million dollar federal grant. In explaining the ASAP program ASAP director L. Cotty Lowry said:

> The law enforcement officer, whether he is a member of a sheriff's department, city police, or Idaho State Police, is usually the first individual with whom the (D.W.I. or driving while intoxicated) person comes in contact. In the case of ASAP, the twenty-six man unit of the Idaho State Police was responsible for 1,124 arrests during the first year of its existence. The members of the ASAP program were recruited from different agencies and each of them received fifty-nine hours of training which emphasized procedures for identification and apprehension of the drinking driver.

Captain Dave Neal, retired, ISP 476, served one year in the ASAP program. "We had great success. Our main mission was to get drunken drivers off of the highways. We worked five weeks of nights and one week of days, which was a little tough on the family, but our success rate was phenomenal."

Before arresting a driver for driving while under the influence of alcohol, the state police first looked for recognizable symptoms of alcohol involvement. These symptoms included weaving on the roadway, driving without lights at night, failure to dim lights, driving unreasonably slow, and overshooting or disregarding traffic signals. Officers were required to, "...observe the driver's action and behavior, write down all observations, and get witness report in writing where applicable."

The ASAP program quickly gained acceptance in the Idaho State Police, and was endorsed by the Idaho Traffic Safety Council, as well as allied law enforcement agencies across the state. The program even received the endorsement of movie star, Tige Andrews. Andrews was an actor who played the role of police captain Adam Greer on the ABC-TV network program, "Mod Squad." Andrews visited cities in southeastern and southwestern Idaho to publicize the risks of drinking and driving, and the steps being taken by the ASAP program to curb drinking and driving.

Hazmat/CVS Specialist Steve Cazier, retired, ISP 559, said the success of the program far exceeded what the federal grant expected from those hired into the program. Cazier was stationed in District 4 as a member of ASAP:

> The people in charge of the grant figured we would average twenty-five to thirty-five DUIs per officer each year, but from the time the program started in August of 1972 just to December of 1972, we far exceeded those numbers. The next year of the program, it was expected we would each get between sixty and eighty DUIs; which all of us again far exceeded. The program considered anyone who arrested thirty or so DUIs in a year as successful. The average for all of us was 100-120 each year and there were many officers who exceeded that number. I was with the program for over five years and those averages stayed about the same.

Corporal Don Furniss, retired, ISP 406, started with the ASAP program in District 5, and served on the program for three years. Furniss agreed the program was a great success, adding the training of ASAP officers was excellent:

> One of the reasons the program was so successful is because we had excellent training and were taught the keys of identifying a drinking driver. However the program involved more than just making arrests. I gave safety talks on the effects of alcohol and we did press conferences about the program and some of the equipment we used.

Sergeant Fred Becker, retired, ISP 425, served four years with the ASAP program in District 3.

> The program worked very well. DUIs were just getting out of control across the state which made the program even more

> immediate. At the time I worked ASAP, drinking and driving was considered more of a social problem instead of a criminal act. The ASAP program helped change that attitude across the state.

The May, 1973 *ASAP Lifesaver* bulletin reported on a press conference and demonstration held for media in the Treasure Valley. The purpose of the demonstration was to acquaint media representatives with the general goals and procedures of the ASAP program. Several media volunteers were first given a series of tests to measure their reaction time, distance perception, and peripheral vision.

The participants were then allowed to drink as much alcohol as they wished in a one hour time period. After their hour of drinking, participants were given a B.A.C. or breath-alcohol content test with the SM-7 alco-analyzer. Following these tests, participants again went through the time reaction and visual tests. According to the report, "Participants showed a consistent reduction in reaction time and visual accuracy as their B.A.C. level reached .08 or above." By the end of 1972, all Idaho State Police Troopers had received training on the SM-7, and every officer completed a one-week school on identifying drunk drivers.

1972 ended for the Idaho State Police with the announcement of another program. The Fatality Accident Reduction Program (FARE) was created in response to Idaho's 7.08 percent increase in fatality crashes in 1972 over 1971. The FARE program received $65,000 from the Traffic Safety Commission, and a study was conducted to determine statistics on when and where the majority of fatality crashes occurred. The study determined the summer months were the deadliest time of year, and Friday, Saturday, and Sunday were the most dangerous days of the year. The most common times for fatality crashes were between 3 p.m. and 6 p.m., and the most dangerous roads in Idaho were determined to be in districts one, three, and six.

> It's obvious patrol officers will have to be concentrated in these areas to be effective. This amounts to the creation of a type of saturation patrol, which has proven effective in other states. These patrolmen will have to concentrate on the violations which are causing the largest amount of fatal accidents. These violations in order of severity are: speed, failure to yield the right-of-way, driving left of center, and DWI (ISP).

The one glitch in the FARE program to many troopers was that it required off duty trooper volunteers.

> The budget for the program will allow one meal per nine-hour shift and only half of the men can be housed in motels and be granted the per-diem allowance when out of their assigned areas. This means that some of the men will have to return home after a shift to keep the expenses down. The object of this requirement is to get more money to the men by spending less on expenses. Volunteer troopers and supervisors will travel to their assigned FARE areas on their own time and will not be reimbursed for travel time. What does this program mean to the men involved? They will sell off a few vacation days but get a little extra jingle in their pockets (ISP).

Although the assigned FARE patrol routes showed a forty-five percent reduction in fatal accidents, and a twenty-one percent reduction in total accidents, the program's funds were not renewed for a second year. Clark Hand stated what the FARE program mostly did, "…was show the Idaho State Police force is drastically undermanned compared to the number of accidents occurring in the State of Idaho…"

10 ✯ Objecting to Management

The Idaho State Police has a history of stepping above the problem and finding a solution

Captain Wayne Longo (retired)

The Idaho State Police had its fair share of problems to solve by the end of 1972, not the least of which was traffic fatalities, a nationwide increase of anti-law enforcement sentiment, and drugs. In March of 1972, in an effort to curb the escalating drug problem in Idaho, the legislature transferred drug enforcement from the board of pharmacy to the attorney general's office, and hired twenty-five new narcotic agents in an effort to curb the drastically increased availability of marijuana, LSD, and heroin in Idaho's communities.

The agents were often referred to as "Parks Narcs" because they were under the supervision of Idaho Attorney General Anthony Parks. The Idaho Bureau of Narcotics and Drug Enforcement was backed by federal funds. Unfortunately, within three years of it existence, the bureau found itself facing several criminal charges which eventually culminated in the dismissal of ten of its thirty-four members, including Bureau Chief Robert King. An independent audit into the charges ended with criminal indictments against some agents, including allegations of armed robbery, kidnapping, assault, arson, perjury, and misuse of public funds. As the controversy concerning the bureau escalated, Parks ordered another independent audit which reached the conclusion that the bureau suffered from, "…a severe lack of experienced supervisors…" by 1975, the Bureau of Narcotics was transferred to the Department of Law Enforcement.

Although the Bureau of Narcotics was not part of the Idaho State Police, this move provided an opportunity for shared training among commissioned state law enforcement officers.

The bureau's goals and objectives were:

> With the assistance of all state enforcement agencies, attempt to materially reduce the drug abuse problem in Idaho. Its primary goal is the detection, arrest, conviction, and imprisonment of all major illicit drug dealers operating within the state. The main objectives are to eradicate the heroin sources and reduce the availability of other controlled drugs and to train and up-grade the skills of all state enforcement officers through continued emphasis on training courses (ISP).

In some of the Idaho State Police districts officers with the Bureau of Narcotics and troopers with the Idaho State Police maintained a "... reasonable working relationship..." in other districts, there was little cooperation, and the feeling of acrimony between the Idaho State Police and the Bureau of Narcotics in these districts lasted for decades.

In one case of cooperation, District 3 Bureau of Narcotic agents, Idaho State Police Troopers, and local law enforcement agencies, in early 1975, netted one of the largest drug busts in Idaho history. Nearly half a million dollars of narcotics was seized, with a total street value of $467,000 and consisting mostly of major controlled substances. Idaho Department of Law Enforcement Bureau of Narcotics and Drug Enforcement Chief A. R. Mason said:

> The amount of drugs involved reflects what can be done by law enforcement agencies committed to halting the illegal sale and use of narcotics. Some of the drug cases we have worked have crossed the boundaries of many state and local law enforcement agencies and we have each contributed something to making the seizures and arrests. Now part of our mission is to demonstrate to the public the problem exists and ask them to work with us to suppress the drug trade in Idaho (ISP).

Regardless of the rising drug abuse rate in Idaho, or perhaps in tandem with it, the Idaho State Police was still desperately trying to reduce traffic accidents. In 1973, the Idaho State Police spent the majority of its training time on learning how to curb the now nationwide pandemic of traffic fatalities. In 1973, 349 people died in traffic accidents in Idaho. Over 54,000 died nationwide and nearly four times that number were maimed or critically injured in traffic accidents. In one single year almost as many people died or were injured on America's roadways as the number of American service members wounded or killed in the entirety of the Vietnam War.

Harold Lee pointed out one of the biggest problems the Idaho State Police faced in the early 70s, was the inability of state patrol cars to 'keep-up' with the 'muscle cars' now available to the public.

> People, especially younger people, were driving cars with 400-horse-power engines and we were in cars with half that horse power. Here you have a new generation of kids with a different attitude than (state police officers) had previously seen, driving these big, heavy muscle cars, and they were not skilled in how road conditions could affect a car's performance. We witnessed a lot of horrific accidents in which speed was the contributing factor.

Jack Brumbaugh recalled one incident with a nineteen year-old driving a 1970 Dodge Super Bee:

> It was nighttime, and he was driving about thirty miles-per-hour when I came upon him. As I started around him he floored it and the race was on, I stayed with him to ninety miles-per-hour then turned my top light on. The race was over and I gave him a ticket. But, the kid didn't learn from this encounter, a week later he was seriously injured when he totaled his car racing a Mustang.

Corporal James Culpepper, retired, ISP 450, said as a Post Falls resident officer the worst part of fatality and major injury accidents, was delivering the news to families of the victims. "I grew up in Post Falls and it was very traumatic to deliver this news, especially to people I knew. In one case I had a boy I knew die in my arms and that's the kind of thing that stays with you the rest of your life."

Cole Watkins recalled two separate accidents in which each claimed the lives of seven people. Watkins said no matter how many fatal accidents an officer investigates, it never gets easier and every fatal crash, "…is a terrible thing. You get where you do what needs to be done and then recover as best you can from seeing that kind of carnage."

Corporal Gordon Mills, retired, ISP 489, investigated an accident near Massacre Rocks that claimed eleven lives. Mills said while this was one of the most horrific accidents he investigated, every fatality he worked, "…left its mark."

Faster cars weren't the only cause of some of Idaho's worst accidents. Wrong-way drivers on the freeway were also the cause of several fatal crashes. The Idaho Department of Highways was baffled at the inability of some motorists to see the freeways' on and off signage. In July of 1973, wrong way traffic on the freeway resulted in three deaths and the serious injury of more than a half dozen others. The Idaho State Police in 1973 issued over eighty citations, and had several arrests of people driving the wrong direction on the Interstate. The arrests were generally of drivers under the influence of alcohol.

The state government reorganization of 1974 brought about some far reaching changes in the administration of the state police. The Director of the Department of Law Enforcement became the appointing authority of the Superintendent of the Idaho State Police. This had previously been the governor's prerogative. This meant the superintendent now served at the pleasure of the director.

Kenneth DeYoung was appointed as superintendent in July of 1974. The Criminal Identification Division was separated out into another division with its own administrator, and the radio maintenance technicians became part of yet another division. The supply employees became part of the State Administrative Division.

Changes brought about by the reorganization, and the policies of Department of Law Enforcement Director John Bender, caused tremendous unrest in the state police during this period. State police captains were not replaced as they retired and promotions became non-existent. Many officers resigned, and a number of positions were left unfilled.

Among the 'Bender Policies' as some troopers referred to them, that many troopers did not like was the enactment of Management by Objectives. In a report to the governor, Bender stated:

> The MBO concept adds the extremely important step of extending to each uniformed member a measure of responsibility for his own job. We encourage and expect each individual to assume responsibility for helping to set his own goals and for determining how he will achieve them. The headquarters staff with input from all levels of the organization have defined goals and objectives that they feel are necessary for an efficient operation. Likewise, each district will determine how much they can do towards meeting the overall objectives. The first line

supervisor discusses with each trooper the overall objectives of the Idaho State Police, the district goals, and agrees on a work plan for the trooper. This work plan should include specific and realistic objectives and priorities for the individual officer (Bender).

For the majority of troopers, this equated to a feeling of 'micro-management' and did not give troopers a clear idea of what the overall objective for the agency was. Many troopers felt this system was basically the beginnings of a quota system that didn't take into account the varied tasks of a state trooper.

Brumbaugh, who served the majority of his career as a resident officer in St. Maries, said in order to be effective in his duties, he had to have latitude in his decisions and in the hours he worked.

> I investigated approximately 125 accidents a year. Accident investigation requires a great deal of time so I might spend most of one month working nothing but accidents, and most of another month working DUIs or other assisting local law enforcement. This didn't always meet with what headquarters wanted. Patrolling isn't about reaching objectives.

Corporal Larry Lehtola, retired, ISP 456, served as the Grangeville resident:

> As a resident you almost always work alone. Resident troopers have a large area to cover and it's imperative for resident troopers to have a good relationship with the sheriff's office and city police. Resident troopers live in the communities they serve, so how they patrol really has to be based on their knowledge of the community, not based on objectives.

Dave Neal described Management by Objective as a numbers game, which in reality had no objective at all.

> Basically, we were asked what we thought we could produce, and asked to pick numbers for how many DUIs we expected to get

> in a year, how many speeding tickets we expected to write, and so on. None of these numbers were based on any kind of statistic. MBO offered absolutely no clear standards, so most of us picked pretty low numbers that we knew we could easily exceed. What this system didn't answer was, how do we compare the objectives of troopers working in, say, Hailey, to troopers working in Twin Falls? Bender also didn't take into consideration training time, investigation time, etc.

For one trooper, whose wish is to remain anonymous, any 'objectives' required by Bender, did not cover every incident a state trooper might face; such as being forced to kill another police officer.

> I was the Cascade resident trooper. It was my weekend off and I got a call from the Valley County Sheriff that some of his deputies were in pursuit of McCall Chief of Police Perkins. I quickly dressed and raced to intercept Perkins who was headed for Cascade. As I got to Cascade, he went through town at about 120 miles-per-hour. He swerved in front of me as I raced to catch up, and I noticed the back window of his car disintegrate. He shot his window out and was shooting at me. He periodically shot at me as he was entering the Banks Canyon. He went into an S-curve and ended up crashing into a vehicle pulling a trailer. He jumped out of his vehicle and started shooting at the people in the vehicle, but they escaped unharmed. Other cars had stopped by now, and he was walking down the line smashing out windows and occasionally firing shots. We tried everything to get him to drop his gun but he wouldn't, so I shot him.

While there was much speculation about Chief Perkins' behavior, no definitive reason for his actions was ever determined. Those who knew him, including the trooper involved in the incident, thought of Perkins as a dedicated, professional law enforcement officer. "No one who knew him expected this," the trooper said.

This trooper remembers the incident was "…beyond traumatic. I was not given any time off or talked to about the incident. This happened on a Saturday and I was back to work on Monday." The trooper said he struggled for many years with this incident, and still occasionally has dreams about it. "The worst part was I received some anonymous threats where individuals swore to avenge Perkin's death. I didn't know if these were prank calls or if they were real. It was a very difficult time for me and my family."

Perhaps among the reasons the trooper was not given time off was that the Idaho State Police could ill-afford to lose any troopers. Along with doing its best to keep Idaho's roadways safe it was also tasked with assisting other agencies. In one instance, this assistance took thirty-five troopers to the Coeur d' Alene area to assist Bonner County authorities in what veteran troopers referred to as the "Indian Wars."

Kootenai tribal members place roadside signs warning motorists of the Kootenai Nation's intent to charge a ten cent road toll. Photo courtesy of the Idaho State Police.

In September of 1974, the Kootenai Nation of Indians sent a message to President Gerald Ford demanding the return of all their aboriginal lands or compensation for them. The tribe said if it did not receive an answer within five days, it would declare war on the United States. The tribe intended to set up roadblocks to enter Boundary County, which was part of the disputed territory, and charge cars ten cents to enter. Several Indians were at different locations on the roads requesting money, but none was collected.

Sheriff Chris Ketner requested assistance from the state police not only to police the Indians, but to ensure that non-Indians showed respect for the Indians and for law and order.

Harvey Riffle said this incident wasn't a war, but added the state police was not going to take any chances:

> The most vivid memory I have of this is all of us lining our patrol cars up and rolling into Bonners Ferry. That was a very impressive sight. We stayed in the basement of the hospital for a couple of weeks, and basically our job was to make sure people weren't stopped from traveling through Boundary County, and to let everyone know we weren't going to put up with anyone breaking the law.

Corporal Phil Broesch, retired, ISP 547, said there had been a few clashes between the Indians and non-Indians in the area, but no real bloodshed.

> The Kootenai Tribe is very small and they have dual citizenship in the United States and Canada. The 'war' was actually a spin-off of national events where a lot of tribes were demanding recognition of their culture, better housing etc. The Kootenai Tribe was poor and they decided to block roads and charge a toll. This interfered with both national and international travel through the area. Our job was to make sure there were no road blocks set up, patrol the area, and to provide support if necessary, to the Boundary County Sheriff.

Broesch said while there were no major incidents in Boundary County, the declaration of war did result in threats against law enforcement. Governor Andrus received letters threatening fire bombings and drive-by shootings of local law enforcement officers and state police. The majority of the threats did not come from the Kootenai Indians, but from other tribes across the nation.

> There was a warning that these (groups who made the threats) knew where local law enforcement officers lived and where their children went to school. I don't know how serious these threats

were, but I sent my family to stay with friends. The situation with the Kootenai Nation eventually cleared up, and the Kootenai Indians did get a lot of what they were requesting.

Broesch added there were a few arrests, and activists Abe Abraham, Chief of the Kootenai Tribe, and Amy Trice, did not encourage bloodshed in the war. "We did arrest one man who was attempting to bring weapons onto the reservation in the trunk of his car, but he was not Indian," he said.

While thirty-five troopers were working to keep the peace in the Indian War to the north, over half of the remaining troopers were sent to Twin Falls to assist with traffic and crowd control. Daredevil Evel Knievel announced on national television he would attempt to jump the Snake River canyon using a steam powered rocket. Knievel had first requested permission to jump the Grand Canyon, but was denied.

Tens of thousands of people came from around the country to witness the jump and lined both sides of the canyon from the Perrine Bridge to the jump site. Idaho State Police troopers were primarily assigned to traffic patrol, which lasted for several days. Knievel was not successful in his attempt.

In July of 1974, Kenneth DeYoung was appointed by Bender as Superintendent of the Idaho State Police. DeYoung and his men faced several new challenges, not the least of which was enforcing the extremely unpopular national 55 mile-per-hour speed limit.

President Ford, in response to growing concerns over fuel supplies, endorsed a policy enacted by President Richard Nixon in 1973, and ordered a nationwide speed limit of 55 miles-per-hour as a fuel conservation measure. The Idaho State Police had long enforced a speed limit of 70 miles-per-hour on the Interstate, and for many the 'double-nickel' became a major social as well as enforcement issue. The double-nickel speed limit stood for thirteen years, finally changing in May of 1987. For the state police, the implementation of the new speed limit meant the organization of Task Force 55.

Task Force 55 was a federally funded program and each state received federal grants and other assistance for the program. The particulars of the program expected law enforcement officers to enforce the speed limit without any allowance for the five to ten mile-per-hour over the speed limit tolerance a lot of law enforcement officers had.

Harold Lee said the double nickel speed limit was unrealistic, especially on freeways. "On long stretches between towns, the speed limit was actually detrimental. As for reducing crashes, it may have reduced the severity of a crash by a tiny degree, but not enough to make a huge difference."

Dave Neal agreed, adding the 55 mile-per-hour speed limit created a horrible time for state patrol officers.

> In those days, we had to share radars because there weren't enough for every officer, so we patrolled in what we called 'wolf packs'. Most of us hated enforcing the double-nickel because we had to keep logs for the feds. They wanted us to show numbers on traffic tickets issued between 56 and 61 miles-per-hour. The feds wanted us to forego the 10 mile-per-hour tolerance a lot of us had. Also, speeding tickets then were not an infraction they were a misdemeanor so out of state drivers had to post bond if they were ticketed. If you ticketed someone in a remote area, you had to take them into the courts. This was a very time consuming process and a lot of the time we might only have time for five or six stops. (sic)

Corporal Don Hiatt, former ISP 407, said how statistics were collected for the 55 mile-per-hour speed limit, was a large part of what made it ridiculous.

> Because this was federally funded, and the money we received was based on writing tickets in that 59-61 mile-per-hour range, we were actually encouraged to let people doing ten to fifteen miles over the speed limit go! I understood what was expected but I didn't worry about the statistics. It caused me a few hits on my ratings, but I didn't let it bother me.

Fred Becker became the TF55 supervisor in 1983.

> All of the troopers I worked with on TF55 were absolutely excellent. My favorite part of working for the Idaho State Police was getting to know the other officers and having a chance to serve with some of the best law enforcement officers in the state.

Despite the dislike of TF55, troopers did like the Idaho State Police selective enforcement program. This program allowed troopers to work the places where statistics showed most accidents were occurring. Troopers were instructed to concentrate enforcement action on the type of violations which were most frequently involved in accidents.

The Accident Investigation Program was also welcomed by troopers. This program required all traffic fatalities be investigated in sufficient detail to provide accurate information to support engineering modifications on Idaho's roadways, and to provide statistical information to agencies interested in traffic safety.

The Idaho State Police recognized keeping statistics helped determine when and where accidents and other crimes were most likely to occur. In 1975, statistics showed that of all the citations issued by the Idaho State Police, fifty percent were issued in the months of May through October. State troopers spent over 40,395 working days on the highways and during those patrols, investigated 5,329 accidents. Troopers wrote 84,182 citations and of those received 76,745 convictions.

Crime in Idaho also rose in all categories except murder in 1975, which kept troopers "...at an extremely fast pace." The largest increases in criminal offences were robbery and aggravated assault, both rose 15.8 percent over the previous year. Burglary, motor vehicle theft, forcible rape, and larceny showed increases as well.

Jack Brumbaugh said by the mid-1970s, it seemed like, "...we were in the Wild West all over again." Brumbaugh added despite the increase in criminal activities, the state police did have something to be grateful for:

> The 1970s brought on a lot better radio system with less deadspots and they were clearer. Our equipment was many times better than it had been ten years earlier. And despite the politics in Boise, it was a great time to be a trooper. We had a mission to accomplish and all of us were doing the best we could to serve the citizens of Idaho.

In December of 1975, Lieutenant Lyle Hall, the District One commander, said his district was looking forward to 1976 because it would be starting out with a full crew of men. "That's something I didn't have in 1975. We're looking forward to 1976 being a good year."

The first six months of 1976 were routine for the majority of state troopers, but a catastrophic disaster on June 5, 1976, would consume over 18,000 man-hours of state police time, and establish once and for all, the imperative need for a statewide police force capable of responding in force to ensure the safety and security of Idaho citizens.

11 ★ Teton Dam

The only source of knowledge is experience.
Albert Einstein

The failure of the Teton Dam sent over 250,000 acre feet of water on a path of massive destruction through towns, businesses, and across farmland. Photo courtesy of the Idaho State Police.

Many Americans rang in the New Year in 1976 with a sense of anticipation for better times ahead. The Vietnam War was over and despite inflation, recession, and energy woes, the country was gearing up to celebrate 200 years of "freedom and democracy," on July 4th.

Idahoans too had plenty to celebrate. The state was enjoying an economic upswing, and in the mid-70s, Boise ranked as America's sixth fastest growing city and Idaho ranked as the fastest growing state. In northern Idaho, the Lewiston Port was completed linking Idaho to the

Pacific Ocean, and in eastern Idaho, one of the state's most "...obviously useful and badly needed projects...," the Teton Dam, was completed.

For the Idaho State Police, 1976 was shaping up to be a 'typical' year. Unfortunately there were plenty of accidents to investigate, drunk drivers to be arrested, and speeding tickets to be issued.

The number of troopers available for these tasks had fallen to 188 commissioned officers; but the moral of troopers across the state was still high. "A lot of times, cars would be called in from other districts to help out with major incidents like the Indian War, or floods," said Harold Lee. "We were a pretty close knit group."

In fact, for nearly forty years, the most common reason state troopers were called to other districts was in response to floods. By 1976, the Idaho State Police had accumulated a tremendous amount of operational knowledge in dealing with large-scale catastrophes; knowledge that on June 5, 1976, would be instrumental in saving hundreds of lives when Idaho experienced its most costly disaster to date.

At 11:57 a.m., the 305 foot high Teton Dam, located forty-four miles northeast of Idaho Falls, in Madison County, abruptly failed, releasing over 250,000 acre feet of water. The failure was initiated by a large leak near the northwest abutment of the dam, about 130 feet below the crest. The dam was designed by the U.S. Bureau of Reclamation and failed as it was being filled for the first time. Harold Lee was in Boise on the morning of June 5:

> I had gone to the dispatch office and I told a dispatcher to go on home that I would cover until the next dispatcher, who was a little late coming in, got there. I received a call from a maintenance man at the Teton Dam site and he told me the dam was leaking. He said crews were on scene attempting to stop the leak, but he felt he should let law enforcement know. A few minutes later, he called me and I could tell he was frantic. He told me the dam had burst. I called Districts 5 and 6 and let them know what was happening.

Dave Neal was among the fourteen men from Districts 5 and 6 who were in the area at the time the dam failed, and participated in the early warning of residents about the impending disaster. In the May-August 1976 *Idaho Department of Law Enforcement Interceptor*, Neal provided this account of the day's events:

11:20 a.m.: Troopers Neal, Grossman, and Harper prepare to apprehend stolen vehicle suspects.

11:30 a.m.: Advisory by telephone by Sergeant Harold Lee advises troopers to be prepared to go to Rexburg area to warn residents that the Teton Dam has sprung a leak.

11:50 a.m.: Troopers are gassing vehicles at the Rigby Highway shop when a call comes through the state police radio that the Teton Dam has just burst. Troopers leave the shop on a code run north and are advised by radio they are to contact Fremont and Madison County Sheriff's offices. Trooper Anderson, already in the area, begins advising residents along State Highway 33 to evacuate their homes.

12:05 p.m.: Trooper Neal and other officers begin to advise residents north of the Sugar City area and south of the dam site that they must immediately leave their homes.

12:20 p.m.: Trooper Neal observes sightseers trying to get into the area to see the flood waters as they approach.

12:25 p.m.: Roadblocks are set up in the Twin Bridges area south of Rexburg to turn back sightseers.

12:30 p.m.: The wall of water begins to approach Sugar City and troopers are concerned about the slowness of residents preparing to leave the area because they are trying to pick up all of their belongings.

12:40 p.m.: Waters enter a portion of Sugar City and as the warning continues to be given to residents by the officers using their public address systems, a vehicle containing three individuals is swept away in a fifteen foot wave, which is not more than twenty yards in front of Trooper Driscoll's patrol car.

1:00 p.m.: Water reaches the edge of Rexburg as law enforcement officers continue a systematic block-by-block sweep, warning residents to move to high ground.

2:00 p.m.: Rexburg is completely under water and Idaho State Police troopers reach the campus of Rick's College where they begin setting up a communication base station. Fences are removed in an area east of the command post to establish a heliport for arriving and departing Idaho National Guard helicopters.

5:00 p.m.: Helicopters begin searching the area with Idaho State Police troopers on board to aid in spotting possible survivors.

7:00 p.m.: Law enforcement officers begin taking all types of small boats into the Rexburg downtown area to search for victims or survivors. Trooper Neal deployed with helicopter crews to search the area for survivors.

By midnight on June 5, darkness ended the search for victims and survivors until daylight (ISP).

The primary mission of the Idaho State Police for the next few weeks was to ensure the security of the people, and the belongings of residents and businesses, within the affected area. Its secondary mission was immediate response to emergency medical needs, and its other duties included the coordination of law enforcement communications for all law enforcement agencies and some state agencies on a twenty-four hour a day basis. Nearly every state trooper was sent to the Teton Dam disaster area during the weeks following the disaster.

Don Furniss was on patrol south of Pocatello when the dam burst:

I was told to return to the district office and be prepared to go to American Falls to warn citizens there. Fortunately, the water moved much more slowly than was anticipated, so when it was determined I wouldn't be needed in American Falls, I was sent to Rexburg. There was so much damage to the main roadways in the area I had to get to Rexburg on a series of back roads. Because I was familiar with the area, I spent most of my time on outside patrols, keeping sightseers out of the area, and responding to emergencies when requested. I believe (the response of the Idaho State Police) was the best it could be. For example, at one point Trooper Andy Anderson went door-to-door warning people even though his own home was under threat and was in fact destroyed.

Harold Barnes was at home working in his yard when he received the call of the dam's failure:

> They called all of us in and by the time I got to Rick's College, the water was in Rexburg. I was on duty for thirty-six hours before I had a chance to sleep. There was some looting at first, but we pretty well shut that down by establishing road blocks all around the area.

Steve Cazier was in Twin Falls when he was notified to respond to the disaster.

> I arrived the day after the flood. I grew up in the area and still had family there, so because I knew the area so well, I stayed for three weeks. Our main mission was to ensure there was no looting and to set up a roadblock system. The flood washed out nearly all of the roads and the entire area around Rexburg was an absolute mess. There was debris all over the place, including dead animals. One of the memories that really sticks out in my mind was seeing the damage the flood did to the railroad tracks. In one area the railroad was twisted like a corkscrew and standing on end. In another area, the railroad was standing on its side and looked like a picket fence.

Gordon Mills said troopers who responded to the disaster were housed at Rick's College and were very well taken care of by the people, many of whom had lost everything in the flood.

> I was at a static checkpoint and basically our job was to keep unauthorized people from entering the area. We did do some roving security to check on reports of vandalism and looting, but there really weren't any major issues with either of these things. Probably the most difficult part of patrolling the flood area after the first few days was the dead animals. There were so many dead cattle in the area and a lot of troopers and residents got sick from the smell.

Larry Lehtola, responded to the disaster from District 2.

> It was a terrible, terrible mess. Our job was to keep looters out and let people know if an area was safe to go into so they could get their personal property. We didn't have much of a problem with looters, but there were a lot of very dangerous areas. In some places there were houses off of their foundations and debris covered everything. Big sections of the highway were out in the middle of fields. I think the worst though, was the dead animals, especially cows, it made a lot of people sick.

The Teton Dam break caused damage in Fremont, Jefferson, Bonneville, Bingham, and Madison counties, and resulted in property damages estimated in excess of one billion dollars.

Considering the extensive damage, it was sadly noted the disaster caused the death of eleven people but authorities initially expected the number of deaths to be much, much higher. One of the main contributors to the low the loss of life was the heroism of the original warning detail that drove their patrol cars in front of the wall of water, warning residents with their public announcement systems. These troopers were Dave Neal, Arnold Young, Robert Lapier, Cliff Grossman, Donald Teeter, Harold Barnes, Michael Hare, Maurice Anderson, Russell Nugent, Joe Driscoll, Thomas Harper, Karl Ljunggren, Ronald Hoodenpyle, and Jack Anderson. There were many instances in which the fifteen-foot crest of water came within feet of the patrol cars as they spread the warning.

Following the disaster, the Madison County Commissioners commended the Idaho State Police for its work in the aftermath of the flood. Keith Walker, Commission Chairman, said without the Idaho State Police and its efforts to evacuate residents lying in the path of the flood waters and the security measures it immediately implemented, "...we cannot even imagine what the death toll would have climbed to and what security problems we might have had."

Regarding the Madison County Commission's request to Governor Andrus for state police assistance, Walker stated he and the other commissioners made a request two or three days after the flood that perimeter security measures be implemented by the state police and the request was immediately granted. "Only the men on the checkpoints know the abuse they were subjected to, but they were tremendous gentlemen in every respect," Walker said:

The state police were the ones with the loudspeakers that gave the warning to residents that the dam had given way, probably saving hundreds of lives, and they were the ones that sealed off the area and thus kept the looting to a very low level. The state police have certainly earned our love and devotion.

Governor Andrus also commended the state police for it service in the Teton Dam disaster:

I want to take this opportunity to extend the sincere thanks to Captain Calvin Bernard, Lieutenant Victor Barfuss, and all other Idaho State Police officers who, along with members of the Idaho Fish and Game Department, have served in Madison County during the Teton Dam disaster. The quick response to the request of local officers offered needed reassurance to county residents while at the same time provided critical security within the flood-ravaged area. The many hours of hard work and personal sacrifice that the 117 officers have rendered are recognized by everyone. Idaho State Police and Idaho Fish and Game officers have assisted a large segment of our state's population at a time of tragedy. On behalf of all of the citizens of Idaho, I extend congratulations for a job superbly done (Andrus).

In the weeks following the disaster, one of the most difficult tasks was identifying the ownership of livestock that survived the catastrophe. The responsibility for this job fell to Brand Board Inspectors, who accomplished the task within two weeks of the disaster. State Brand Inspector Burns Beal said about 5,300 cattle were killed by the rampaging waters. The brand board accounted for approximately 15,000 head of cattle that survived.

Beal said the most dramatic cattle losses occurred at the Meyers Feedlot just north of Sugar City. There were about 5,000 head of cattle in the lot at the time the flood waters hit. The water destroyed many of the fences in the lot, as did cattle trying to escape. Beal said curiously, many of the younger cattle survived while the mortality rate of older cattle was much higher. "The rushing wall of water in some cases carried cattle fifteen to sixteen miles and I was surprised that so many survived."

Governor Andrus and the leadership of the Idaho State Police received many letters of appreciation and commendation from individual citizens and local governments of the counties affected. The Idaho State Police had once again proven itself as a cohesive, well-trained law enforcement entity, able to accomplish its mission in the face of extreme adversity.

In 1977, Governor Andrus resigned his position as Idaho's Governor to take a position as Secretary of the Interior under President Carter. John Evans was appointed governor and replaced John Bender as Director of the Department of Law Enforcement with Kelly Pearce in May of 1977. Fourteen new troopers were hired to fill vacancies.

Governor Evans said his motivation for the firing of both Bender and DeYoung was the fact that state policemen were lobbying in the legislature against programs devised by Bender and DeYoung. Evans said this lobbying took time away from the Idaho State Police's main mission, which was patrolling Idaho's highways.

Evans appointed Bender as Drought Coordinator, and allowed DeYoung to finish his time with the Idaho State Police by "…moving him to another position in the department. DeYoung is looking at retirement down the road not too far…" Evan's added: "We are not turning anyone out to pasture so close to retirement. We have to have some compassion and this is the best scenario for everyone."

In September of 1977, Idaho State Police Troopers received news that was guaranteed to boost the morale of every officer. Pearce announced the "skunk" was coming back.

> Visibility is the primary reason we will be returning to the "skunk" stripes. We think we can bring about better compliance of the law by driving a highly-visible automobile rather than one that just kind of blends in, and frankly, that's the situation we have right now. The change is also being made for reasons of officer morale and cost. The cars we have now are light blue with white tops and doors. Our new cars will be the traditional black with two white stripes (ISP).

The change was indeed welcomed by state troopers, many of whom felt the "skunks" were an Idaho State Police trademark.

Sergeant Larry Tomlinson, retired, ISP 555, said the evolution of equipment used by the Idaho State Police was usually excellent, with the exception of the blue and white cars. "They were no good. I know everyone I worked with loved getting our black and whites back."

Brumbaugh said the return of the "skunks" was a huge sigh of relief, "We should have never changed to blue and white. It was a bad idea and a political one."

Duane Owen said the black and white cars "…separated us. They were distinctive and every one of us was so proud to have them back."

With the return of the black and whites, the Idaho State Police also considered the possibility of using airplanes to help patrol Idaho's highways. Many troopers were concentrating their patrol efforts in areas with high accident rates, which meant hundreds of miles of Idaho's roadways were sporadically patrolled.

The National Safety Council still considered Idaho one of the most "undermanned" states in terms of state police, (in the mid-70s, the council recommended Idaho needed at minimum ninety-two more officers), and the use of radar detectors and citizen band radios, or CBs, were being used effectively by motorists intent on exceeding the 55 mile-per-hour speed limit without getting caught by "Smokey the Bear."

Pearce believed one answer to the perpetual manpower problems faced by the Idaho State Police was the use of aircraft in patrolling Idaho's highways.

> This program could be effective in controlling high-speed traffic and truck traffic on selected areas of the Interstate highways. Aerial surveillance would be carried out using an unmarked plane carrying a pilot and a trooper. The plane would fly between 1000-1500 feet and the airborne patrolman would use a stopwatch to time vehicles driving between marked points on the highway. The airborne trooper can then radio to ground units when a speeding vehicle is spotted (Pearce).

Pearce said it would be difficult for motorists to spot an airborne patrol and since the aircraft would not be using radar, radar detectors would be ineffective in warning speeders. Pearce cited three reasons the air patrol was vital to the safety of Idaho's citizens. The increasing fatality rate topped the list, lack of "citizen responsibility" in adhering to the 55 mile-per-hour speed limit was second, and the ability to cover a much larger area than a patrol car was third.

The airplane program was never instituted, primarily because it was considered too costly.

Duane Owen recalls CB radios and radar detectors were among the most popular devices of both truck and automobile drivers in the 1970s, which meant Owen and other troopers had to come up with new techniques and procedures of their own to battle speeders. “I had my own CB and I often listened to the truckers and motorists talk. Because so many folks had radar detectors, I didn’t always use my radar. I used a stopwatch and hand calculator which was very effective.”

Owen said he computed the speeds of passing vehicles over a marked course on which he had previously calculated a distance and speed guide number. “I would select a road near an Interstate exchange and work out a speed formula for time and distance between two obvious markers such as large signs.”

Owen’s call sign was “Big O” and he said for the most part, truckers and motorists treated state troopers with respect on the CB.

> Truckers and sometimes cars would make ‘Smoky broadcasts’ (letting other drivers know a state trooper was in the area), but sometimes they would use the CBs to alert us of traffic hazards or drunk drivers. Travelers would also check in to ask about weather conditions or road conditions. Every once in awhile, someone would get abusive, but for the most part CB users were good to us. Several times CBs were used to get us to the scene of an emergency.

In July of 1977, the Idaho State Police celebrated another first, when Joan Pincock was hired as the first female trooper. In the July 13, 1978 issue of *The Idaho Statesman,* Pincock was quoted as saying: “It’s quite an honor and privilege to be the first female trooper hired in the state.” Pincock went on to say she planned to, “…do my best for them.” Pincock added she felt that most of the other troopers had accepted her as a trooper.

The same year, two women, Elizabeth Bilger, Pocatello, and Jodi Mogensen, Payette, were hired as weighmasters by the Department of Law Enforcement Commercial Vehicle Division, and became the first full-time, commissioned, active duty female police officers in the Department of Law Enforcement. Both women received the same training as other weighmasters.

In the 1975-1976 Annual Report to the governor, Pearce stated the Idaho State Police continued to upgrade its accident investigation program by ensuring every trooper was sufficiently trained.

> All accidents should be investigated to sufficient detail to provide accurate information required to justify engineering modifications, selective enforcement programs, and to provide statistical data to agencies interested in traffic safety. By utilization of federal grants, the Idaho State Police has maintained an in-service program of training for all personnel (ISP).

In February of 1978, the Idaho Senate approved a bill that, had it passed into law, would have seriously handicapped the Idaho State Police and other Idaho law enforcement entities in controlling speed limits on Idaho's roadways.

The senate approved a bill banning the use of radar speed control devices. The bill was sponsored by Boise Republican Senator Lyle Cobbs. Cobbs said he sponsored the bill because of two separate stories he heard about people being killed by radar when the radar waves hit pacemakers. Cobbs said there was very little known about radars and their effects on people. Senators who voted against the ban contended the radars were not a health hazard to people, but not allowing law enforcement to use radars would certainly result in safety hazards across the state.

Cobbs later requested the bill be held from going to committee until he could gather more information on the validity of the stories he had heard. Several Idaho State Police officers and other law enforcement entities were prepared to testify against the bill when it was tabled by the House Transportation Committee. The bill was never resurrected and radar continues to be used by Idaho law enforcement as the main means by which officers determine vehicle speeds.

In May of 1978, Thomas Proctor was appointed as Superintendent of the Idaho State Police. Proctor was a twenty-two year veteran of the Los Angeles Police Department, and initiated numerous changes in the Idaho State Police.

Hats were changed from the previous light blue Stetson style to the dark blue Montana peak style, which is still used today. A new uniform shoulder patch and hat badge was adopted. Both items were designed by Corporal Thomas Wilson. New stainless steel revolvers and speed loaders were issued. New leather replaced belts and holsters, and new light bars replaced the bubble style lights on top of patrol cars.

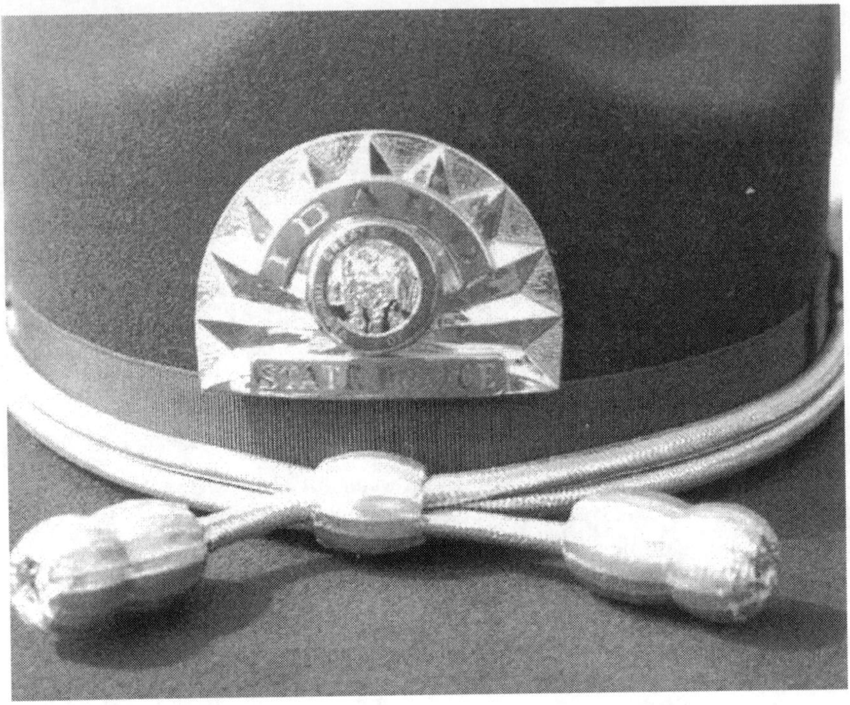

Uniform changes under Colonel Tom Proctor included changing the trooper's head cover from the light blue Stetson to the dark blue Montana Peak. Photo courtesy of the Idaho State Police.

Proctor said the state police was, "...looking for a new image, and modernizing." Some of the changes were made for reasons of officer safety. In the October 20, 1978 issue of *The Idaho Statesman,* Sergeant Arlo Larsen and Sergeant Tom Thompson modeled the old and new looks for state troopers, including the safety necktie that comes apart when it's grabbed. In the article, Proctor added the uniform change was the first the Idaho State Police had since the late 1930s.

Proctor also re-instituted a reserve program. In the late 1950s and through the mid-1960s, the American Legion Auxiliary supplemented the patrol force by assisting with traffic patrol and other functions. The program was discontinued in 1969 when active participation waned.

The reserve program recruited interested civilians to become volunteer officers. Uniforms, training, and equipment were furnished to the reservists, and a reserve procedure manual was provided to volunteers. Perhaps most importantly to the troopers under his command, Proctor hired fourteen more troopers. The manpower of the Idaho State Police had been seriously reduced by attrition and other factors during the previous two years.

While most troopers welcomed the changes brought about by the new leadership of the Idaho State Police, the trooper's primary mission, reducing fatalities on Idaho's roadways, remained an extremely difficult task. Regrettably, troopers themselves were not immune to the hazards of the highway. Corporal Rick Wright was on a traffic stop when a truck driver, who was later found guilty of driving under the influence, crashed into the rear of Wright's patrol car. Wright was thrown through the windshield and suffered a severely broken leg.

Trooper James Barber was injured after his patrol car collided with a pickup during a high speed chase.

Sergeant Ronald Kirtley, retired, ISP 409, was seriously injured when his patrol car was struck head-on by a drunk driver. Kirtley suffered severe breaks in both legs.

> I was hired in 1972 to go to Lewiston as part of the ASAP program, I was on about eighteen months when I got hit head-on by a drunk driver. I really don't remember the accident, but I spent thirty days in traction at Saint Joseph's Hospital. I remember not long after I got home, I received a pink slip in the mail telling me I had been terminated from employment with the Idaho State Police.

Kirtley said the state did not have a program in place to assist employees who were injured in line-of-duty accidents so injured troopers, without enough saved vacation or sick leave to get them through recovery, found themselves out of a job. Kirtley credits District 2 Lieutenant, Manny Newell, with helping Kirtley and his family get through the first year following the accident.

> After my accident, the Department of Law Enforcement did develop a long-term disability plan to assist troopers injured in the line of duty, but it didn't help me with my situation. About a year

after the crash I came back to the state police as a dispatcher. I did that for about two and one-half years and was then able to go back to regular patrol.

For Ronald Kirtley and his brother Sergeant Ross Kirtley, who is currently serving with the Idaho State Police Executive Protection Unit, being a state trooper has an even deeper meaning than their own dedication to service. Ross Kirtley is the third person in his family to have car number 409.

> Our father hired on as a state trooper in 1955 and when he retired my brother, Ron, took dad's car number. I took the number when my brother retired in 2003. Car 409 has belonged to a Kirtley for sixty years and I'm very proud of that. Dad left big shoes to fill and I'm very proud of my family's service.

Throughout the 1970s, several other troopers were injured in the line of duty, though none as seriously as Ron Kirtley, but in August of 1979, the Idaho State Police experienced the loss of another state trooper to a fatality crash.

Corporal Douglas Dean was killed while responding to what he thought was a fatal crash. Dean's patrol car careened off of a curve in the Warm Springs Mesa subdivision of Boise, and over a thirty-foot embankment. Dean was thirty-five years old and a native of Emmett. Dean left behind a wife and three daughters. Dave Neal said Dean's death was a 'wake-up' call for every trooper.

> When Doug was killed, I saw him in his coffin with his uniform on, and it had a huge impact on me. It really brought home the fact we (troopers) are all in this together and when an officer is lost it deeply affects every one of us. Officer safety has always been important to me and Doug's accident was another reminder of how serious law enforcement officers need to be about officer safety.

Troopers mourned the loss of their fellow officer and were once again reminded of the hazards faced by law enforcement officers; hazards that would drastically increase for every Idaho law enforcement officer in the coming decades.

12 ★ Drug Threat

Nothing makes one feel so strong, as a call for help.

Pope Paul VI

Reducing the horrific increase and severity of automobile crashes was on the top of the Department of Law Enforcement and Idaho State Police agenda throughout the 1970s. However, the threat to Idahoans in the form of illegal drug traffic grew progressively worse as the decade drew to a close.

The creation of "Parks Narcs" under the Attorney General's office proved state officials were taking the threat seriously, but the unfortunate antics of some of the original drug enforcement agents caused a setback in the state's drug enforcement capabilities.

The Bureau of Narcotics and Drug Enforcement was created and placed in the Department of Law Enforcement in 1975 and by 1977 the bureau was fully staffed. In the 1976-1977 Annual Report to the governor, Director Pearce said the newly selected agents were highly qualified and motivated for undercover activities and drug enforcement.

The first major objective of the bureau during the year was to upgrade the enforcement capabilities of local law officials through training schools. At the beginning of the year it was intended that schools would train officers in basic drug enforcement knowledge and investigative techniques so that greater effort could be maintained at low-echelon drug trafficking. Changes in the enforcement program increased local effort towards second-echelon traffickers in illicit drugs and the result was a change in the training agenda to more advanced technology in drug investigation and undercover operations (ISP).

Special Agent in Charge, and former Idaho State Police Captain Wayne Longo, (retired), was hired by the Idaho Bureau of Narcotics in 1976. "At the time Idaho didn't have many entities working narcotics. By the beginning of the 1980s, we were starting to investigate some really big cases."

Pearce said these types of cases were, "...detailed, time consuming, and difficult to conclude."

> Drug trafficking, with each succeeding year, becomes more sophisticated and difficult to infiltrate. Intelligence data on suspected suppliers and traffickers must be developed so that confidential informants can be used to the utmost. The great numbers of tourists, visitors, and transients to the state that delve into drug use and supply quantities of narcotics while in the state, increases annually. These individuals are difficult to detect and apprehend due to the short period of time in the area. This is particularly true in resort areas and the larger metropolitan cities of Idaho.

Special Agent in Charge Merrill Kelley, retired, said drugs available to users by the mid-70s were extremely potent and drug dealers were constantly coming up with exotic new ways to 'push' their exotically named goods.

> I made one of the first large purchases of marijuana in the state. It was about 100 pounds of marijuana out of Bellevue, Washington. I met the seller in Lewiston. Marijuana was the big thing when I started but within a short time, LSD became available. After that, we really started seeing a lot of different drugs: Mexican Cross Tops, Red-Devils, Rainbows, and of course one of the worst, Black Tar Heroin.

In 1975, Kelley was tasked with starting a Bureau of Narcotics region in the Twin Falls area. By 1977, Kelley and three agents were assigned to this region.

> The bureau had established units in Boise, Pocatello, and Coeur d' Alene, but it was early recognized the Twin Falls area, was becoming a hub for drug traffic. It was a big task, but we had really great people in our region. One thing a lot of people don't know is that undercover officers are the only ones who can legally participate in the commission of a felony such as buying drugs.

Taking drug traffickers off the street was the duty of the bureau's agents, but keeping them off the streets fell to Idaho's judicial system. In a report to the governor, Director Pearce expressed dismay at the judicial system's propensity to impose light sentences on drug traffickers.

> The cooperative effort with other state's narcotic agents resulted in numerous large quantity busts of traffickers. These confiscations and arrests made an impact on the supply sources to many areas of the state and reduced availability of many hard drugs and marijuana. With the high profit motive in the smuggling of drugs, greater risks are now taken by traffickers. Courts, through their handling of cases and the light sentences imposed upon conviction, do little to deter the drug traffic problem in Idaho.

Although the fatality crash numbers in Idaho were far too high for any form of celebration, Idaho State Police troopers were grateful for the success of both the Selective Enforcement Program and school safety programs, which were credited with a noticeable decrease in Idaho's high accident rate.

One of the most successful of these school safety programs was started by Corporal Rich Wills, retired, ISP 550.

> In 1975, I was giving a safety talk at the Glenns Ferry School. When I finished my presentation, I noticed a group of kids across the hall in another class room and they were really laughing and having a good time. A few minutes later a man came out of the room and he had a dummy. I asked him about his presentation and he said he used ventriloquism in his talks because everyone loves a dummy.

Wills recalled the man had some old 95 records, which he offered to Wills to help him learn to become a ventriloquist.

> Along with the records he gave me a dummy and it didn't take very long to learn ventriloquism. I started using the dummy, which I named Crash, in the younger elementary grades and the

kids just loved him. I got three other dummies which I named Otis, Dopey, and Roger. Eventually, I also got a black Crash.

Rich Wills and his dummy "Crash" give a safety presentation to elementary students. Photo courtesy of the Idaho State Police.

As the program gained in popularity, Wills began giving presentations to schools statewide.

Headquarters received 40 to 50 letters a week from kids, parents, grandparents, etc. so I ended up going off the road and was transferred to headquarters. I spent half of my career teaching with the dummies. Sometimes the program caused a few issues because the district commanders were a little territorial, but it was a very successful program.

Wills said he gave presentations to every school in Idaho at least twice and also taught the program to officers in seventeen other states.

It took eight years to do every school once! But the kids really enjoyed it. The best part of teaching this way is that a dummy can say anything and it's funny. With the dummy I was always able to shut down the class clown, and there were a lot of kids who tested that.

Wills and his dummies are, to date, the only Idaho State Police program to receive a Presidential Commendation Award.

My wife, Connie, my daughter, Kimra, and my son, Kyle, and I all traveled to Washington D. C. President Clinton and Attorney General Janet Reno presented the commendation to me and other officers from different states who were receiving commendations, on the White House lawn. It was really a neat experience.

The decrease in traffic fatalities eased the patrol burden of state troopers, but with the state's continued budgetary shortfalls, assistance requests from other law enforcement agencies increased dramatically. In an effort to provide more cohesive support to both allied agencies and state troopers, Proctor implemented the first tactical response team in the history of the Idaho State Police. The team consisted of five members and was called the Special Operations Squad (SOS).

One of the first missions the SOS participated in was the fishing dispute between the Nez Perce Tribe and Idaho Fish and Game in the Rapid River area near Riggins. The dispute centered on treaty fishing rights for Chinook salmon. In June of 1979, the U.S. Interior Department, and the Idaho Fish and Game ordered an emergency suspension of the Nez Perce Tribe's treaty fishing rights because Idaho was experiencing the smallest spring run of Chinook salmon in its history.

Over a four year period, numerous disturbances in the Rapid River area raised the potential for major conflicts. The rift was resolved when the Idaho Fish and Game lifted the fishing ban and allowed the tribe to resume its ritual fishing.

Duane Owen recalls an incident at the hatchery that highlights the issue:

We nicknamed the dispute between the Nez Perce Tribe and the Idaho Department of Fish and Game the 'Fish Wars'. The Tribe was claiming treaty fishing rights and they were spearing

> fish out of the Rapid River hatchery. Fish and Game officers were not armed in those days, but a lot of the Tribe members carried guns and knives, so there was some understandable concern on the part of the Fish and Game that if they attempted to stop the Indians, it might result in injury. I remember one incident in particular. A group of Indians were asked to leave the hatchery but refused. When I arrived, there was a shouting match going on between the Fish and Game people and the Indians. I got out of my car and levered a shell into my 12-gauge shotgun, and the Indians moved away.

Owen said this was not his preferred method of dealing with a situation.

> I think being shot at or having to shoot at someone is an ever-present thing in an officer's mind. My approach was to be a silver-tongued devil! I always figured there was someone out there who could whip me every day of the week and twice on Sunday so I always tried to treat people with respect and understanding.

Along with the SOS squad, Proctor created the Executive Protection Service, a twelve-man detail made up of Idaho State Police troopers, to provide protection and security for VIPs visiting in the state.

Corporal Arnold Young, retired ISP, 517, said prior to the formation of the unit, the governor occasionally had a trooper assigned to him for protective details, but if large scale protective services were needed, troopers were assigned by the districts.

> The Executive Protection Unit consisted of two troopers from each district and we received training in Boise from the Secret Service and the FBI. Usually not all of us were called in to provide protective services but when there was a big event like a governor's conference, we all attended.

In 1981 following the attempted kidnapping of Governor Evan's son, John Evans Jr., a permanent Executive Protection unit was formed, and a trooper was permanently assigned to the governor.

According to the May 16, 1981, *The Freelance Star,* Charles Lopez, 21, Bryan Spurgeon, 22, and Russell Piper, 19, all of Burley broke into the home of John Evans, and held him for about twenty-five minutes. Evans's wife was able to escape the home through a window and ran to a neighbor's house for assistance.

Police responded to the home and arrested Piper at the scene. Lopez and Spurgeon were arrested a few hours later. All three were charged with first degree kidnapping, first degree burglary, aggravated assault, and use of a firearm in the commission of a felony. All three received fifteen year sentences for the crime, but Piper's sentence was later reduced to one year in jail.

The creation of two new units, and the continued battle against traffic deaths, kept state troopers extremely busy, but on July 23, 1979, state police responded to another major riot at Idaho's new prison. Overcrowding, unrest and a hot summer were blamed for sparking the riot. The prisoners burned buildings and cars at the penitentiary and state police officers from across the state were called to secure the area perimeter when it appeared a massive breakout might occur. The uprising was quelled within eighteen hours, with minor prisoner injuries and no further deaths. Rioting prisoners caused nearly two million in damage to the facility.

In August of 1979, Proctor resigned his position with the Idaho State Police to join his family in Utah. Victor Barfuss was appointed colonel. Barfuss and his troopers faced a number of challenges, including more budget cutbacks. Barfuss said despite being down thirty troopers, the state police would, "...get the job done..." adding the number one priority for his men was traffic patrol.

Unfortunately, every law enforcement agency in Idaho was struggling with cutbacks and budgetary issues. Arnold Young said he became the lead investigator in a homicide that occurred in Ashton, where he was stationed as a resident officer, because the city police and sheriff's department were working other cases with limited manpower when the shooting occurred.

> I was assigned as the lead investigator when Clinton Buckland shot his mother-in-law, Laura Hatch on Main Street in Ashton. I had received the same basic homicide investigation training as everyone else when I was at P.O.S.T. but my actual experience in homicide investigation started with the Buckland case. I depended on the expertise of the sheriff and my supervisors to keep me

going in the right direction. The case took quite a long time, but we successfully prosecuted Buckland.

In an October 19, 1979, *Post Register* article, it was explained that Buckland shot his mother-in-law, who had "taken up with his father, Vern Buckland," when Vern Buckland and his ex-wife Barbara Buckland got into a fight in front of the Derby Club. Buckland claimed the shot was intended to be a warning shot to break up the fight between his mother and father, and that shooting Hatch was an accident. Buckland was found guilty of second degree murder by a five-woman, seven-man jury.

Young said while the main role of state troopers is traffic patrol, troopers are often called to assist other law enforcement departments on cases ranging from drug enforcement to homicide investigation."…It isn't often a trooper takes the lead on these investigations, though…"

Steve Cazier recalls an incident in which his investigation of a traffic accident helped solve the murder of a state police officer in California.

I was working in the Twin Falls area and there was a blizzard on US 93. I don't recall the year, but it was mid-late 1970s. I responded to an accident between a semi and a pick-up truck. When I arrived at the scene, I put one driver in the back seat of my car and the other driver in the front seat of my car to keep them warm. The driver of the pick-up was Carl Russell Carson. When I ran the plates on his pick-up, the pick-up came back stolen. I arrested him for auto theft and when I took him in to book him into jail, officers from Ventura, California were on the phone and told me Carson had killed a state policeman in Ventura.

Cazier said Carson had been in the Air Force and didn't like it, so he was headed to Montana to live, "…off the land." Carson soon realized he would not be able to survive Montana's harsh winters so he was returning to Nevada.

When I was handcuffing Carson I noticed the Army jacket he was wearing had lumps and bumps all over in it. He had knives wrapped in tape and bullets in the pockets of the coat. I also found six P and P bullet cartridges and a typical law enforcement type gun in the pick-up. When I interviewed Carson later, he admitted that he had lain in wait for an officer at the college campus in Ventura because he knew if he was going to live alone he would need another gun.

Cazier said after shooting the police officer, Carson stole the officer's weapon and patrol car and drove it to an oil field where he stole the pick-up.

In the interview Carson said he had intended to shoot me and the truck driver, but people living nearby had heard the crash and had come out of their houses to see what was going on. That scared him so he decided not to shoot us. Carson was charged with first degree murder and found guilty. I spent a few days down in California testifying at his trial.

One bright spot on the beleaguered Idaho State Police horizon in 1979 was the establishment of the federally funded Bureau of Motor Carrier Safety selection of Idaho as one of four states to show that a program of increased truck inspection would curb the spiraling truck accident rate. The program was dubbed the Idaho Motor Carrier Inspection and Weighing Demonstration Project. The program utilized both ISP and civilian inspectors.

Cole Watkins said one thing many people don't fully understand about traffic law, is that traffic laws are often created because of pressure from entities other than law enforcement, such as insurance companies, and organizations like Mothers Against Drunk Drivers.

Laws come into effect because of pressure on lawmakers, and a lot of the time that pressure comes from entities other than law enforcement. The Motor Carrier Safety Act (MCSAP), like the Alcohol Safety Action Program, was started because of catastrophic truck accidents. The federal government and insurance companies wanted the program and Idaho was one of the states chosen to pilot the program.

The success of the MCSAP pilot project in Idaho prompted Congress to formulate a federal grant-in-aid MCSAP program nationwide in 1982. Increased truck inspections for weight, height, and other safety issues soon uncovered another reason why the interstate trucking industry should come under closer scrutiny: drug trafficking.

Steve Cazier recalls one case he worked while a member of the MCSAP program, in conjunction with the Idaho Bureau of Narcotics:

> The operation was called Rubber Ducky. I was part of the MCSAP program, and I worked with narcotics agents to buy drugs from truck drivers. Our goal was to try to stop commercial vehicle transport of drugs. Basically we would go to truck stops, and undercover narcs would attempt to buy drugs from truckers. The program lasted about a year and we had several successful arrests.

By the end of the 1970s, troopers across the state were engaging in more drug related arrests than they had in previous years, and the Idaho Bureau of Narcotics, which had recovered from its shaky beginnings due to the "Parks Narcs" fiasco, was beginning to conduct more and more arrests in Idaho of both drug pushers and drug users.

Arnold Young remembers one incident in which he confiscated an estimated sixty pounds of marijuana that was growing near Ashton. Young received a call from a deer hunter who had stumbled onto the marijuana grow in Fremont County. Young recovered fifty-eight plants which had grown to over six feet tall and had been carefully planted, cultivated, and watered. Young said the plants were nearing their maturity when they were discovered and there was evidence some of the plants had been harvested.

Director Pearce recognized by the end of 1979, that budget shortages across the state would tax the traffic enforcement and crime prevention ability of all law enforcement entities. The state police was seriously undermanned with thirty of its authorized positions unfilled. Pearce requested the 1980 legislature to allow him to hire twenty-three civilian dispatchers for the state police's six district offices. Pearce said this would enable him to free twenty-three trained troopers from dispatch duties, and put them back on the highway.

> This would be about one-fourth of the additional troopers needed to bring the Idaho State Police force to the level recommended by the National Safety Council nearly ten years ago. Since the National Safety Council's study was released,

Idaho's volume of traffic, highway mileage, population, and registered vehicles have increased, so even more troopers would be required to meet acceptable standards.

The National Safety Council's study showed Idaho should have 327 troopers and twenty-seven supervisors to meet the highest police standards, or 239 troopers and twenty supervisors to meet acceptable standards. Pearce told legislators he would be happy to have the minimum acceptable force, which would mean hiring eighty-eight additional troopers and one supervisor.

> Today the authorized strength of the Idaho State Police is 210 officers, but this includes dispatchers, clerks, and troopers. There are 151 field troopers authorized but the force is currently down to 139 troopers. The way the trooper schedule works out there aren't any troopers on the road between 3 a.m. and 6 a.m. It's best if people don't foul things up and have an accident between those hours (Pearce).

The budgetary issues which forced the Idaho State Police into a manpower shortage were partly caused by the voter approved one percent lid on property taxes. The legislature adopted an Idaho State Police budget that forced the elimination of twenty-eight troopers through attrition. Colonel Barfuss said the cutbacks not only hurt the state police, but hurt every citizen in the state.

> When I first became a trooper, I was only the twentieth trooper in the state. I lived with that, and I don't like it but I can live with this. The troopers are living with it and their productivity and work is higher than ever. My hope is that the public will see what's happening on their highways and they will see the need for more troopers.

Barfuss' hope for better times ahead fell short as the decade of the 1980s began. As it had so many times in the past, the Idaho State Police faced natural disasters, increased alcohol-caused fatality accidents, and increased illegal drug related incidents.

13 ★ External and Internal Eruptions

Individual troopers can, and definitely do, make a difference.
Sergeant Harold Lee, (retired)

St. Maries was one of the hardest hit areas in Idaho with ash fallout when Mount Saint Helens erupted on May 18,1980. Photo courtesy of the Idaho State Police.

On May 18, 1980, at 8:32 a.m. Pacific Time, the deadliest and most destructive volcanic event in U.S. history struck in southwestern Washington. The eruption of Mount Saint Helens killed fifty-seven people, destroyed 250 homes, forty-seven bridges, fifteen miles of railway, and 185 miles of highway.

The elevation of Mount Saint Helens was reduced from 9,677 feet to 8,365 feet. The blast was heard hundreds of miles away and prevailing winds distributed the ash cloud hundreds of miles from the volcano. All of the states in the Rocky Mountain Region from New Mexico to British Columbia, Canada, received some of the ash fallout. In all, over 540 million tons of ash fell on an area of over 22,000 square miles.

Witnesses in northern Idaho recalled how a few hours after the blast, the sky darkened and changed from an azure blue to an ominous orange-red. As ash began to fall, covering some parts of Idaho in as much as five inches of ash, Idaho State Police troopers faced an unprecedented crisis.

Larry Tomlinson, said troopers had to deal with a lot of stranded cars and in some instances closed roads.

> It was really a mess. We had to modify the air intake on our cars, and even doing that we had to change our air filters every few hours. I went to Moscow to help with clean up and it was quite a job. I don't know how many inches of ash fell in the area but I remember in many areas the ash stripped the paint right off of cars.

Don Hiatt said he was on patrol when the volcano erupted.

> There was this huge black and gray cloud coming, and it was really eerie. Within a few minutes of seeing the cloud, ash started falling. Street lights were coming on and it wasn't very long before it got pretty dark. Coeur d' Alene ended up with a fair amount of ash, but not as much as other places. Still, we patrolled several days in dust and ash. We had to wear masks and one or two inches of ash covered everything. It was a terrible mess.

Jack Brumbaugh was a resident officer in Saint Maries, which was one of the hardest hit areas in Idaho.

> I was working the night shift and it was that afternoon that the ash really started coming down. I looked at a map of the fallout in a newspaper later, and in Idaho, in an arc from Plummer to Saint Maries is where the most ash fell. I'd heard about the volcano exploding that morning, but I never dreamed the ash would come this far.

Brumbaugh said as the ash started falling, people panicked and everyone was in a hurry to get home.

> We couldn't stop people from going where they wanted to go, and we sure couldn't slow them down. ITD had put snow plows out trying to get the stuff off of the roads but the ash was so fine it just ended up blowing all over the place. That night I dug ash out of the air cleaner in my patrol car several times but it didn't matter. The ash ruined the engine of my car and I ended up having to have the engine rebuilt.

Many northern Idaho residents struggled with car problems caused by the ash fallout. Farmers reported thousands of dollars in damage to farm equipment, and for weeks after the fallout, cars stalled on roadways because of ash clogged engines.

> That year we actually had the wettest spring we'd had in a long time, so that helped to knock the ash down some, but it took several years before it was no longer noticeable. For three or four years after the eruption, when someone felled a tree the ash would come down. A lot of the ash ended up blown into barrow pits along the highway and if a car crashed and ended up in the barrow pit, it would stir up a bunch of ash. It created a terrible mess and I sure don't ever want to go through that again.

Along with natural disasters, troopers also had to deal with 'internal eruptions.' On January 1, 1980, the Idaho State Police instituted a new Officer's Performance Evaluation that many Idaho law makers, and indeed many state troopers, felt was nothing more than a quota system.

The performance evaluation, or Officer Activity Report as it was called by the leadership of the Idaho State Police, was implemented to comply with a new state law that required specific data before a state employee could be given a merit pay increase.

Idaho State Police leaders expressed in strong terms the evaluation was nothing like a quota system, but many law makers and troopers disagreed. A Coeur d'Alene newspaper headline read: "New quota system has state policemen boiling over." An Emmett newspaper headlined: "Police quota unacceptable."

Colonel Barfuss explained the system as a way in which the 136 troopers could gain points, and merit increases to their pay, for the number of contacts they made. Barfuss said troopers did not have to issue speeding tickets to get points, but could make points giving safety talks, recovering stolen vehicles, and through motorist assists.

Each trooper was issued a form that listed the estimated point potential for the number of speeding tickets or other violations in each trooper's area. Barfuss further explained the system recognized troopers in larger urban areas would have to issue more tickets or give more safety presentations in order to obtain the same points as troopers in rural areas.

Deputy Director of Law Enforcement John Rooney said the activity report was a necessary tool in evaluating troopers because it could be used to show, "...some troopers just aren't working very hard..." Rooney claimed those troopers were the ones spreading the rumors that the new system was a quota system.

Troopers and law makers however, argued any kind of point system actually hampered a trooper's ability to judge situations and determine the ever-changing enforcement needs of their patrol area. This was especially true of resident officers.

Arnold Young was the Ashton resident for a large part of his career.

> It's very important for a resident officer to become part of their community. Ashton is fifty miles from the district office and I worked very closely with the sheriff's office and the city police. It was necessary for me to have latitude in deciding my patrol times and although my main job was traffic patrol, I was also called in quite a bit to assist local officers.

By the end of 1981, the state police was told to stop the quota system. Deputy Director Richard Hutchison of the Idaho Personnel Commission said using the quota system was, "...something that is being done but not sanctioned," adding the official state policy did not provide for ticket quotas to be part of the evaluation process. A legislative committee said the system needed to be overhauled because it was, "...affecting officer's job satisfaction."

The quota issue wasn't the worst problem state troopers faced at the dawn of the 80s decade. The state police reserve program was dropped due to liability concerns and training issues and the nation was facing a fuel crisis. Limited fuel supplies and high gasoline prices drastically changed the habits of motorists. Although essential agencies like the state police were able to get the fuel they needed, no organization was immune from the rising fuel costs.

Prices soared from under .50 cents a gallon to over $1.25. Patrol cars were downsized and stationary patrols became a new enforcement technique.

If budget shortfalls, increased highway fatality rates, and shrinking numbers of officers to enforce the law weren't enough, law enforcement officers across the nation saw a drastic increase in officer line-of-duty deaths throughout the 1970s.

The decade of the 1920s was the nation's deadliest decade with 2,318 officers lost, an average of 232 each year. The decade of the 1970s was the second deadliest with 2,295 line-of-duty deaths, an average of 229.5 deaths each year. In 1980, 206 officers died in the line-of-duty and law enforcement officers across the nation hoped for an even more extreme decrease in the coming decades of officer line-of-duty deaths. 1981 would mark the last year until 2001 that line-of duty deaths exceeded 200 officers. Sadly, Idaho added two officers to the 1981 total.

In January of 1981, Idahoans, and law enforcement officers across the state and the nation, were shocked at the news two Idaho Fish and Game officers had been murdered after confronting backcountry trapper Claude Dallas over game violations. Conley Elms and William Pogue went to Dallas' remote camp in southern Owyhee County to determine if Dallas had violated game laws. Both were gunned down and then executed by Dallas.

Rich Wills participated in the search for Dallas, and was among the officers who arrested Dallas fifteen months later.

> Initially the Fish and Game learned of Dallas' poaching activities from the owner of the 45 Ranch. The ranch owner's son, a cowboy on the ranch, had ridden by Dallas' camp and saw deer and bobcat. The bobcats and deer were taken out of season, and he reported it because the cowboy himself wanted to trap bobcat when the season opened. In hopes of getting Dallas to stop poaching and move out of the area, the cowboy told Dallas the fish and game often came into the area. Dallas said he would 'take-care' of any fish and game officers who came after him.

Wills said in fear for his own life and that of his wife the ranch hand left the area. The man also called fish and game and told them of Dallas' threat.

On January 5, 1981, Pogue and Elms went to Dallas' campsite and a short time later a friend of Dallas', Jim Stevens, showed up. Stevens had come up from Winnemucca, Nevada with groceries for Dallas. Dallas' camp was on the Owyhee River and since he wasn't at the camp, Pogue and Elms walked up the river to search for him. When they found Dallas they took his .22 caliber pistol from him, unloaded it, and gave it back to him. For whatever reason, they didn't search him, and Dallas had a .357 magnum pistol concealed.

Wills said Pogue and Elms discovered Dallas had poached bobcat and deer, and informed Dallas they were going to arrest him.

Dallas then pulled his .357 magnum pistol and shot both officers. After shooting them with his pistol, Dallas used a .22 caliber rifle and shot both of them in the head execution style. He later told officers the reason he did that was because, "it was inhumane for them to suffer."

Jim Stevens claimed he did not witness the initial shooting of the fish and game officers, but he did witness the execution with the rifle. Stevens also said he 'reluctantly' helped Dallas dispose of the bodies of the officers.

Conley Elms was a very big man. They tried to load him on a mule to take him out in the desert and bury him, but he was too heavy for them. They drug Elms down to the river and dumped his body there. They took Pogue out into the desert and buried him.

Wills said Owyhee County Sheriff Tim Nettleton and he made a pact after the shooting that they would work together and do whatever it took to find Dallas. Both had traveled to the site where Pogue and Elms were murdered.

It was a terrible thing to see. After that, Nettleton and I agreed we would be a part of bringing Dallas in. We didn't know when we would catch him, but we knew he would eventually be found and since both of us had been involved in the incident from the beginning, we wanted to follow through.

Along with assisting in the search for Dallas, Wills also had the responsibility of feeding the cattle in the remote Owyhee canyon the ranch hand had deserted.

The ranch owners were terrified Dallas would want revenge on them because they turned him into fish and game. About every two days I had to go feed the cattle. It was eerie going into that canyon by myself because we still hadn't captured Dallas and I wondered if he was somewhere out there planning to ambush me. I was able to get another officer to help me a few times.

After fifteen months, an anonymous tip finally led officers to Dallas' location.

Because Nettleton and I agreed to be there when they brought Dallas in, when we learned he was in the desert in northern Nevada we headed there. The FBI brought in a helicopter with an assault team to bring him in. My role was to take pictures for the FBI. I set up out in the desert with a deputy from Nevada. The deputy gave me a rifle and a pistol. As it turned out, the FBI SWAT team was dropped off at the wrong house so Dallas took off in his pick up. He was headed in the same direction as we were set up. As he drew closer, Dallas bailed out of the passenger side of his truck and a round caught him in the ankle. He shot at us a couple of times but he never hit anyone.

Wills said the FBI arrested Dallas, and he, Wills, was able to interview Dallas on the way back to Idaho.

Dallas went on trial and was able to convince his jury that the shooting had been in self defense. He ended up with a sentence of thirty years in prison after being convicted of two counts of voluntary manslaughter and a gun charge. In 1986, he escaped from prison in Idaho, and was on the run for almost a year. He was captured in California in 1987.

Of curious note, Dallas managed to convince a jury in his escape trial that he had to escape out of fear for his life from prison guards. "He is the only man in the history of the penal institution to be acquitted on an escape charge," Wills said.

Even decades after the incident, whether or not Dallas murdered Pogue and Elms in self-defense has had a polarizing effect on Idaho citizens. Some found the murder despicable and without any justifiable cause, while others felt Pogue in particular had overstepped his authority and behaved like a bully.

Dallas was released from prison, and there was some concern he might come after the law enforcement officers who caught him. I had a few concerns, but after awhile I just quit worrying about it. I don't know where Dallas is now. There are rumors he went back to northern Nevada.

By mid-1981, state troopers had one positive thing to celebrate. In July of 1981, the Idaho State Police was named, "…among the best dressed police units in the United States." The Idaho State Police uniform was tagged one of the best eight designs in the country out of 368 reviewed. The National Association of Uniform Manufacturers and Distributor in New York judged the uniforms. Director Pearce said the uniform conveyed an image of seriousness of purpose.

In September of 1981, Pearce resigned as director, and the department of law enforcement's public information officer, John Rooney, was appointed Director, Department of Law Enforcement. Barfuss remained as the colonel of Idaho State Police.

1981 proved to be a better year for state troopers in terms of traffic fatalities, than it had been for several years. Traffic fatalities, which had cost 331 people their lives on Idaho roadways in 1980, dropped to 293 in 1981. This would be the last time Idaho experienced so many fatalities until 2003, when the death toll again rose, to 293.

Troopers and state police leadership realized by the end of 1981 that the state's financial crunch was going to have an effect on all state employees. Faced with a near $600,000 budget shortfall, caused by lower than anticipated receipts from title fees and other registrations, Director Rooney was forced in early 1982 to lay off seventeen Department of Law Enforcement employees. Of that seventeen, fifteen were troopers. The Idaho State Police was already twelve people short due to attrition. These positions had not been filled because of a 1981 hiring freeze. Following the lay-off, the Idaho State Police had a force of 163 people, which included civilian employees, and was down twenty-three percent from its peak of 212 employees in 1972.

While the lay-off of troopers affected the morale of many state officers, most echoed the sentiment that there was still a job to do, and troopers would simply have to step up and get it done. For Steve Cazier, the lay-off opened up another opportunity.

> My wife worked for Mountain Bell, and we had to transfer to Pocatello in order for her to keep her job. The state had lain off a bunch of guys so there were no transfers available. I was asked if I wanted to take over as the District 5 dispatch supervisor. At first I didn't want the job but I took it. I was a dispatch supervisor for three years before I went back to patrol. When I first started as the supervisor, I realized there was no manual on how dispatchers were trained, so I came up with a dispatch manual.

Bob Wright said the lay-off affected every district.

> The lay-off hit the Idaho State Police pretty hard. We already didn't have the numbers we needed, so losing more troopers curtailed our abilities in many areas. It wasn't good for the state or for Idaho State Police but we continued to what we were hired to do.

Along with the lay-off, the Department of Law enforcement also lost operation control of the Idaho Ports-of Entry when the Department of Transportation convinced legislators to place the Idaho Ports-of-Entry system under the Department of Transportation. The passage of House Bill 645 set July 1 as the date for the change and 189 Department of Law Enforcement employees now answered to a new boss.

The change forced many commissioned law enforcement officers in the ports-of-entry to choose which agency they would stay with. Several troopers were forced to give up law enforcement careers when it appeared staying with the ports-of-entry was more advantageous.

In District One, already struggling with manpower shortages, troopers were stunned to learn they would be down yet another officer when Harvey Riffle was nearly killed by a speeding car. Riffle was struck by the car while working an accident scene on the bridge entering Sandpoint.

A truck hauling sheet glass had tried to cross a bridge, but the bridge girders were too low and the glass struck the girders. Riffle had nearly completed his investigation when he was struck by a car. Riffle said he recalled very little of the accident.

> I remember I was on foot and southbound on the bridge. I was going to check if it was safe to start releasing traffic. The next thing I remember was waking up in the Spokane Hospital. I had two broken legs and a pretty serious head injury. I was told I'd been unconscious for four days. I also found out later my family was told I wouldn't make it to the trauma center in Seattle, which is why I was sent to Spokane. The folks who took care of me at the scene didn't think I would make it even to Spokane. I spent three weeks in the hospital and many months after that recovering.

Phil Broesch said he had been dispatched to help Harvey with traffic control.

> When I got up there, Harvey had pretty well cleaned the area up. I went to the north end of the bridge to stop cars. I had my lights on but a speeding car come around the curve and blew past my lights. A few seconds later I saw Harvey lying on his back on the roadway. The car skidded to a halt. I called for help and got the driver out of the car. I arrested him for reckless driving, but he was never prosecuted.

Riffle was thrown over fifty feet. His gun was thrown over ninety feet. Riffle said he felt very lucky to survive his accident but with the severity of his injuries, he was uncertain if he would ever be able to return to patrol duties. As was the case with Ron Kirtley, the state had still not developed any long term disability benefits for injured officers.

> There were really no options for troopers seriously hurt in the line of duty back then. If you weren't physically able to do the job, or the state felt you weren't able to recover in a short period of time, you were out of a job. I was lucky and very grateful I had so much support from the community after the accident. I was also lucky I was able to eventually recover and go back to work.

While troopers in District One were feeling the effects from a loss of manpower, there was still a tremendous amount of work to be done and the state police leadership was working to determine how to prioritize the duties of its troopers. One mandate would not be changed, however, and that was the instant response of troopers to assist other agencies when requested.

One such request for assistance came from allied law enforcement in Coeur d' Alene, when it was reported a Greyhound bus had been hijacked.

Corporal Brad Strom, retired, ISP 510, said the incident is widely referred to as: The Great Greyhound Bus Caper.

> We got a call from the Shoshone County Sheriff's Office that an individual had jumped from the window of a Greyhound bus that was being hijacked by three armed men. The person who escaped the bus told officers at least one passenger had already been shot and killed. At that time, the District One commander was Lieutenant Skinner. Skinner confirmed with the sheriff's office that the report was legitimate. Phil Broesh and I were sent east up Fourth of July Canyon, and sure enough, we saw the bus. Everything we had been told matched with the bus's identification. By that time, every state police car in the district, along with Bureau of Narcotics agents were called out.

Strom said about twenty-five police cars got behind the bus, while Skinner placed two unmarked cars at the Post Falls exit to block the Interstate and stop the bus.

The driver of the bus noticed the two narcotics agents blocking the road, and later said because both of them had long hair and beards, he thought they were hijackers. The narcotics officers had shotguns aimed at the bus so when the driver came to a stop, he bailed out of the bus. Inside the bus one of the passengers, a man who was going home on leave from the Navy, also thought he was facing hijackers so he got in the driver's seat of the bus and proceeded to plow through the two narcotics officers cars that were blocking the Interstate.

Strom said that act of aggression quickly accelerated the incident and Skinner, in an attempt to stop the bus, shot out the back tires of the bus while other officers shot out the front tires.

At some point it was realized the hijackers might not understand they were surrounded by police, so Skinner ordered all of us to, "light-up," (turn on emergency lights), and let the hijackers know they had nowhere to run. We positioned a couple of marked cars in front of the bus and that's when the Navy man realized we were not hijackers. We ordered everyone to exit the bus with their hands-up and as people came out we were asking questions about who the hijackers were, how many people were injured etc. It was at that moment we realized the whole thing was a giant hoax. One of the clearest memories I have of the incident was when a fairly elderly lady from Great Britain stepped off the bus. She looked me right in the eye and in her very British accent informed me: "This type of thing could only happen in America."

Strom said while the incident is generally looked on in hindsight as quite funny, at the time it was anything but.

We later discovered the man who had reported the hijacking was actually an escaped mental patient. He was so convincing in his story that no one initially considered the possibility of a hoax. As funny as the story is now, though, it could have actually ended in disaster. When the shooting started to take out the bus's tires, had everyone opened up, it would have been a massacre.

Strom said the bus caper wasn't the only "crazy" case he found himself in the middle of in 1982.

> I was also called in to assist Shoshone County when some miners decided to build a catapult and shoot rocks into the town of Wallace. We got the men arrested, but they did manage to cave in the tops of a few buildings and cause some other damage in town. None of the people we arrested provided a motive for why they were shooting rocks off of the mountain, but at least no one was injured in the incident.

By the fall of 1982, manpower limitations and other issues forced the state police to do away with its motorcycle patrol program. Several of the troopers involved in the program had suffered injuries in accidents, and although the motorcycles were extremely useful in patrolling Idaho's narrow mountain roadways and the more congested roads in urban areas, weather conditions permitted their use for only a few months out of the year. With the end of summer 1982, the motorcycle patrols were discontinued and the motorcycles were sold at public auction.

In November of 1982, the state police celebrated another first in its history when Patricia Stewart became Idaho State Police's first female trooper with full patrol duties. Joan Pincock was the first female trooper hired by the state police in 1978, but Stewart was the first to assume full patrol duties.

Stewart started her career with the Idaho Department of Law Enforcement, as a secretary at DLE headquarters in 1976. She also worked with the motor carrier program and in 1979 decided to test for the position of state trooper.

As 1982 came to a close, the Idaho State Police's financial situation began to stabilize and in the early spring of 1983, sixteen new recruits were hired, filling vacancies in the 188 positions authorized by the legislature. However, the state police was still woefully undermanned. In an effort to further stabilize the state police, and prevent future cutbacks, state police employees voted to form the Idaho State Police Association.

The association was the first formal statewide organization formed by the state police, although each of the six patrol districts had its own separate organization. Formation of the Idaho State Police Association was an alternative to another idea which had been talked about by state police employees in the interest of job security: unionization.

One mandate of the association was to lobby in the legislature during budget hearings, and bring to the attention of legislators that Idaho, once again, had the highest traffic fatality rate of the seven northwestern states.

Sergeant Fred Rice, ISP 433, said the association has evolved and grown over the years, but its primary mission remains the same, giving a "voice" to state police employees.

> When the association was first formed, one of its primary missions was to offer association members a venue for expressing their opinions and concerns. Initially the association was only open to troopers, but with the reorganizations of the state police in 2000, it was opened to all employees. Over the years, the association has evolved to fit the needs of current employees.

Rice said some of the initial concerns brought to the attention of Department of Law Enforcement and Idaho State Police leadership, centered on officer safety issues.

> Troopers on the road recognized the need for better equipment, ranging from better flashlights to cages in cars, and they were able to express those needs through the association. The leadership of the state police has always been receptive and supportive of the association and it's helped improve conditions for all employees.

Rice added the association is successful because, "Over the years many, many people have volunteered to help raise money for association projects, and serve as board members representing their districts."

While the association gave state troopers more clout in shaping the direction of their agency, the state police was still plagued by far too few troopers and an ever increasing demand from Idaho lawmakers and Idaho citizens to make Idaho's roadways safer. One answer to this problem was the creation of the "recon program."

Rice said the recon program was started in 1982.

Joe Fisk, Tom Thompson, and Willis Brownlee were the first troopers to be trained in recon. They were trained by a Minnesota State Trooper, whose brother was a physicist. By 1983, there were about twenty of us in the program. In the beginning there were a lot of physicists and engineers, who didn't believe we could do recon, but the program we have focuses strictly on what happens in traffic accidents and it has been very successful. The Idaho State Police was among the first in the nation to start this type of recon program.

Rice explained the recon program uses the law of physics in the process of investigating and determining how an accident took place. "Recons collect, identify, and analyze roadway evidence such as road gouges, tire marks, and debris locations, to determine the information used in mathematical formulas that help us "re-create" the accident."

Master Corporal Wayne Scoggins, retired, ISP 481, said although being a recon is highly rewarding it's also often mentally and emotionally challenging.

The recon program is extremely important because it provides answers to questions. Like investigating any fatality, it can also be difficult especially on a resident officer because sometimes you're called to an accident and it's someone you know. One of the most difficult recons I did was on the accident that killed my middle son's girlfriend. She was only sixteen. I investigated two other fatality crashes in which I knew the people.

Master Corporal Bob Laumann, retired, ISP 569, said another important aspect of crash recon is that along with solving the cause of an accident, it teaches how accidents might be prevented.

A lot of information, including the use of seatbelts, and where to place air-bags in cars, etc., were discovered in part through recons done on fatality crashes. It is important, however, for troopers interested in becoming recons to understand there is a downside. Investigating crashes will eventually catch up with you. A person can only deal with blood and guts for so long, and then they have to pay an emotional, mental, and sometimes physical toll. I'm sure the toll is very different for every trooper, but I think the troopers serving now need to know it will affect them eventually.

Rice added that every year since the recon program began, the Idaho State Police has solved at least one major case that ended in a conviction.

> Sometimes a crash recon just eases the mind of family members, but of equal importance, we learn something from every recon. Over the years we have developed the program so that recons can not only do fatality crashes, but can diagram crime scenes such as homicides. Recons are a very valuable tool to both patrol and investigations.

Willis Brownlee said introducing the recon program into the state police was beneficial to all Idaho law enforcement entities.

> I recall a few accidents that weren't properly investigated because the officer didn't have proper training. With the recon program, we are able to assist other agencies. To be a recon, a person has to have certain abilities, such as math skills, and an interest in that type of work because it's very demanding. Personally, I found the recon program rewarding and I especially enjoyed instructing the program.

With the recon program in place, the Idaho State Police may have had the means to investigate fatality accidents and assist with homicides and other crimes, but it still lacked the manpower it needed to provide the coverage recommended by the National Highway Safety Administration.

And while fatality accident rates throughout the 1980s remained below the 1970s average, Idaho experienced an increase in other costly and often deadly crimes, most of which could be traced back to what President Richard Nixon in as early as 1971 called, "America's public enemy number one." Drugs.

14 ✮ Drugs, Drunks, and Death

Character is, in the long run, the decisive factor in the life of individuals and of nations alike.

Theodore Roosevelt

For decades, law enforcement entities across the nation have battled the increased use and abuse of illegal drugs. In 1969, illicit drug use became so prevalent across the nation President Richard Nixon called for a national anti-drug policy at the state and federal level. In 1973, Nixon created the Drug Enforcement Administration to coordinate law enforcement efforts at all levels. Every U.S. president since Nixon has supported and reinforced America's anti-drug policies. However, despite the efforts of law makers and law enforcement, drug use and abuse is still on the increase across the nation.

Statistics show twenty-five percent of all deaths in America can be directly attributed to drug use. Nearly seventy-five percent of all deaths among people ten years old to twenty-four years old result from one of four causes – motor vehicle crashes, other unintentional injuries, homicide, and suicide. Unfortunately a large number of people in this age group engage in behaviors such as drug use and drinking, that increases their likelihood of death from one of these four causes.

Detective Jim Hopkins, retired, said these statistics are further proven by the success of drug cartels importing drugs into the United States.

> Statewide, nationwide, it's the same sad story. The demand for drugs is so great the drug cartels can import it by the tons and tons and find a market. The demand for drugs never seems to decrease. Face it, with drugs there is a tremendous amount of tax free money to be made in the drug business. That alone ensures the drug problem in this country will remain extremely difficult to stay on top of, let alone overcome.

Hopkins added Idaho is known as a marijuana export state, and because much of the state offers remote locations and agriculture areas where marijuana is easily cultivated, controlling marijuana grows is a huge challenge for Idaho law enforcement. In the following account, Hopkins was a Bureau of Narcotics agent. In 2000, the Idaho State Police became the umbrella organization for all commissioned state law enforcement officers.

> The Bureau of Narcotics did a large number of drug busts in the 1980s and 1990s. One year we harvested 155,000 marijuana plants statewide. In one single bust, we harvested 48,000 plants and we tied that bust to the Mexican Mafia. We made twelve arrests in that case and all but one of the people arrested was a Mexican national. The plants on this particular bust were over six feet tall and the area they were located was extremely remote. We had the Idaho National Guard come in with their Blackhawk helicopters and we used slings to load the plants out to a flatbed. That was the largest single seizure in the United States that year. It was also a very difficult operation because we worked in 100 degree temperatures and were in an area infested with rattlesnakes.

Former Special Agent in Charge and Idaho State Police Captain Edwin Gygli, retired, said in 1981, the Omnibus Crime Act was passed and developed to fight organized crime. In 1982, Idaho formed the Marijuana Eradication Program (MEP) team, and Bureau of Narcotics agents from across the state assembled to go after drug grow sites.

> We formed a task force and every district in the state worked hard toward that common goal, which was going after higher echelon drug traffickers in Idaho. We were issued undercover driver's licenses, which we used to conduct purchases, etc. It was a lot of undercover work and although it was dangerous at times, we all understood and accepted it was necessary. Back then, we weren't required to wear a wire as long as there were two agents there to witness the transaction, which was another reason we formed the MEP team.

Gygli recalled one operation in the early 1990s that quickly became one of the Bureau of Narcotics' most important and successful investigations. The operation was named Satin Doll.

> Satin Doll involved a group of Los Angeles gang members who were part of the 38th Street Gang. The gang literally flooded cocaine into Pocatello. They were led by a man named Reyes. What really gave them away was they were buying a lot of property and vehicles and they were paying in cash. We ended up indicting about thirty people. The ones who were found guilty got an average of thirty years fixed in federal prison.

Detective Lieutenant Gary Kaufman, retired, said all major drug cases, like Satin Doll, take a long time to build, and a tremendous amount of undercover work.

> I've been on quite a few cases where from start to finish, we invested two to three years. It's not uncommon, especially when we're investigating large scale cases with a lot of players. Unfortunately, when we bring down one organization, there is always another organization willing to step in and take over the drug trafficking trade.

In a letter to Gygli, Special Agent Clark Rollins, and other members of the Bureau of Narcotics who worked on the Satin Doll case, United States Attorney Maurice Ellsworth commended agents for their, "... outstanding leadership," in the arrest of the gang members involved.

> Bureau of Narcotics officers Ed Gygli and Clark Rollins were critical to the successful arrests. The cooperation and assistance of the Idaho State Police and use of state police headquarters as a briefing and command post also contributed to a smooth operation. Many Bureau of Narcotics and other law enforcement personnel were involved in the operation. I appreciate the ongoing cooperation and assistance of the Idaho Department of Law Enforcement in our Organized Crime Drug Enforcement Task Force (OCDETF) program. The Department of Law Enforcement is a key player in assuring the success of many OCDETF cases throughout the state. Please convey my gratitude to the Bureau of

Narcotics officers and other employees of the Department of Law Enforcement who are doing an outstanding job in responding to the problem of illegal drugs in Idaho.

Along with increased drug abuse among Idahoans, Idaho State Police troopers were experiencing a dramatic increase in drunken driver arrests.

Colonel Barfuss retired from the Idaho State Police, after thirty-two years of service, in August of 1982. Colonel Calvin Bernard was named as his replacement, and when asked by the press what plans he had for the state police, Bernard said he would make one of his top priorities the battle against the drunk driver. Bernard had several other changes to the Idaho State Police in mind, but in the 1983 Annual Report to the governor Bernard first focused on the various successes of his state police:

> The Idaho State Police had a very rewarding and exciting year. There were several first time accomplishments, new equipment issues, and a major enforcement emphasis was begun on the intoxicated driver. The total Idaho State Police effort in law enforcement has proven again and again an asset to the state of Idaho.

1983 wasn't just a year of firsts for the Idaho State Police. Idaho citizens were also facing some 'firsts' in the form of new laws on a proposed change to the legal drinking age, and a proposed change to the minimum blood-alcohol concentration a driver could have before being charged as driving while under the influence.

Opinion concerning the proposed change in the legal drinking age in Idaho from nineteen years old to twenty-one years old caused fierce debate among Idaho citizens and lawmakers. National statistics showed in states where the legal drinking age was raised to twenty-one years of age, traffic deaths due to drinking in the sixteen to eighteen year-old age group had been reduced by over one-third. Many against the change, however, feared the change would not keep teenagers from drinking, but would instead cause them to, "…find more remote areas to drink, and resort to obtaining alcohol through theft or other illegal means…" Others argued if teenagers were old enough to be drafted into military service, they were old enough to drink.

Despite opposition to the proposed law, Idaho law makers passed a DUI law in 1983 that set .10 percent blood-alcohol concentration as the "per se" legal limit. The "per se" clause made a test result at this limit sufficient evidence for a conviction. The result was that more people were arrested for DUI, but the Attorney General's office reported an increase in court trials as people pleaded not guilty to the charge, concerned about the harsher penalties imposed by the law.

Another spark to the controversy surrounding the new DUI laws was the announcement the Idaho State Police would conduct a series of sobriety checkpoints. In August of 1983, the first checkpoint was set up on SH75 near Red Top Meadows in Blaine County. Blaine County was selected for the roadblock because it had a higher-than-average alcohol-related accident problem during the late night hours.

The objective of the state police was to aggressively seek people who were intoxicated and arrest them. News media organizations were called in to report on the roadblock in hopes of getting the word out to Idahoans the state police was determined to enforce the state's drinking and driving laws.

Many prosecuting attorneys and defense attorneys, however, felt the use of sobriety checkpoints was unconstitutional, and would be challenged in court using the Fourth Amendment's right against unreasonable search and seizure as a basis to overturn convictions. The Idaho Trial Lawyers Association weighed into the debate stating, "...in order to make an arrest, the arresting officer has got to have probable-cause to believe the individual has committed a crime. That goes for any crime including driving under the influence."

Because of the controversy surrounding the use of roadblocks, the state police scrapped the roadblock idea and instituted Emphasis DUI Patrols in September of 1983. The first of these patrols was held in the Burley-Rupert area, where statistics showed a higher than normal number of DUI accidents occurred.

Unlike the roadblock system, troopers did not stop motorists at a designated point. Instead motorists were stopped only if they committed a traffic infraction, such as speeding, tailgating, improper lane change, etc. Nine troopers participated in the emphasis, and over 190 motorists were stopped in the two five-hour periods of the patrol. The patrol proved successful with eighteen DUI arrests and forty other citations issued for traffic violations, including several for excessive speed.

The emphasis patrols helped the state police utilize standardized field sobriety tests, or FSTs, to determine probable cause for arresting drunk drivers. The tests were recommended by the National Highway Traffic

Safety Administration, which had commissioned the Southern California Research Institute to conduct studies on the most effective sobriety-test methods. The studies found the best methods for detecting impaired drivers, are the horizontal eye-gaze nystagmus, the walk-and-turn, and the one-leg stand. All three of these tests still form the basis used by the Idaho State Police and law enforcement entities across the nation, as probable cause to administer additional tests to suspected DUI drivers.

Duane Owen recalls the training received by troopers to deal with DUI drivers as, "top-notch."

> We received a tremendous amount of training on identifying drunk drivers. The (Idaho State Police leadership) recognized the horizontal gaze nystagmus was especially effective in determining whether or not a person was under the influence, and every trooper was trained on it. The field sobriety tests we used then were extremely effective, and they're still effective today.

The Idaho State Police instituted another program called Report Every Drunk Driver Immediately or REDDI, with tremendous success. Bernard said by mid-1984, sixty-five people had been arrested for DUI as a result of tips via the REDDI line.

> Drivers who might otherwise have gone on to kill or injure themselves or others were taken off the roadways because of tips from the REDDI line. The REDDI line has also been used to inform troopers of accidents and other highway emergencies. Although the line is not the cure-all to the DUI problem, it has proven itself well worthwhile.

While the DUI emphasis patrols proved to be a successful tool in the state police battle against drunk or aggressive drivers, the issue of too few troopers to enforce traffic laws on Idaho's roadways remained. With only 115 uniformed troopers, it came as little surprise to the leadership of the state police that the traffic fatality death toll for Idaho in 1983, with 263 people killed, was once again on the rise.

Along with increased DUI patrols, the Idaho State Police formed a special detachment of troopers to conduct "trucker safety checks." The results of these checks were startling; one-third of truckers flunked. The most common problem troopers found were out-of-adjustment brakes, and falsified log books.

Fortunately the success of the MSCAP pilot program in Idaho convinced the Federal Highway Administration to continue with its truck inspection program. Lieutenant Rich Humpherys was responsible for the pre-planning of the Idaho MSCAP, and the state certification designating the Idaho Department of Law Enforcement and Idaho State Police as the lead agency for the program was signed by Governor John Evans.

The troopers in this program were to inspect commercial vehicles for safety compliance, check equipment and driver violations, and were trained in the recognition of hazardous material violations and how to respond to hazardous material accidents.

Captain Bill Reese, ISP 585, has worked in the Idaho State Police Commercial Vehicle Safety program for twenty-two years.

> Prior to MCSAP, Idaho piloted the Bureau of Motor Carrier Safety program. This program went from 1980 to 1982 and was very successful. The program is still funded by MCSAP grants. Sometime in the mid 1990s, we changed the name to Commercial Vehicle Safety, (CVS), because people know what that means.

There were three major differences between the MCSAP pilot program and newly instituted MCSAP program.

Reese said the CVS program then and now has very little turn-over because of officer satisfaction.

> The Idaho CVS program is considered by federal auditors as a model program. Our last audit was held in 2010, and was conducted by a group of auditors who were known for their, "take no prisoners," approach. These auditors are paid to find problems and we had very few. My personal attitude is there is always room for improvement, but one of the reasons we have very little officer turn-over in CVS is because this program has always strived to be the best and our troopers receive excellent training.

By the early 1980s the leadership of the state police realized Idaho State Police troopers also needed more training. Thus another important first for the Idaho State Police was the introduction of a new approach to trooper cadet training. The Idaho State Police Stress Academy began in May of 1983.

The rigorous course demanded the utmost in physical, personal, and mental performance from the cadets. All seventeen of the cadets who started the course finished and graduated to become patrol officers. A special graduation ceremony was held at the Capitol Rotunda, with Governor Evans administering the oath of office.

Dave Neal said one of the major reasons for starting the academy was officer safety.

> At the time the academy was started state troopers had six weeks of P.O.S.T. training and whatever training they received at the district level. The state police recognized it needed better training, especially in officer safety issues such as felony stops. The academy really pushed officer survival, state troopers taking on a better image, and advanced certification in areas like crash reconstruction.

The Idaho State Police still conducts a stress academy. Neal says the academy has proven its value in many areas, especially officer safety issues, over the years.

> The academy is also excellent at weeding out people who are not really ready to be a state trooper. The state saves a lot of money by not hiring people who are unprepared. I believe the Idaho State Police is one of the best trained law enforcement entities in the nation.

For state police 'old-timers,' the stress academy was welcomed because it offered training many of them hadn't received when they were hired. Detective Les Stimpson, retired, said the state police had created a trooper-in-training program in 1969, but the stress academy offered advanced training that with the changing times became even more important.

> The difference between the 1970s and the 1980s in dealing with the different enforcement issues troopers faced was education. The Idaho State Police got a lot more involved in

training its troopers and that training was second to none. Troopers learned everything from accident recon to officer safety.

Wayne Scoggins said the stress academy lives up to its name.

> When I was hired, the stress academy was held at Gowen Field and it was exactly that, a stress academy. My class had two tactical officers and it was very much a military based 'bootcamp.' We were up at 5:30 a.m. every morning doing physical training, classroom instruction, practical exercises, etc. Anytime we spoke to a TAC officer, it was just like the military; yes sir, no sir, ask permission for everything. The leadership of the state police understands the stress troopers have to deal with, and they found with the stress academy a way to train troopers to better deal with it.

Among the most exciting changes in 1983 for state troopers, was the purchase of twelve Ford Mustangs. These high performance vehicles had 5.0 litre engines and manual transmissions. Troopers assigned to the Mustangs received extensive hands-on driving instruction prior to their patrol assignment. The troopers who received the car said the car handled a lot better than any of the state police's previous vehicles. Each district received two of the cars. In his report to the governor, Bernard stated:

> The Mustangs are becoming increasingly popular among state patrol agencies. These cars have more spunk than our other cars and exceed 140 miles per hour in test drives. They still get good gas mileage. The Mustang gets about sixteen miles to the gallon, better than the eight to ten miles per gallon current patrol vehicles get, so there's an economy factor as well as a performance one with these cars.

The Mustang was able to accelerate from zero to fifty miles per hour in 6.3 seconds, and could run a quarter-mile in 15.5 seconds. The Mustang could go as fast as most sports cars. The Idaho State Police hoped the Mustang would be a major deterrent against people who thought they could outrun the state police. The Mustangs were also a hit with the public, and very popular in parades. Other patrol vehicles purchased in 1983, included forty-seven Plymouth Gran Fury cars.

As 1983 drew to a close Idahoans faced another natural disaster in the form of an earthquake. On October 28, shortly after 8 a.m. one of the largest earthquakes in the continental United States shook Idaho. The epicenter of the quake was near the base of Idaho's tallest peak, Mount Borah. Measuring 7.3 on the Richter scale, the tremor was felt virtually statewide. Two children in Challis died when the rock facing on a storefront collapsed, crushing them.

Idaho State Police troopers faced numerous rock slides in roadways around the area, and artesian fountains erupted, flooding hundreds of acres of farmland. One spring that served as the source of water for the Will Ingram Cattle Ranch completely dried up. Nearly 200 homes received minor to moderate damage, 11 commercial buildings were destroyed, and 39 homes received major damage. Harold Barnes recalled his experience during the earthquake.

> I had stopped a motorcycle for speeding and suddenly the motorcycle started swaying violently. It was a huge bike, so that was a little disconcerting. A short time later, a call came over the radio about the earthquake. I was sent to make the loop from Salmon back to Idaho Falls. Although there was no real damage to the roads, there were a lot of rock slides over the roads. In the Mackey basin, there were numerous geysers spouting out in the fields. Amazingly, the next day they were all gone.

Captain Danny Bunderson, ISP 439, said it took several days to clean up the worst of the damage from the earthquake on roadways, although it took significantly longer to clean up damage to homes and property.

> I was working when the earthquake hit, but I didn't get to respond immediately. I sent some troopers to see what needed to be done. Fortunately, although it was a large earthquake, it hit in a very rural area so thankfully we didn't have a huge death toll although it did kill two children in Challis. The biggest issue we had to deal with was rocks on the road. Thankfully, overall the damage was pretty minor.

By 1984, the Idaho State Police priority was once again on DUI enforcement and the new DUI law. Special DUI emphasis patrols were held throughout the state. Several of the state police districts reached record high numbers of DUI arrests with these emphasis patrols adding to an already ambitious DUI enforcement effort. Brad Strom said the DUI emphasis patrols were instrumental in lowering the number of fatality accidents across the state.

> The state police got really serious about the DUI emphasis patrols in about 1984, so we started running a lot of DUI emphasis patrols. We would have anywhere from five to eight cars working in an area. I remember one weekend we worked an emphasis in the Island Park area. That weekend, we arrested 38 DUIs. That was a record then, and probably still is.

The emphasis patrol technique worked equally well with other types of traffic enforcement. Utilizing officers of the Task Force 55 program, speed emphasis patrols were also conducted. Speed emphasis patrols were employed across the state, and their efforts proved extremely successful, showing an overall reduction in motorist speeds.

The reduction in speeding motorists was considered a major reason for the drop in traffic accident fatality rates in 1984. Although the 241 lives lost on Idaho's roadways were still far higher than anyone in law enforcement liked, it was the lowest fatality rate for Idaho in twenty-one years.

In January and February of 1984, the state police faced another flood disaster. When extremely heavy mountain snowpack began to melt, many parts of the state were faced with record runoff, which resulted in flooded highways, farmlands, businesses, and homes. The Idaho State Police aided in evacuation, traffic control, and other emergency coordination.

Although law enforcement was called in numerous times to assist with evacuations and other patrol measures, Idaho citizens also worked hard to avert what could have been one of Idaho's worst natural disasters. The winter of 1983-84 slammed Idaho with record snowpack in the mountains, far exceeding weather report expectations.

The cities of Burley and Oakley were under particular threat of being overrun by flood waters, as the lower Goose Creek Reservoir threatened to overflow its banks. An overflow of the reservoir would have resulted in the loss of thousands of acres of farmland and massive flooding in the cities of Burley and Oakley.

Local officials and towns-people devised a daring plan to divert the water from the dam by widening and extending over nineteen miles of an existing canal, and by digging twenty-four miles of new canal in just three days through existing farmlands. The herculean effort diverted the potential flood waters into Murtaugh Lake and the Snake River.

Folks living in Salmon weren't nearly as lucky. Ice jams, the most notable of which was on the Lemhi River near Salmon caused tremendous damage, and led to a federal disaster declaration. An extensive ice jam formed in the Lemhi River just above the confluence with the Salmon River around the town of Salmon. Initial ice jam build-up began on December 22, in the Salmon River. On January 19, the flood damage began.

After the flood waters receded, ice up to three feet thick remained in many homes and ice nearly five feet thick remained around homes and along streets. Most of the damage was concentrated in Salmon and in adjacent agriculture fields. Only minor injuries were reported but 325 people were displaced and eighty-one homes were severely damaged.

The summer of 1984 did bring a more enjoyable duty to state troopers, when the Idaho State Police became the official escort of the Olympic flame as it traversed the state in June on its way to Los Angeles for the opening ceremony.

By July, the Idaho State Police found it had another mission to prepare for: the National Governor's Conference, which was held in August of 1985. A new unit was formed in the state police, the Support Services Division, led by Captain Tom Thompson. Thompson's first mission was to plan security for the conference.

In August, a contingent of ten people from the Department of Law Enforcement and the Idaho State Police traveled to Nashville, Tennessee to observe the way the Tennessee Highway Patrol handled the influx of dignitaries and the security problems created by the conference. Among the security measures taken, was the reactivation of the Special Operation Squad as the Idaho State Police Crisis Response Team.

Along with providing security for the National Governor's Conference, the Crisis Response Team (CRT) became an invaluable asset to law enforcement entities across the state. The creation of the CRT provided an opportunity to hone the specialized skills of the state police; skills that would save a number of lives in the coming years.

District 3 Patrol Officers, mid 1960s. Back row: Gerry King, Bill Green, Manny Newell, Walt Kirtley, Homer Garrett. Middle row: Victor Barfuss, Pappy Baker, Marvin Wright, Chet Sterling, Wally Pidgion, Jack DeWalt. Front row: Ed Given, Don Ikenberry, Bill Morgan, Don Royce, Jack Sweet, Jack Tucker. Photo courtesy of Don Ikenberry.

District 1 Port-of-Entry, early 1960s. Back row: Jim Fehling, Ray Thornton, Jon Prendergast, George Hicks, Gene Betts. Front row: Harry Anderson, Frank York, Bill Manning, Irv Sisson, Harvey Riffle. Photo courtesy of Jim Fehling.

Pappy Baker, taken in 1957, the car is a 1955 Chevy. Photo courtesy of the Idaho State Police.

1959 Ford patrol vehicle. Photo courtesy of the Idaho State Police.

Idaho hosted both the National Boy Scout Jamboree, and the World Boy Scout Jamboree. Photo courtesy of the Idaho State Police.

Idaho State Police Troopers celebrated the return of the "Skunk." Troopers vehemently disliked the blue and white color scheme for their patrol cars. Photo courtesy of the Idaho State Police.

Along with investigating fatal crashes, Idaho State Police troopers were tasked with investigating plane crashes until the creation of the Federal Aviation Administration in 1958. Photo courtesy of the Idaho State Police.

Lieutenant Lyle Hall left, presents Ron Eggleston, Derald Harmon, Jim Fehling, Harlan Bush, Ed Applington, Willis Brownlee, and James Smith with their Basic Certificate Award in 1971. The certificates were given after troopers completed requirements, such as attending P.O.S.T., or for time in service if the troopers were trained through the Port-of-Entry system.

A.E. Perkins, an unidentified man, and Dean Bennett with a mock patrol car set up outside of Boise in 1962. Photo courtesy of the Idaho State Police.

Middleton High School Superintendant Tom Tuttle, and Idaho State Police Trooper D. E. Kelly stand in front of a display board Trooper Kelly used during a safety presentation at the school. The display shows pictures of fatality crashes on Idaho's roadways. Photo courtesy of the Idaho State Police.

Harold Lee and Harry Anderson inspect a car at Forest Brothers Wrecking Yard in Coeur d'Alene, circa late 1950s. Photo courtesy of Jim Fehling.

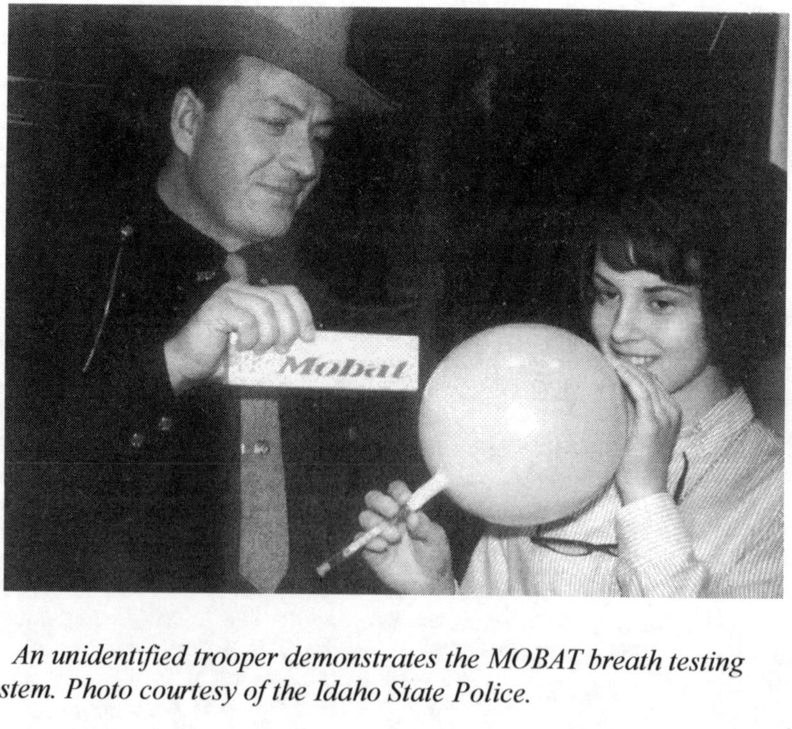

An unidentified trooper demonstrates the MOBAT breath testing system. Photo courtesy of the Idaho State Police.

Prior to 1980, Idaho State Police troopers also had to serve as dispatchers. Photo courtesy of the Idaho State Police.

The MCSAP motor home was used as a command center in several situation in which the Idaho State Police was involved. Photo courtesy of the Idaho State Police.

15 ★ Crisis Response

We make a living by what we get, but we make a life by what we give.
Winston Churchill

In July of 1985, Superintendent Bernard retired from the state police after thirty one years of service. Rich Humpherys was named as his successor. In the 1985 Annual Report to the governor, Colonel Humphreys said the highlight of the year, was the Idaho State Police involvement in providing security for the National Governor's Conference.

The Crisis Response Team Badge was designed by Colonel Ralph Powell when he was assigned to the team. Photo courtesy of the Idaho State Police.

Never have so many Idaho State Police officers, not to mention the personnel of other branches of the Department of Law Enforcement, worked so closely on a project. The opportunity to combine the individual skills of our officers to achieve a common goal was highly rewarding and contributed to an enhanced sense of unity amongst our troops.

The National Governor's Conference provided other benefits to the state police, including specialized training and improved equipment. Humphries said the state police contributed nearly 17,000 man hours to the conference, with nearly half of that time in preparation and training.

> The security at the conference was flawless. The satisfaction that each state police officer enjoyed because of the accomplishments that each had achieved through their individual efforts will probably never be equaled. No other event in the state's history has seen such a concentrated gathering of law enforcement personnel. Careful planning and long hours paid off and the National Governor's Conference was held with no threats to the safety of the many attending dignitaries (Humpherys).

The National Governor's Conference and the creation of the Crisis Response Team also provided the Idaho State Police the opportunity to upgrade its communication system. New solid-state radios were installed in patrol cars, and a number of hand-held radios were added. The seven officers of the Crisis Response Team were given specialized weapons and tactics training.

Past CRT Commander, Dave Neal, said although the Crisis Response Team was activated specifically for the conference, it wasn't long before the team was being called to assist with drug raids and other critical incidents.

> Prior to the creation of the CRT, the state police had the SOS team, but they really didn't get great training and their equipment was cobbled together from what the state police already had available. The CRT received much better training and better equipment. Our initial training was a two-week school at Gowen Field. It was good training but where we really learned the most, was from the after-action reviews we held following every incident we were involved in. We made it a priority to talk about what went right and what went wrong so we could constantly improve.

Delon Jones was among the first members of the CRT, and the last original member to leave the team.

I was the CRT sniper team leader. I went through Marine sniper school in 1982. It was a very tough course and out of the twelve people who started training with me, only two of us made it. I was the lead sniper for the CRT for fifteen years. There were a few times when things got pretty tense, but I really enjoyed my time with CRT.

Wayne Longo said having the CRT available to assist in critical incidents was a 'real boon' to Idaho law enforcement agencies.

Throughout the decade of the 1980s we were seeing increased drug activity across the state. In October of 1986, the CRT was called in to help District 1, the Idaho Bureau of Narcotics, ATF agents, and the Bonner County police officers when we raided a methamphetamine distribution ring on a Hoodoo Valley ranch.

Longo, who at the time of the raid was the supervisor of the Bureau of Narcotics team in north Idaho, said a husband and wife, and four other men were suspected of distributing methamphetamine and other narcotics.

During the raid we found over a pound of meth, an ounce or so of cocaine, and several firearms. The CRT approached the house and outbuilding from the rear of the property and several state police patrol cars and unmarked sedans carrying investigators approached from the front. It was a very successful operation and we were able to make several arrests.

Colonel Ralph Powell, ISP 403, said by the end of the decade, the Idaho State Police Crisis Response Team had established its own identity and, in addition to responsibilities to its own department, was frequently called out to support smaller law enforcement agencies that did not have this type of resource. Powell was a sergeant during his years of service with the CRT.

I served with the CRT for five years, and was the CRT Assault Team Leader. On February 21, 1989, I submitted a proposal to

Major Tom Thompson for an ISP-CRT shoulder patch that would identify us as “Idaho State Police Crisis Response Team, and detail on the patch what we represented.

Powell submitted several hand-drawn logo drafts for consideration, and the patch bearing the Bald Eagle and lightning bolt, scope cross hairs, and sword, was selected as the CRT badge. Powell explained the meaning behind each symbol:

> The Bald Eagle and lightning bolts symbolize that we are an elite group. We can strike as fast as lightning, yet be as quiet as a bird in flight. The eagle also symbolizes strength and loyalty. The scope and cross hairs symbolize accuracy and sureness of our objectives. It also symbolizes confidence and exactness as well as the faith and trust that the public displays in our abilities. The sword symbolizes strength and endurance. Like the edge of the sword, our skills have been honed to acute perfection and piercing accuracy. Like tempered steel we are unyielding in our resignation and diligence to complete the task.

Throughout the 1980s, another threat was increasing in north Idaho – violence perpetuated by groups affiliated with the Aryan Nations.

On September 15, 1986, a bomb exploded at the home of Reverend Bill Wassmuth, a human rights advocate, and leader of the Kootenai County Task Force on Human Relations. On September 29, three more bombs exploded in Coeur d’ Alene. Two businesses, The Luggage Rack and Jax Family Dining were bombed, as was the Federal Building. A fourth bomb was found undetonated on the roof of the Federal Building. The bombings triggered a massive investigation by federal and local police. No one was killed in any of the bombings, but a large number of people were evacuated from other public buildings as officers searched for more bombs.

Phil Broesch said the Aryans had been tied to several violent acts in other states, but this was the first time they attacked, “basically in their own back yard.”

> The Aryans were pretty active during the time of the bombings because they were preparing for the World Aryan Congress. When the bombings occurred, I was out by Post Falls and all of the

sudden I was clocking cars doing ninety-five-a hundred miles-per-hour. I pulled a couple of cars over and realized they were feds, or ATF agents and U.S. Marshals responding to the bombings. I finally gave up running radar.

Longo said the bombings were intended to start a neo-Nazi race war. The bombings were planned as part of a hit-list of murders and robberies by imprisoned members of The Order and a neo-Nazi group known as The Order II or the Bruder Schweigen Strike Force II. The group was led by David Ross Dorr.

The Order II was supposed to use the bombings as a diversion to rob the National Guard Armory for automatic weapons and explosives, but the quick response of law enforcement forced the group to abandon its plans. We already knew the group had been involved in counterfeiting, and we were preparing warrants for that and for firearms violations.

Longo said Bureau of Narcotics agents, and Idaho State Police Troopers worked with federal agents in serving search warrants on the people responsible for the bombings. Police arrested Robert Pires, David Dorr, Debbie Dorr, Edward Hawley, and Olive Hawley. All five were charged with several federal charges including conspiracy, and counterfeiting.

Broesch said this raid was one of the largest he ever participated in.

They had placed bombs in various places around Coeur d' Alene, including in the home of a Catholic priest. Thankfully, the bombs didn't kill anyone, but no one knew how many bombs had been planted or where all of them were. We spent several extremely tense hours before the situation was under control.

While increased criminal activity, especially in the northern part of the state, was keeping troopers plenty busy, troopers were also receiving extra training and instruction on the ins and outs of their upgraded equipment. The state police continued to strengthen its role in the enforcement of commercial vehicle safety through the MCSAP program. By mid 1985, the program grew from eight troopers to twelve.

With the increase of troopers to the MCSAP program, commercial vehicle inspections topped 6,700 for the year and commercial vehicle accidents were down in Idaho. The accident rate per million commercial vehicle miles traveled dropped from 2.83 in 1984 to 2.55 in 1985. The overall number of accidents also dropped in Idaho from 2,026 in 1984 to 1,421 for 1985.

Humpherys described another new program started in District 1 at the end of 1985:

> We are excited about a new program that the Office of Highway Safety has initiated. District 1 has been isolated as having the second highest accident ratio in the state – second only to the much more densely populated Ada County – because of this, the Office of Highway Safety has agreed to fund an additional six troopers for District 1. The program, called STEP (Selective Traffic Enforcement Program) will be focusing on those violations that seem to be causing the accidents.

The trend toward a stronger, more modern state police force meant even more changes for the Idaho State Police in 1986. Humpherys reported the state police graduated two academies, which returned the state police to its authorized strength and announced the successes of the newly formed auto theft unit.

> Stolen vehicles are a major problem within the state, with over 1,700 vehicles stolen in 1986. The success of the auto theft unit is continuing to increase with over $500,000 in stolen property recovered to date. This has been accomplished by only four state police troopers.

Sergeant Brent Bunderson, retired, ISP 511, worked auto theft prior to the auto theft unit being formed.

> I was working a pilot program with the state police in auto recovery and the pilot program was extremely successful. The headquarters staff called me to Boise and I presented a vehicle

theft prevention overview for them. They determined I would become the first vehicle theft investigator for the state. Within a short time, the state police formed a unit with an investigator in each district.

Captain Danny Bunderson was one of the first troopers assigned to the newly formed unit.

My brother, Brent, really pushed the program because he could see there was a real need for this type of investigation in the state. We worked a lot with local agencies, most of which simply didn't have the manpower to conduct these types of investigations. One thing we discovered early in the program was that a lot of the time these cases would start out with a stolen vehicle and then mushroom into a much larger investigation.

Brent said members of the unit received training in areas such as title fraud, odometer fraud, and how to restore numbers on automobiles and guns using acid.

We worked some very large cases that resulted in the recovery of millions of dollars in property and in some pretty high-profile convictions. One case I worked involved a mob family out of California. This case basically involved a variety of criminal activities and the investigation into this case went clear into Canada. The leader of the family and others were arrested and convicted on several charges.

Brent said he also worked cases that began as auto-theft investigations and ended with solving homicides.

One case involved a murder in Las Vegas. I stopped a vehicle south of Pocatello. The man in the vehicle was arrested for DWOP. I found the numbers on the vehicle didn't match with any of the information the driver had, and when I searched the vehicle I found a gun, a stun gun, and a knife. We also found blood in the vehicle. When we traced the vehicle I found out the owner had

> been murdered the day before and his car stolen. Another case involved a murder out of Hollywood, California. I saw a vehicle sitting in an unusual place with out of state license plates. I ran the license plate and it came back stolen. I ended up in a short pursuit with the vehicle and arrested two men and a woman. The woman confessed to some of what they had been doing, including the murder of a man. She said they had tied a man up to a tree under the Hollywood sign and shot him in both legs. Eventually the man died of exposure.

Brent recalled one of the largest investigations he worked on involved a salvage company out of Wendell.

> We had been tracking some stolen vehicles and discovered a ring that went from Springfield, Missouri to Portland, Oregon. Desert Sky Salvage out of Wendell was their Idaho connection. We served a search warrant on the outfit and it took us about four days to complete the search. We found evidence of over 5,000 stolen vehicles. We also recovered stolen guns, blank Idaho titles, and a huge amount of removed vehicle identification plates. That case ended with several convictions.

In the 1987 Annual Report, Humpherys reported the auto theft unit nearly tripled its successes over the previous year. Humpherys further reported auto thefts were on the increase, with over 1,900 vehicles stolen in Idaho in 1987.

On May 4, 1987, a major change to Idaho's traffic laws was announced when the much debated 55 mile-per-hour speed limit was repealed on rural interstates within Idaho. Of the 608 miles of interstate highway in the state, the speed on 570 of these miles increased to a maximum 65 mile-per-hour limit. The increase in speeds did not result in a large increase in traffic fatalities.

Cecil D. Andrus, who had served as Idaho's governor from 1971 to 1977, returned to the governor's chair in 1987. Andrus replaced Department of Law Enforcement Director John Rooney with Mack W. Richardson, Jr. Following Richardson's appointment, the command structure of the Idaho State Police was reorganized.

The purpose of the reorganization was to provide a better coordination of resources. Many troopers with a rank of lieutenant or higher were promoted one rank. This resulted in the commanders of all six districts now having the rank of captain, and added a lieutenant, or deputy commander, to each district.

The intent of the reorganization was to provide a better sharing of responsibility within both the district and headquarters command structure. With the change, the Idaho State Police now had a colonel, a lieutenant colonel, with the title of deputy superintendent, three majors, two field operations commanders, a MCSAP captain, and a support services operations commander. The reorganization also freed the twenty-one district sergeants for increased field supervision.

Colonel Humpherys further noted throughout 1987, the Crisis Response Team continued to, "…prove its value."

> The Crisis Response Team during this year demonstrated its professionalism and abilities by responding to the continued problems surrounding the Aryan Nation Church in northern Idaho. The CRT traveled to the Coeur d' Alene area on several instances. The CRT also assisted the Bureau of Narcotics in the service of warrants. In addition, a variety of tactical problems has required other agencies to call on the CRT for its assistance.

In early 1988, Humpherys announced the formation of two more programs within the MCSAP. For the first program, a federal grant was obtained to fund six new truck accident reconstruction experts. The six troopers were selected from across the state. Idaho was one of the first states in the nation to be selected for the Safety Net Program. It was the first state allowed to implement a heavy truck accident investigation unit.

The troopers selected for the program underwent a comprehensive three-week reconstruction and heavy truck reconstruction program. These troopers were tasked with the responsibility of investigating every major truck accident in the state to determine if accidents correlated with safety inspection violations, driver error, and/or drug or alcohol involvement. The success of the program was so complete it was funded again in 1989.

Because of the program's success, the Idaho State Police was the first state police agency in the nation to have computer-aided accident reconstruction as a backup to the usual methods of reconstructing an accident. The program was called COMCRASH by its inventor, Tom Ravensdale of London, England.

Information gathered by troopers at the scene was entered into the program, which generated a report with graphs and charts that showed a cause analysis of the accident. The program saved hundreds of man hours in reconstruction time. An indirect result of the grant was the establishment of the Institute of Traffic Studies at Boise State University by Ravensdale, which lasted for several years and provided a training facility for reconstructionists.

The second program was the creation of a Hazardous Material Specialist. This program was authorized by the legislature, and Corporal Jack Anderson of Pocatello was named the first Hazmat specialist to receive advanced hazardous materials training within the state. He was further mandated by legislative authority to train other police agencies within the state to properly respond to hazardous materials accidents.

Among the reasons for the creation of hazardous materials specialists was because Idaho was a repository for trans-uranic waste being shipped into Idaho. But in October of 1988, Governor Andrus informed the Federal Government that Idaho would no longer be a repository for this waste, which was being shipped into the state from other locations in the country. Andrus mandated the Idaho State Police to stop and inspect all suspected loads entering the state and turn them back at the border. By February of 1989, the federal government backed down and informed Andrus it would cease shipping waste into Idaho until a compromise could be reached.

In the 1988 Annual Report, Humpherys recognized the contribution of the MCSAP, calling troopers assigned to the program, "...critical to Idaho State Police operations." He also recognized the STEP program for reducing serious injury and fatality crashes on northern Idaho's highways.

> With the increased tourism in the state and continued recreational development, the Coeur d' Alene area is experiencing ever increasing traffic flows. Despite this increase, our Selective Traffic Enforcement Program troopers continue to help hold the accident rate down. Coupled with our enforcement efforts across the state, a number of safety presentations and displays were given.

On July 1, 1988, the Idaho State Police and other law enforcement entities across the state were given a major tool in the law enforcement toolbox when the Forensic Section was transferred to the Department of

Law Enforcement and became the Idaho Bureau of Forensic Services. Statewide, law enforcement now had one of the greatest developments in the history of criminal investigation, headquartered in Boise.

Rick Groff, Idaho State Police Forensics, retired, said the history of forensic services began in 1963 when the Idaho Department of Health, Division of Laboratories, was formed under the leadership of Darrell Brock, D.P.H. Brock established an analytical unit for the analysis of blood and breath alcohol for the Idaho State Police.

> In 1969, this service was extended to local law enforcement agencies through a grant from the Governor's Traffic Safety Commission. This service was eventually provided from other laboratories within the Health Department around the state. In 1968, the legislature funded a drug identification laboratory in the Board of Pharmacy. Operation of the laboratory was transferred to the Division of Health in 1970.

Groff said in 1972 that Robert Dews moved from the Washington State Patrol Crime Lab in Seattle to Boise to assume management of the drug laboratory. Eventually, the alcohol analysis units statewide were combined with the drug laboratory to create the Forensic Section of the Division of Health. The Forensic Section originally provided services from Boise, Coeur d' Alene, Idaho Falls, Pocatello, and Twin Falls. Dews was the first manager of that system. However, by 1982, the Forensic Section moved its operations to the three locations that currently provide services: Boise, Coeur d' Alene, and Pocatello.

> Dews had experience in forensic disciplines besides blood alcohol and solid dosage drug analysis. Under his leadership, the Boise laboratory at the Health Lab on Old Penitentiary Road expanded into other forensic disciplines such as trace, serology, firearms, and toxicology. After Dews left the forensic section, I managed the laboratory in Boise for a number of years and the Forensic Section while it was a part of the Department of Health and Welfare.

The Boise laboratory started with one part-time person performing blood and breath alcohol but by 1980 the laboratory had eight staff members. Groff said the Coeur d' Alene laboratory also started out with one part-time person performing blood and breath alcohol testing in 1969. In 1974, Bob Martin, who worked in the Forensic Section in Boise, transferred to Coeur d' Alene and offered drug analysis to law enforcement agencies in the northern part of the state.

> He was the sole analyst for three years until the state hired Wally Baker in 1977. The services provided at that time were basic serology, drug analysis, and blood and breath alcohol analysis. Toxicology services were offered to law enforcement beginning in the late 1970s.

As with the Boise and Coeur d' Alene labs, the Pocatello laboratory started out with one part-time person in 1970, and the laboratory covered the eastern one-third of Idaho. In 1974, it was staffed with two chemists. They performed examinations in controlled substance analysis and blood and breath alcohol. During its first ten years, the laboratory slowly expanded its services to cover analyses in conventional serology, arson, and crime scene investigation.

One of the challenges that the forensic laboratories now faced under the umbrella of the Department of Law Enforcement, was the inability to retain a bureau chief for more than eighteen months to two years. When Colonel Ed Strickfaden completed the transition of the Department of Law Enforcement to the Idaho State Police in 1999, one of the changes he made was to elevate the position of Idaho Department of Law Enforcement Forensics Bureau Chief to the rank of Idaho State Police Major. He then promoted Colonel Ralph Powell, who was a captain at the time, to the rank of major with the understanding Powell would have to serve in that position for a minimum of three years. Powell said:

> This was a new chapter for me, not only moving into a position where I would exclusively supervise civilian scientists, but one where I would have a contractual obligation to do so for a set number of years. In my interview for the position I outlined a five-year plan for crime labs, so I didn't hesitate to agree to Colonel Strickfaden's terms.

Powell continued as the Forensic Services System Director for an unprecedented eleven years. A most significant accomplishment under his tenure was successfully stemming the constant exodus of Idaho State

Police trained scientists to other laboratory systems because of poor wages. Powell requested, and completed a "Hay Study," reclassifying full time positions and moving these positions up on the pay scale as much as four pay grades. Additionally, realignment of disciplines also created career ladders that encouraged forensic scientists to stay with the Idaho State Police.

For the Idaho State Police and other law enforcement entities, these services would prove invaluable in the coming years as advances in forensic technologies provided ever more reliable methods not only of identifying criminals, but for proving innocence or guilt through scientific methods.

In 1974, another significant asset to the Idaho State Police and other law enforcement entities across the state was formed, The Bureau of Criminal Identification (BCI). Dawn Peck currently serves as the Idaho State Police BCI Manager.

> BCI is responsible for a number of programs that assist Idaho's law enforcement. For example, we are the criminal history repository for the state. This repository is two-fold. We keep criminal data on individuals, which is a data base that describes the person, and we process all arrest fingerprints in the state Automated Fingerprint Identification System (AFIS). This information is available to the complete criminal justice system nationally. We also search latent prints from crime scenes through AFIS and if a match is made, we send the results back to the submitting agency's examiner or to our forensic specialists for final verification.

In 1989, Peck added, Idaho was one of the founding members of the Western Identification Network.

> We share this AFIS with seven other western states: Alaska, Washington, Oregon, Montana, Wyoming, Utah, and Nevada. As the BCI manager, I sit on the Western Identification Network board. The board sets policy and I ensure the policy is followed.

BCI, like forensics, has continued to grow and improve with advances in technology.

Our duties have expanded with technology, but that same technology has made it possible for BCI to complete its various missions without having to significantly increase the staff size. I remember when I first started all of our criminal histories were entered into the database manually. I started in the criminal history division and there was at least five years worth of arrest fingerprint cards and dispositions that needed to be entered. We started an intern program with Boise State University and were able to get six interns to help. Currently BCI has a staff of thirty-one and we're able to keep pace with demand because we now have automation in our areas of responsibility. We conduct criminal history compliance reviews where we meet with law enforcement, prosecutors, and the courts to ensure they are submitting their fingerprint and criminal history information correctly.

Along with maintaining the criminal history data base and AFIS, the BCI conducts applicant background checks, maintains the Idaho sex offender registry, maintains the administration and operational activities of the ILETS system, maintains the Idaho missing persons clearing house, the Idaho AMBER alert program, and compiles a yearly uniform crime report.

We do applicant background checks for both government agencies and civilian employers. These background checks are used for a number of reasons, including employment requirements and regulatory and licensing needs. BCI became the managing agency for the state sex offender's registry in 1993, all of the sex offender registration information is sent to BCI. We do notification to offenders and to law enforcement if offenders are not in compliance. We also do all of the affidavits if defendants fail to do what they are supposed to or are applying for expungement from registration duties.

Peck says ILETS is a carry-over acronym for the Idaho Public Safety and Security Information System.

ILETS is the telecommunications system that links Idaho law enforcement entities to one another, the FBI, and criminal justice agencies in other states. We manage all agency connections and conduct all of the training and auditing for this system. ILETS is the system over which all regulated information flows. We conduct field training on the system across the state and every entity that uses the system receives training at least once a year. Everything we do with ILETS is in support of law enforcement and other criminal justice entities that are lawfully authorized to receive information from the system.

In 1996, BCI started Idaho's missing person clearing house. The BCI manages the data base, and coordinates with other agencies, including the National Center for Missing and Exploited Children to maintain the missing person data base and to coordinate the AMBER alert program for the state.

Currently the BCI maintains the registry of 3,864 sex offenders, 129 active missing persons, 23,957 Idaho warrants, 923 Idaho protection orders, and 6,800 no contact orders. In 2012, the bureau processed 72,000 applicant fingerprint cards and 71,000 criminal fingerprint cards. Peck said the BCI will continue to harness advances in technology as they become available.

In the 1988 Annual Report to the Governor, Humpherys acknowledged the benefit of technological advances, adding as the Idaho State Police became more diverse and efficient in new technologies it was in a much better position to serve the citizens of Idaho.

Technological advances, however, couldn't always serve Idaho's law enforcement officers in terms of officer safety; the unpredictable and all too human threat remained.

16 ✯ Psychology

A hero is no braver than an ordinary man, but he is braver five minutes longer.

Ralph Waldo Emerson

Ed Strickfaden and Sean Daly discuss tactics for capturing the Pratt brothers.

On January 12, 1989, Forest Service Officer Brent Jacobson was shot and killed while attempting to apprehend two robbery suspects during a severe snow storm in Bonner County. Corporal Sean Daly, retired, ISP 579, said Jacobson had volunteered to help local authorities track the robbery suspects because he was experienced in tracking and cold weather conditions.

> The two suspects were James and Joseph Pratt, and they were involved in a home robbery in Sagle. The Pratt's crashed very close to my home, so my home was used as a safe house for my neighbors. We initially received a call from the Bonner County Sheriff wanting help in the manhunt. Me, Ed Strickfaden, Terry Ford, James Culpepper, Phil Broesch, Steve Richardson, and Michael Sutton responded to help.

Court records state Joseph Pratt and his brother, James Pratt, disguised themselves in black masks and clothing and went to a residence in Bonner County with loaded firearms, on the night of January 11, 1989. The Pratts entered the residence, bound some of the occupants with tape and forced others to look for money.

Sheriff's officers arrived while the Pratts were still inside the residence. Both suspects shot at people in the residence, and at law enforcement officers, but none of the shots resulted in injury to any of the occupants or officers. The Pratts fled, taking one person in the house with them as a hostage. They released the hostage shortly after fleeing.

An automobile chase followed in which the Pratts exchanged more gunfire with police. The Pratts drove to a wooded area where they crashed their vehicle and subsequently fled on foot. Police searched for the Pratts in snowy weather throughout the night and into the afternoon of the next day.

Bonner County Sheriff's Deputy Steven Barbieri and Jacobson eventually located the Pratts near the Smith Creek area and ordered them to surrender. It remains unclear who fired first, however, a gun fight followed in which Jacobson was shot to death. The Pratts fled the area and eventually surrendered at a nearby farmhouse.

Daly said law enforcement officers from the state police and the Bonner's County Sheriff's Office searched the several summer homes in the area where they suspected the Pratt's might be located. The Pratt's were located in one of the homes, but fled out the back door as officers arrived. The state police then followed the Pratt's into the forested area searching for the suspects by following their tracks where the men had fled along a power line cut.

> It was getting dark as we headed over a ridge in the area and Strickfaden stopped us because he was afraid we were going to walk into an ambush. We went back to the command post and we were there a short time when Terry Ford came on the radio saying there had been shots fired. Within a short time, we found out Jacobson had been shot.

Ed Strickfaden said he felt very strongly about pulling his men off of the manhunt because the changing situation of coming darkness and positioning, provided a perfect opportunity for the Pratt's to ambush any pursuing officers.

> There was about fifteen inches of snow on the ground and we were following their tracks. They went over the top of a ridge and it was starting to get dark so I felt we wouldn't be able to work any tactics against the suspects. In fact I figured with the coming darkness and their being over the ridge, the tactical advantage was with the suspects. I pulled my men out and we went back to the command center. I told the sheriff we had pulled out and why we had pulled out. I recommended to the sheriff that we let the Pratt's spend the night in the snow and freezing cold, while we secured the area and then had our CRT come and work them in the morning. The sheriff agreed to get the CRT on the way but at about the same time, the sheriff got a call from one of his deputies.

Strickfaden said the Bonner County Sheriff received a request from one of his deputies to continue the pursuit.

> The sheriff decided to allow his men to continue until dark. I talked to the sheriff and again explained to him why I had decided to pull out, and I was very forceful in my argument that he also call his men back. He decided to allow them to continue the search until dark, and they walked into an ambush. Initially there were reports that Jacobson was shot but officers said they heard

> moaning coming from the area where the ambush occurred. So we thought Jacobson was wounded and needed our immediate help.

Jacobson was in front of another local deputy when he spotted the suspects in ambush and radioed the other officer to take cover. Jacobson identified himself and was immediately engaged in a gunfight. One deputy was able to return fire and wounded one of the suspects. Strickfaden said

> When we found out Jacobson had been shot, we went up a logging road that was above the area where the shooting took place. I told troopers and deputies to turn on all of their lights and to rack their shotguns and make a lot of noise. My objective was to make the Pratt's think there were a large number of officers closing in. My other objective was to give Daly and myself a chance to come in from the flank to search for Jacobson. The noise the officers made did spook the Pratt's and they left the area. Daly and I entered the forest on their flank, staying about twenty yards apart as we silently maneuvered our way around the hillside not knowing what to expect. We knew that we had to reach Jacobson as he might be wounded and in need of immediate medical care. When we found Jacobson it was clear he was deceased.

Daly said the suspects ran to a farmhouse where they were taken into custody the next morning. Phil Broesh was among the troopers responding to the farmhouse.

> The Pratt's were on the front porch and both of them were in pretty rough shape. Jim Culpepper grabbed the younger brother and I cuffed the older brother. James Pratt had been shot in the leg and we transported him to Bonner General Hospital. I remember at the hospital someone told James Pratt one of the officers they shot at was dead. I'll never forget his response, "If he ain't dead he aughta be the way he sounded."

Both brothers were convicted of first degree murder and several other felonies. James Pratt was originally given the death penalty, but his sentence was commuted to life four years later. Joe Pratt was sentenced to life. Jacobson was forty-one years old and the third U.S. Forest Service law enforcement officer to die in the line-of-duty. In 2011, Jacobson was posthumously awarded the Idaho Medal of Honor.

Jacobson's death was among the incidents that convinced the leadership of the state police that with the continued increase in traumatic occurrences faced by Idaho law enforcement officers, the need to assist troopers in dealing with post-episode traumatic stress—which often follows incidents such as officer involved shootings or fatality crash—was a necessary officer-safety tool.

In the winter 1989 edition of *Idaho State Police Magazine*, Humpherys announced the state police had instituted a policy requiring all officers involved in a shooting or other highly traumatic incident to undergo psychological counseling.

> Officers are typically an independent breed, self-sufficient and of the attitude that they can handle anything. Often that's good, but in dealing with the trauma those kinds of incidents bring, there is no shame in admitting a need for help. This policy is designed to help officers understand and cope with the emotions they will experience following incidents of this kind.

Dave Neal said there are two kinds of officer survival. "The first involves what is needed to survive the incident the second is what is needed to survive after the incident." In the article "Armed Encounters-Officer Survival," winter 1989 *Idaho State Police Magazine,* three troopers discussed how they survived both the incident and the trauma that followed.

Corporal Steve Hobbs, retired, ISP 475, is one of the few state troopers to have been involved in more than one armed encounter, two of them in a span of just a few months. In July of 1989, Hobbs assisted a county agency on a family disturbance call. The husband had beaten his wife and was firing on officers with a rifle. Ultimately one deputy was pinned down and officers were forced to return fire to protect the pinned down deputy. At one point the man did put down his weapon, but he picked it up and resumed firing. Officers were forced to shoot the man.

The second incident occurred in September of 1989. A city police department received a call of an armed man breaking into his estranged girlfriend's residence. The man had shot and wounded the woman with a 12-gauge shotgun. The woman was able to flee to a neighbor's residence. Hobbs said within a short time of arriving at the scene, it became obvious the man was attempting to commit suicide-by-cop.

> It was a strange situation from the very beginning because we arrived at the scene and saw the neighbor, it was his house the woman had ran too, and he was standing outside armed. We initially thought he was the suspect so we deployed our cars and positioned ourselves in a defensive position around him. From behind us we hear a guy ask, "Are you looking for me?"

Upon realizing their mistake, the officers scrambled for cover. The suspect continued to urge officers to shoot him, while officers attempted to talk the man into surrendering his weapon. Officers were unable to convince the man to surrender his weapon and after a short time, the man committed suicide.

Hobbs said it doesn't matter how seasoned or "tough" a trooper is, every officer pays a price in the aftermath of a traumatic incident.

> You go into shock. I don't care how tough you are or anything else. It may not happen right away. I was in shock from both incidents for at least two days until it hit me what had really happened. After the first shooting I didn't really see anything wrong. I felt fine and thought there was no problem. But three days later I fell apart.

Hobbs said he was grateful his leadership required him to see a psychologist following the incidents.

> Back in the old days, you were left alone. They stuck you in a car and if you were the shooter they took your weapon away which made you feel like you'd done something bad. Now the philosophy is different. They have someone with you looking after you. Because I've been involved in these types of traumatic incidents and got help, I realize how important it is to give this help to others involved in similar incidents.

Corporal Jay Komosinski and Sergeant Fred Rice were also interviewed for the article and recounted their experiences.

Komosinski was providing assistance to a county agency which was involved in a pursuit with several armed robbery suspects. Officers boxed the suspects in at a dead-end road but one man fled the scene with a shotgun. Komosinski arrived on scene as the officers were taking a suspect into custody. Komosinski spotted the armed subject further down the road but when he went to radio to pass the information to officers approaching from another direction, the man opened fire.

Komosinski grabbed his shotgun from his patrol car, but realizing a shot fired from his position might hit motorists on an adjacent highway, opted instead to perform a flanking maneuver using the shadows of homes for cover. Although one suspect urged the other to give up as there was no escape, the suspect responded, "No, someone is gonna die." Komosinski fired on the suspect, wounding him. Officers captured the suspect as he was crawling again for his weapon.

When asked what the most valuable lesson he learned from this incident was, Komosinski said getting psychological help was important, but added his training was also paramount in surviving both the incident and the aftermath.

> It pays to train. Prior to coming with ISP, I would've never "double-tapped" (a shooting technique where two successive shots are fired instead of just one.) I might not have grabbed my shotgun and I wouldn't have used cover as much. But because of my experience at the academy, where instructors constantly teach good techniques, I developed good habits. It's also important that the academy training be followed up by good refresher classes. When you are in a stressful situation, you revert back to your training. If you're trained properly then you're not going to have a problem. But if you're making a lot of mistakes in your training, they're definitely going to manifest themselves two and three times over in an actual situation.

The incident in which Rice was involved appeared at first to be a routine traffic stop. An NCIC check on the driver stopped for speeding showed the man was wanted in Florida on multiple felony counts. Rice called for backup and began a felony stop when the man decided to drive off and a pursuit ensued. Rice was joined by Corporal Robert Conner who was driving one of the state police Mustangs. Conner pulled alongside the fleeing pickup at an off ramp. The man turned in front of the Mustang actually driving up and over the hood of the smaller car, disabling it.

As the man attempted to back off the wreckage, Rice decided to terminate the pursuit and rammed the pickup with his patrol car. The subject reached for a gun and turned toward Conner, who had been knocked unconscious in the crash. When the suspect realized Rice had his own weapon drawn and leveled at the suspect, the suspect surrendered.

When asked if counseling for troopers who had been involved in shootings or other traumatic incidents was necessary, Rice said although he was not forced to shot the subject, seeing a fellow officer in mortal danger made counseling absolutely imperative.

> I found myself in a position of denial. In other words, "I'm a macho cop, I can handle the situation." I think we all try to be that. When we arrive at a situation, we're supposed to handle it because we're trained to, but I think sometimes we try to start living that in our own minds. I had some definite problems that I needed to face over this ordeal. The first couple of weeks I thought I was handling everything quite well and I was given the opportunity to seek counseling if I wanted it. I almost turned it down but I didn't, and I'm so glad I didn't.

Dave Neal said its imperative officers involved in traumatic incidents get help after the incident.

> When we're talking about traumatic incidents and officer survival, we're talking about the whole package; the actual physical encounter and the tactics used to survive, as well as following up on the emotional side of the encounter so that we can keep that officer a healthy, functioning person for the rest of his career.

On February 20, 1989, the Idaho State Police kicked off a year-long celebration of its fiftieth anniversary. A ceremony was held in the governor's office and Governor Andrus signed a proclamation, proclaiming Idaho State Police Week.

Steve Cazier presents Governor Andrus with an Idaho State Police 50th anniversary commemorative pistol.

In a letter to the employees of the Idaho State Police, Governor Andrus said, "Idaho owes heartfelt thanks to you."

Any historian reflecting on the factors that have made Idaho great would certainly have to include the immeasurable contribution made by the Idaho State Police. All Idahoans owe a debt of gratitude to the many men and women who have served with the ISP during the past fifty years. The entire role of the Idaho State Police trooper is based on service. You have patrolled the highways of our state, rendered aid at accident scenes, provided directions or roadside assistance, apprehended

> intoxicated drivers, and protected motorists through the enforcement of traffic laws. You have provided aid during major emergencies and natural disasters. You have protected the public by capturing dangerous criminals.
>
> You have enhanced safety, speaking in our schools and before civic, community, and business groups. Wherever and in whatever form duty has called, you have always been prompt to serve. Your image of dedication, integrity, courage, and courteous service is a source of pride for all Idahoans. As you celebrate your golden anniversary, I'm certain our citizens will join me in a well-deserved salute to your accomplishments, and a heartfelt thank you for your sacrifices on our behalf. Truly, Idaho is a better place because of the Idaho State Police (Andrus).

Steve Cazier presented Governor Andrus with a fiftieth anniversary commemorative pistol that was manufactured through commission with the Smith and Wesson Company. Cazier was instrumental in getting the commemorative pistols for troopers who wanted them.

> I wanted a commemorative gun, but there wasn't anyone working on that so I took it over. I asked the the Idaho State Police Association if they would support doing it. It was decided we could offer payroll deductions for people who wanted to buy a gun. Smith and Wesson required a minimum of 226 guns be purchased in order for them to produce the weapons. I ended up having to personally buy several guns, but we finally got enough orders. The commemorative guns were a .357 magnum revolver.

The year-long festivities included special displays of vintage cars and uniforms, and a fiftieth anniversary logo was created by Phomma Keopanya, from Twin Falls High School. The logo was stamped on state police envelopes and incorporated into a pin worn by troopers throughout 1989. Keopanya received a one hundred dollar savings bond for his winning entry, and rode to Boise in a state police vehicle to participate in the proclamation ceremonies at the governor's office.

The Idaho State Police was also recognized nationally in 1989 for having one of the best dressed police forces, and for having one of the best police vehicles. State troopers were honored by the National

Association of Uniform Manufacturers and Distributors with the Outstanding Achievement Award.

The state police had earned this award in 1981. The state police patrol vehicle won third place in the Law and Order Magazine best police vehicle contest. Idaho's famous "skunk" car took honors for unique design and for being readily identifiable as a state police vehicle.

Idaho legislators approved nine more trooper position in 1989, including three hazardous materials specialists and six trooper positions. The hazmat troopers were assigned to instruct hazmat handling and respond to all hazmat incidents either to assist local authorities or to conduct the investigation.

Humpherys said with the ever increasing problems of hazardous materials and radioactive waste encompassing the state, it was imperative the state police maintain a strong hazmat specialty force to strengthen the state's ability to recover costs of toxic spill cleanup and other damages. Steve Cazier said the hazmat team was very well trained. "We were given excellent training and a lot of it. They wanted us to be specialists and be able to assume incident command in the event of a hazmat incident."

State police leadership also announced the establishment of the Idaho State Police Auto Theft Unit. The unit had the responsibility of investigating auto theft within the state. The Idaho State Police had previously established an operating unit under Director Rooney with four officers working part-time patrol and part-time theft investigation. With the formal establishment of an auto theft unit, six troopers were trained with a sergeant appointed to oversee the investigators.

Brent Bunderson said despite the numerous successes of the auto theft unit, it only existed for a little over a year.

> In early 1990 because of budget requirements, the unit was disbanded. I stayed active in vehicle theft and served as the Regional President of the Association of Auto Theft Investigation. I helped create the Wasatch Front Vehicle Theft Association, which is headquartered out of Salt Lake City, Utah. This association is still in effect in Idaho, Wyoming, and Utah. I was fortunate that I got to continue working auto theft until I retired from the state police in 2002. There was a tremendous need for an auto-theft unit then, and I believe there is still a need for one.

By 1989, the state police Crisis Response Team found itself responding to a variety of critical incidents across the state. Ed Strickfaden commended the CRT for its assistance to District 1 during the annual Aryan Nation conference in north Idaho in April of 1989.

The CRTs assignment consisted of crowd and traffic control, and of handling any critical incidents that might occur during the Aryan Nation skinhead conference in Hayden Lake. Although no incidents required the special skills of the team, it was gratifying to see such a professional group of officers work so diligently at the tasks assigned. It was largely due to the team's efforts and professional demeanor that set the stage for this very successful law enforcement operation.

The Idaho State Police Crisis Response Team in 1988: Back row: left to right-Craig Harris, Steve Jones, Ralph Powell, Delon "Papa" Jones, Dave Neal. Front row: left to right-Mike Nauman, Lamont Johnson, Wayne Marsh, Dan Tiller.

Strickfaden added the CRT had come to the aid of north Idaho several times over the previous three years to assist with the Aryan Nation conference.

> I believe it speaks very highly of the team and their reputation that local law enforcement was willing to entirely turn over any critical situation to them for resolution. The CRT members are excellent representatives of the Idaho State Police and everyone on the team is dedicated to superior performance.

Jerome County Prosecuting Attorney John Horgan, in a letter to Director Richardson, commended the CRT for its assistance to Jerome County on a drug case.

> Merrill Kelly and his crew were working on a narcotics group in our area. One of the suspects to be arrested was reputed to possess at least one semi-automatic pistol. The suspect was also reported to have a propensity to use that weapon. Merrill made the decision to call in the experts. Your CRT did a tremendous job. The suspect was arrested and he did have a pistol in hand. Several other rifles and shotguns were removed from the suspect's home (ISP).

In July, the CRT was called in to assist Twin Falls County with a hostage situation. Delon Jones said the standoff between the suspect and officers lasted forty-three hours.

> The CRT was called in when Jesus Bautista Mejia took both of his daughters hostage. I was recovering from knee surgery, but I responded because I was the team's sniper. They were trying to talk him out, but he wasn't having any of it. Every time he stood up or came near the window he had one of the girls held in front of him. Sometimes when he came to the window he'd hold a gun to the child's head. After we'd been there for some time, I was told if I had a head shot to take it. About every 20 minutes for the next four hours, I took my weapon off safety, but he finally gave himself up. It was a very tense standoff.

Dave Neal said the stand-off started when police were called to a domestic dispute at the Mejia's house.

> We tried to talk him out of the house but he refused. We decided to deploy gas, but he heard us coming and he came out the door holding a gun to his oldest daughter's head. He had her in front of him and his other daughter behind him. He went into another house down the street a couple of blocks. It was his wife's cousin's house. We couldn't risk shooting him because we were afraid of hitting one of the girls or another officer. He stayed at that house for several hours and then finally gave up.

Neal said this incident was one the CRT used to enhance its training and hone its skills.

> As a team we had developed Alpha, Bravo, and Charlie plans for various situations. Bravo was always the gas plan, and gas is a very effective tool to ending these types of incidents. But, because of the failure in this particular case—meaning Mejia was able to escape because the way we employed the gas, he was not affected by it—we learned we needed to employ gas into the building and any possible exit points, such as back doors.

In December of 1989, the CRT was recognized for its expertise by the Oregon State Police. In a letter to Neal from Reginald Madsen, the Oregon State Police Deputy Superintendent wrote:

> The Oregon State Police wishes to extend its appreciation for your assistance during our SWAT team training in Baker City. Our personnel advised you took time from your busy schedule to aid in critiquing our general and scenario training. This is an invaluable aspect of our training and it is greatly appreciated.

Neal said another of the reasons the CRT was successful in developing relations with allied agencies, was because of its attitude toward quickly establishing incident command.

> We were not there to take over a situation. We were there as a tactical solution if a tactical solution became necessary. The police chief or sheriff remained in charge of the incident and before we made a decision to act, we were all on the same page about what the plan was.

State police assistance was also requested in late summer of 1989, when numerous troopers were called in to assist on the Loman Complex Fire.

Captain Rob Storm, ISP 593, said troopers were called in to assist with road blocks around the area and to provide security at firefighter camps.

> The Loman Fire was the largest fire in the nation at the time, and was threatening homes and structures. The Boise County Sheriff requested our assistance and along with providing road blocks and traffic assistance, we were also there because of the huge camp of firefighters. There was some concern about violence in that big of a camp and our goal was to be very visible and keep away any potential for trouble.

The fire raged from July 29 through August 11, and twenty-nine state troopers from Districts Three, Four, Five, and Six worked 787 man-hours in the Lowman area. Storm said the state police mission was successful, but added the downside to the assignment was, "… everything stank of smoke. Our uniforms stank, our cars stank. It took a long time before the smell was gone from our cars."

On December 4, 1986, nearly every state trooper in District 3 was called in to assist when a riot erupted in the cellblock housing the most dangerous prisoners of the Idaho State Correctional Institution. This cellblock was known as Unit 8 Tier B. The rioting prisoners destroyed the cellblock by smashing windows and walls, tearing out electrical fixtures and wiring, setting fires, and flooding units.

Steve Cazier said because of the fear of a mass breakout, troopers were assigned to separate inmates as they exited certain areas of the prison.

> One of the inmates got stabbed at the start of the riot, and at the same time prisoners started fires in one of the cell blocks. As guards sent the prisoners out of the block, we gathered them into small groups and kept them separated which helped quell the rioting.

Ronald Kirtley said the prisoners made a complete mess of the prison.

> We set up a perimeter around the prison and the prisoners were really making a mess of things inside the prison grounds. There was an auto body shop at the prison and some of the prisoners were driving cars from the shop into buildings. There was also a large pile of wood the prisoners were using for different building projects and they ended up burning all of that. We were able to ship the maximum security prisoners out to other states, but the rest of the prisoners had to be housed in tents after the riot.

Rob Storm described the experience as, "…completely surreal."

> We separated law enforcement officers into groups of eight to ten in a team and then we assigned search grids to each team. The teams were assigned to clear each cell block. Half of the team was to arrest prisoners, the other half of the team was to provide cover. I was a cover officer. As we came across prisoners, we would search them, cuff them, and then take them out to the central yard. It was an extremely surreal experience. Smoke was pouring out the cell blocks and there was a lot of yelling. The lights were dim and it was kind of like being on a movie set.

By 1990, the leadership of the Idaho State Police reported the state police held the traffic accidents on Idaho's roadways to its lowest number in twenty-six years. The auto theft unit was also complimented for its significant achievements. The six investigators assigned to the unit recovered ninety-nine stolen vehicles and various other stolen items valued at over $800,000. The unit completed 725 agency assists to city police departments and sheriff's offices.

Of particular note, Humpherys reported alert troopers recovered over $8,000,000 worth of illegal drugs. Humpherys said the huge amount of drugs recovered was only a small portion of the estimated amount transported across Idaho, adding the state police could be even more effective in reducing traffic accidents, drug trafficking, and auto theft if there were sufficient troopers to conduct twenty-four hour patrol.

> Another year has passed and we still do not have a twenty-four hour patrol on any portion of Idaho's roadways. This will continue to be a major goal of the state police as we look at 1990 and beyond. The state police recognize Idaho is quickly changing. A sound economy and increased tourist travel is bringing more citizens to our state. As the population increases, so do the number of calls for service from the public and from other police agencies.

Ed Strickfaden was the District One commander during that time period, and he recalls along with an increase in drug and other arrests, his unit was also facing issues with corruption among elected officials in Shoshone County. While the particulars of the case cannot be discussed here—as some officials who were allegedly participating in the corruption scheme were found not guilty—Strickfaden said the case was investigated by the FBI and through that investigation, several activities that contributed to the increased crime rate in northern Idaho, "...were brought to a screeching halt."

> We worked with the FBI on an undercover corruption investigation in the Kellogg-Wallace area. The conclusion of that investigation ended the corruption. Whore houses were shut down, as were several other illegal enterprises. Unfortunately, the FBI wasn't able to convict everyone involved, but the case did go a long way toward cleaning up a very bad situation.

Wayne Longo was the Special Agent-In-Charge in District One when the corruption scandal was under investigation.

> Shoshone County had some serious wrong-doings going on and I was basically ordered to keep my detectives out of the county. We were helping the FBI conduct surveillance on drug dealers that were being protected by some elected officials, and

also on some fairly large gambling activities. The FBI was not successful in prosecuting some of those involved, but the investigation did end a lot of the corruption.

The positive confirmation from Idaho citizens, of pride toward the Idaho State Police as it celebrated its fiftieth year, reinforced in troopers and the leadership of the state police a determination to continue their record of impeccable service. That determination would help to carry the state police through one of its most difficult and demanding decades: the 1990s.

17 ★ Officer Down

We've done so much, with so little, for so long, that now we can do almost anything with next to nothing.

Idaho State Police Colonel Rich Humpherys

In 1970, Idaho's population was a little over 700,000 citizens. By 1990, the state's population topped the one million mark, but the number of Idaho State Police patrol officers available to keep Idaho's roadways safe, remained at the 1970s level with just 137 officers to cover Idaho's thousands of miles of state and federal roadways.

In 1990, the Idaho State Police force had fewer officers per capita than any of the surrounding states, and was also the lowest paid state police force of any of the surrounding states. But despite those figures, what really bothered troopers and their leadership, was the inability of the state police to provide twenty-four hour coverage.

In 1972, the National Safety Council recommended the Idaho State Police have a total staff of 350 troopers. With under half of that number in 1990, the state police was tasked with increased challenges in areas ranging from traffic control to illegal drug enforcement activities.

In his column, The Eagle's Nest, in the summer 1990 edition of *Idaho State Police Magazine,* Humpherys reminded his employees at least they had the tools they needed to do the job.

> Our goal is to give each officer the best tools we can provide. But, we also must live within our budget. We're often forced to make difficult decisions about what we'd like to have and what we can afford. For the most part, I believe we're doing a commendable job. Our officers have equipment as good as, and in many cases better than our similar-sized counterparts. In some cases – computer technology for instance – we're ahead of many law enforcement agencies.

While the leadership of the state police felt the organization was moving in the right direction, troopers across the state were not as well pleased with some of the department's policies. One "unwritten" policy in particular that troopers did not agree with was that state police officers were encouraged to adopt a policy of tolerance, such as not writing citations for traffic or other violations, towards members of the governor's staff, state legislators, sheriffs, etcetera

The policy caused serious trouble for Department of Law Enforcement Director Mack Richardson. In news articles across the state, Governor Andrus expressed anger over the policy and promised, "...disciplinary action," if it were proven that Director Richardson had ordered troopers to not issue citations to legislators.

Idaho Code does allow that senators and representatives, "...in all cases, except for treason, felony, or breach of the peace, shall be privileged from arrest during the session of the legislature, and in going to and from the same..." but does not specify that legislators cannot receive written citations for traffic violations.

Upon hearing that troopers were told not to ticket legislators, Governor Andrus said he would not hesitate to fire the persons responsible for directing troopers to give special treatment to lawmakers and other high-ranking state administrators.

Eager to clarify to his troopers the department's stance on the issue, Colonel Humpherys sent a memo to all of his districts:

> The following information is to reinforce and put into writing what I relayed to you verbally on November 4, 1990. The following enforcement policy is in effect immediately: All Idaho State Police officers are to treat all citizens fairly and equally in that no one is above the law. The type of enforcement action taken is determined by officer discretion based on the circumstances present or known at the time of the contact. If there is any question about this order, contact me immediately.

On November 8, 1990, Governor Andrus announced he had asked for the resignation of Richardson and had also requested Humpherys, who had announced a January 1, 1991 plan to retire, to leave earlier so the governor could seek his successor immediately. The governor further announced he would soon be reorganizing the state police.

> It has become increasingly clear over the last four days that management problems exist in the department and in the state police. I will not tolerate, nor will the people of Idaho tolerate any policy of special treatment of anyone. My review of the facts in this regard leave no doubt those instructions were issued by the director of the department to that effect. The state police officers on the highways have no doubt done what they were instructed to do (Andrus).

The governor had flown to northern and eastern Idaho to interview troopers directly about the policy they had been told to enforce, and in order to ensure the troopers would feel comfortable in discussing the issue with him, did not allow supervisory personnel to be present.

> The Idaho State Police is a highly professional, talented and capable organization. All the troopers are asking is to be allowed to do the professional job they are trained to do. This unfortunate and unacceptable incident should in no way reflect on the individual members of the state police. They were not responsible.

Colonel Humpherys retired as he originally planned in January of 1991. Ronald Moore was named superintendent of the state police. Richard Cade was appointed as the Director of the Department of Law Enforcement following Richardson's resignation.

With the flap of "...forced favoritism," behind them state troopers got back to the business of keeping Idahoans safe, and among the top items on their agenda was arresting DUI drivers, encouraging citizens to buckle-up under Idaho's new seatbelt law, and supporting other law enforcement agencies with the resources of the Crisis Response Team, which responded to six critical incidents in 1991.

Dave Neal said in March of 1991, the CRT responded to a request from the Boundary County Sheriff's Office when two members of the Hells Angels Motorcycle Gang held two Canadian Port of Entry personnel hostage. The subjects were later captured by the Royal Canadian Mounted Police. In April of 1991, the team responded to a request from the Filer Police Department on a shots fired call. The subjects surrendered after an eight hour standoff when CS gas was deployed.

In June of 1991, the CRT responded to three requests including one from Butte County Sheriff's Office on an armed, barricaded subject, who surrendered after eight hours, and one from the Washington County Sheriff's Office on an armed, barricaded subject in New Meadows, who surrendered after twelve hours. Both deployments ended when the CRT deployed CS gas.

Butte County Sheriff Cary Van Etten commended the CRT and other state police officers for their support during the incident. In a letter to Captain Pat McDonald, District Six Commander, Van Etten said:

> I would like to take this time to thank you and your men for the assistance rendered in the situation we had in which an armed man barricaded himself in a house after severely beating his girlfriend. It is quite comforting to know that the manpower that arrived to assist is available to the small departments such as ours, not to mention the expertise exemplified by the personnel at the incident. The training and practice required to plan and execute the operation in such a professional way was quite impressive to me and other observers.

The third June incident in which the state police and its CRT members were involved in was, "deeply personal" to every trooper as it involved the shooting of one of their own.

On June 15, 1991, Father's Day, Corporal Steve Hobbs was shot when he stopped an out-of-state vehicle for speeding near the Utah Border.

Hobbs, a five year veteran of the state police and one of the only state troopers ever involved in more than one shooting incident, said he was in an area of the Interstate where radio communications were, "…hit and miss, but mostly miss."

> I was down near the Utah border which is a notoriously bad radio area. I stopped a vehicle for speeding, but I didn't check out on the stop because I knew I didn't have good communication. I was walking up to the car and I remember I did everything I had been taught to do. I touched the trunk to see if it was open and also to clear the car by looking in the back seat. When I was in training, I was taught to never go past the A-post until you look inside the car. When I started to make my pivot around the A-post

the driver started shooting. He had his gun held up against his chest.

Steve Hobbs was pulled from his burning patrol vehicle by Floyd Veibell, a motorist who stopped to assist Hobbs. Photo courtesy of the Idaho State Police.

The driver was Shawn Kerrigan of Milwaukee, Wisconsin. Kerrigan was driving a stolen 1989 Dodge Omni, and was heading for Mountain Home to see his sister. He was traveling seventy-five miles-per-hour in a sixty-five mile-per-hour zone.

He shot at me four times and hit me three times. The first shot hit me in the left shoulder and skimmed along my vest and lodged in my tricep. One bullet went through my right arm into my chest and exploded. I still have shrapnel around my heart, and later on I found out I still had the bullet in my tricep. Another bullet was stopped by my vest. The fourth bullet missed me. I knew I was in serious trouble, but I tried to go after the guy.

Hobbs was critically injured, but managed to get back to his patrol car and began to pursue Kerrigan. Shock and loss of blood caused Hobbs to fade in and out of consciousness. Losing control of his vehicle, he crossed the median and came up on the eastbound side of the Interstate. A few moments later, Hobbs went back into the median where his car was stopped by the tall sagebrush. Kerrigan, who later admitted he thought Hobbs was dead and other officers were coming after him, exited the Interstate at the Juniper rest area. Kerrigan fled into the trees and said he planned to have a shoot out with officers if he was pursued.

Hobbs said he called for help on his radio, which was received by District 4 Dispatcher Dee Silver.

> She told me later that I was screaming into the radio for help. I was able to tell her I was south of Sweetzer. She dispatched Delon Jones, who was working up on Interstate 86 and was about seventy miles away. Delon had one of our Mustangs, which was a pretty fast car, and he told me he was going around 140 miles-per-hour to get to me.

In the meantime, Hobbs was in his vehicle with the top lights still on. The heat from the car's catalytic converter set the sagebrush and subsequently his car, on fire.

A few moments later, a family stopped to assist Hobbs. Floyd Veibell, his wife Jeanene, their son Bryan, and his wife Shari, and their daughter Anette, and her husband, Grant Redden, along with their seven young children were traveling home to Utah from Idaho in two vehicles. The family saw the patrol car and the smoke. The family stopped and Floyd pulled Hobbs from the burning car.

A few minutes later, Michael Bryson and his wife, Dena, of Clinton, Utah, arrived at the scene. The Veibells and Redden began administering first aid. Concerned the burning patrol car might explode, Hobbs' rescuers moved him to the opposite side of the highway and truck driver, Arthur Roberts, of Fort Pierce, Florida parked his truck between the patrol car and Hobbs as ammunition in the patrol car began exploding.

Hobbs said several other people stopped to assist, and some of them attempted to put out the fire while others assisted with administering first aid. John Cook, and his wife, Joanie, and brother, Bill Dennison, arrived at the scene several minutes after the Veibells. Cook was an EMT and Dennison was an EMT in training. Cook had his EMT equipment bag with him and provided essential life saving assistance to Hobbs. Ten minutes later Gerald and Jacqueline Jeppsen arrived at the scene in their vehicle pulling a fifth-wheel trailer.

> The Jeppsens were asked if they would transport me in their travel trailer, and they agreed. The Jeppsens and a bunch of my other rescuers took me to Snowville, which was about eleven miles away. Once we got there, someone called an air ambulance and I was taken to McKay/Dee Hospital in Ogden, Utah, where I spent several weeks.

On June 16, a multi-agency manhunt was assembled to search for Kerrigan, who had been identified because he left his wallet in the vehicle he abandoned at the Juniper Rest Area. Kerrigan had covered several miles on foot, but was caught after asking a BLM crew for water. The BLM crew recognized Kerrigan and reported the sighting. Within minutes, Idaho Fish and Game Officer Tom Poczkalski and Mini-Cassia Search and Rescue team member Bruce Spaulding apprehended Kerrigan without incident.

Kerrigan later pled guilty to the shooting and was sentenced to a forty year fixed term sentence in the Idaho State Penitentiary. For Hobbs, the long journey to recovery was filled with even more tragedy.

> I am so grateful to my rescuers. They did everything they could to save me and I will always, always appreciate that. But unfortunately, things didn't end as I hoped they would. I really thought I would be able to recover and get back in a patrol car someday. But, that didn't happen, and because the state didn't have any sort of long-term disability program, I didn't have too many resources to help me out. The law has since changed, but at the time I was shot, basically the philosophy was you either die or you get better and go back to work, there wasn't really anything in place for people who were disabled.

Hobbs said he worked for a while as a brand inspector, and then at the Cottrell Port-of-Entry. Eventually, he became a school resource officer with his wages shared by the Minidoka Sheriff's Office, the school district, and the state.

It took me a long time to realize I wasn't going to get better. I was going to be disabled for the rest of my life and would never be a state police officer again. That was especially hard because other than my family, nothing meant more to me than looking out my window and seeing that black and white in my driveway. Probably the worst thing that happened to me was that I'd lost so much blood I had traumatic brain injury. My temper was on a hair trigger and I was suffering from serious PTSD. My wife and I ended up divorcing, and for a long time I would wake up thinking I'm going to get better, but of course I didn't.

Steve Hobbs shakes hands with the actor who played Hobbs in the Rescue 911 dramatization of Hobb's story. Photo courtesy of Idaho State Police.

Hobbs said the state did send his family to a psychologist but the doctor's daughter was diagnosed with cancer and the doctor quit seeing patients. Hobbs added although the Idaho State Police worked with a variety of different agencies and a disability package was put together to support him and his family:

We sort of fell through the cracks on the psychological help, and because the state didn't have long-term disability for injured officers, it didn't take long to exhaust the money they did have

> available. I ended up with no income, and I feel like I was never fully compensated for my disability.

Hobbs said he didn't blame the state police for his predicament, and added he was grateful his incident lead to legislation that would help a state trooper if one were injured in the future.

Over twenty years has passed since the incident. Hobbs' story was featured on the television show *"Rescue 911,"* and he says he has, "... gone through dramatic changes," since the incident.

> I took me a long time to realize I wasn't going to get better and I needed to accept I would always be disabled. Once I realized that, it was like a ten-ton weight was lifted off of my shoulders. I have since learned how to ask for help, and how to rely on other people when I need to. Once I realized I could do that, it was like a one hundred and eighty degree flip from where I had been.

Although he has come to terms with his disability, Hobbs says no matter how many years have passed he still misses being a state trooper. On September 14, 2012, the Idaho State Police District Four building was dedicated as the Fontaine Cooper building in honor of the first Idaho State Police officer killed in the line of duty. Hobbs was a guest speaker at the dedication and in addressing the Cooper family said, "...even knowing the outcome, and I believe Fontaine Cooper would say the same, I would do it all over just to once again serve as an Idaho State Police trooper."

If any of those serving in the leadership of the state police were complacent about officer safety prior to the Hobbs shooting, none were complacent after the incident. Hobbs was asked several times to speak to state police trainees about his experience and what they should learn from it. In the summer, 1992 *Idaho State Police* magazine, Hobbs was interviewed and in the interview was asked: "You talked to cadets at the recent academy. What did you try to impress upon them?" Hobbs answered:

> I wanted them to know that they have to have a desire to get home. When you do this job, it's just that, a job. You need to make sure that your family is your number one priority. I also told them that yes, you can get shot out here, but you can live through it...

Hobbs said as soon as he turned on his lights to stop Kerrigan, Kerrigan had it in his mind to shoot Hobbs. Kerrigan later stated he had considered shooting, "…the tall officer in the Mustang," (Delon Jones), when Jones got out of his car at the rest area where Kerrigan had left the stolen car. Kerrigan also considered committing suicide, but abandoning that idea, threw his gun into the brush and left the area on foot. The gun was never recovered.

Dave Neal said as painful as incidents such as Hobbs' shooting might be, these experiences do offer important opportunities to learn critical information that enhances officer safety.

> We have learned a lot of things over the years about officer safety, and unfortunately a great many of them were learned the hard way. A cop is always behind in the decision when it comes to a shooting, and through officer shootings, we have learned officers need to take care of themselves first, not rush after the suspect if they flee. It's a very important lesson. An officer's first thought should be providing self first-aid to ensure they survive their injuries, not, "I'm going to get the guy who did this."

In the same interview as mentioned above, Hobbs was also asked, "Is Idaho changing? Are we heading for increased violence in this state?" Hobbs' answer was chilling, and unfortunately quit accurate.

> Yes, things are changing. People are beginning to think that guns are the way out. You stop these people on drug interdictions and ninety percent of them or more are carrying weapons to protect their stash. We go to bar fights all the time that involve weapons. It used to be just knives, now it's guns. People say they hear firecrackers going off in their neighborhoods, so we respond to the call to find out someone's been shooting off .22s or .38s or even higher caliber weapons. In Rupert just a while ago, someone had a high-powered rifle they were shooting off in town. People are getting more and more involved in weaponry out here. Officers need to be more aware of their own safety as well as the safety of those they are trying to protect. (sic)

The state police was doing what it could with what it had to keep troopers safe, but along with more people considering guns, "...as the way out." More and more Idahoans were becoming involved in the use and sale of illicit drugs. In the mid-1980s, cocaine seemed to be the drug of choice for many of Idaho's drug abusers. By the early 1990s methamphetamine was the rising star. Law enforcement agencies across the state were desperate to get this drug off the streets. "All drugs are a bad deal," said Wayne Longo. "But meth is the worst."

In early 1991, the state police announced two of its newest employees had been "hired" for the specific duty of assisting officers with drug detection. K9s Annie and Finni were funded under the Federal Highway Administration's MCSAP program. Annie was assigned to Corporal Gary Brush in District 5, and Finni was assigned to Corporal Kevin Butler in District 3.

The primary mission of the K9 teams was to stem both illegal narcotics use by commercial vehicle drivers as well as to be vigilant for narcotics smuggling aboard commercial vehicles. Both the dogs and their handlers received extensive training, and within their first year both dogs were credited with assisting officers in recovering almost $250,000 total street value of drugs, including marijuana, methamphetamine, and cocaine.

Master Corporal Terry Ford, retired, ISP 587, also received a K9 partner, Code Red Rose. A state police news release, stated Rose, a twenty month old black Labrador retriever, joined the state police to sniff out narcotics in the state's five northern counties. Following is an excerpt from the press release:

> Rose has already aided state police officers in uncovering marijuana and methamphetamines, but she is also trained to detect hashish, cocaine, and heroin. She completed a six-week narcotics detection class in Stanwood, Washington before joining the Idaho State Police. Her abilities were demonstrated during the training in Washington, when her nose found a locker with marijuana growing equipment on Camano Island that wasn't part of the training exercise. Officers were able to obtain a search warrant and seize the locker's contents. She is credited with a total of 100 successful searches of cars, buildings, open areas, luggage, and buried narcotics. As a commissioned state trooper, Rose will be available to aid law enforcement agencies.

Ford said in the first year he and "Rosie," as he called her, worked together they discovered over $140,000 street value in cocaine, marijuana, and other drugs.

> The best part of having a dog for drug interdiction is that you never get skunked. With a K9, if there are drugs you're going to find them. I went to a lot of different districts with Rosie and we were very successful. I was also the one who started the program in District One of taking K9s into schools to search for drugs, and that program was really successful. Rosie was the first dog in this area (northern Idaho) that a judge took judicial notice of, meaning defense attorneys couldn't question her capabilities.

Ford was among several K9 handlers who helped pass laws in Idaho for better protection of police animals.

> Senator Gary Schroeder and Bob Taylor, who owned a kennel in Sagle, were the two who started the push to make it a felony to kill, harm, or harass a police dog, police horse, or search and rescue dog. There was a lot of concern that as police dogs became more effective against crime their lives would be targeted by criminals. A misdemeanor wasn't enough of a deterrent. It costs a lot of money to train these dogs and the laws on the books at that time basically made it a minor crime to hurt one. The bill we pushed through recognized K9s as police officers, and made it a felony to hurt these animals.

Ford said his favorite part of his career with the state police was working with Rosie.

> I was very upset when the state police did away with its drug dog program because I think it was hugely successful. Rosie gave great probable cause in our war against drugs and doing away with the program was a huge hit to the state police.

Although unhappy with the loss of the drug dog program, Ford said as a law enforcement officer, "the Idaho State Police was still the best place to be; there was good, there was bad, but I always felt like I was part of a family." Ford was especially touched by the support he received when Rosie died in February of 2003. Rosie had served the state for seven years.

During that time, Rosie located and law enforcement seized illegal drugs and narcotics with a street value of approximately five million dollars. Rosie's accomplishments and those of other K9s past, present, and future, serve as a reminder that we can accomplish great things for the citizens that we serve.

Terry Ford and his dog Code Red Rose, or "Rosie".

The feeling of belonging to a family is a common theme among law enforcement entities nationwide, and October of 1991, law enforcement officers finally had a way to honor law enforcement officers who died in the line-of-duty. Thousands of law enforcement officers from across the nation gathered in Washington D.C., for the dedication of the National Law Enforcement Memorial. The memorial honors federal, state, and local law enforcement officers, whose lives were lost in service.

At the time of the memorial's dedication in 1991, 12,561 names, including thirty-five Idaho officer's names, were carved into the memorial which features two curving 304-foot-long marble walls.

P.O.S.T. Academy Executive Director Larry Plott (retired) and Trooper Jay Komosinski represented Idaho at the dedication ceremony. Jody Pogue, the widow of slain Idaho Fish and Game Officer William Pogue, and his daughter, Jody Turner, also attended. In the Winter 1991 *Idaho State Police* magazine, Plott described some of the day's events.

> The dedication began with a procession in which more than 10,000 participated. The procession began on Capitol Hill at noon. Marching were representatives of law enforcement organizations from almost every state, as well as survivors. In addition, the procession included horses, K9 officers, bagpipe units, antique police vehicles, and hundreds of motorcycles and police cruisers…At 1 p.m. on October 14, the roll call of fallen officers began at the memorial site. In this ceremony, 160 readers, representing every state, read each of the 12,561 names of fallen officers engraved on the memorial's walls. The roll call lasted throughout the night of October 14, ending just before the actual dedication ceremony on October 15, and was followed immediately by the playing of "Echo Taps."

Those attending the memorial voiced the "sincere hope and prayer," no more names would be added to the wall. Unfortunately, those hopes and prayers have not been realized. Since 1991, new names are added each spring, and to date, the National Law Enforcement Memorial has over 19,000 names on it.

18 ✱ Weaver Case

In valor there is hope.

Tacitus

The cabin where Weaver and his family lived during the Ruby Ridge stand off. Photo courtesy of the Idaho State Police.

In the 1992 Annual Report to Director of Law Enforcement, Richard Cade, Idaho State Police Colonel Moore said the priorities of reducing traffic fatalities; increasing arrests for drivers under the influence of alcohol or drugs; and increased emphasis on educating youngsters in the kindergarten through sixth-grade levels on seat belt safety, were established.

Unfortunately, our driving under the influence arrests were not increased. This perhaps can be attributed to extensive personnel commitments for other activities requiring law enforcement resources such as the Ruby Ridge incident in northern Idaho. In any event, driving under the influence violations and seatbelt enforcement will continue to be priorities to division employees during the years ahead.

For members of the CRT, 1992 started with a request from the Gooding Police Department. Gooding Chief of Police Steve Spence requested the CRT to assist in serving a high-risk search and arrest warrant. This was the first of six high-risk operations the CRT participated in during 1992.

Dave Neal said Joseph C. Palczynski had barricaded himself in an apartment and was armed.

> The stand-off lasted about twelve hours then we deployed CS gas. Palczynski tried to climb out of the second-story window of the apartment and we captured him. I learned about a year later, Palczynski was killed in a standoff with the Baltimore Police Department.

In a letter to Colonel Moore, Chief Spence said he deeply appreciated the team, adding, "...It is really comforting to have the team in place for local agencies to call upon when needed."

> Palczynski, of Baltimore, Maryland, was wanted on several Maryland state, and federal charges, including escape from a mental hospital, federal firearms charges, and threatening to kill police officers. I deeply appreciate the response of the team and want to commend the entire team, for a job well done and the professionalism they displayed during the operation and arrest.

In March, 1992, a request from District Two sent the team north to assist with an armed subject in a semi-truck. The subject ended up committing suicide. July took the CRT to Valley County, when the Valley County Sheriff's Office requested help with an armed and barricaded subject. The subject surrendered after deployment of CS gas. A request from District 5 was also received in July when three prisoners escaped while being transported.

But the incident that would take up hundreds of man-hours, involve troopers from across the state, and pitted the CRT not only against Idaho's difficult terrain, but also against an armed and dangerous separatist family, was the request for state police assistance when U.S. Marshal William Degan was shot and killed on August 21, 1992.

The Ruby Ridge Incident, as it is widely referred to now, actually began in October of 1989, when Randy Weaver, a former U. S. Army Green Beret, allegedly sold two sawed-off shotguns to an undercover agent from the Bureau of Alcohol, Tobacco, and Firearms.

Weaver was suspected of weapons trafficking with the Aryan Nation white supremacist group and in January of 1991, Weaver was arrested for making and possessing illegal firearms. Slated to appear in court in February of 1991, Weaver never showed. Instead, Weaver barricaded himself, his wife, Vicki, and their children, Sara, 16, Sam, 14, Rachel, 11, and Elisheba, 10 months, and their friend Kevin Harris, in his two-room cabin near Ruby Creek, which was accessible only by one steep road.

The shoot-out on August 21, 1992, began when six U.S. Marshals went into the area around Weaver's cabin to scout the area to determine suitable places away from the cabin to ambush and arrest Weaver. The marshals, dressed in camouflage, were equipped with night-vision goggles and M16 rifles. Three marshals, including Degan, formed the reconnaissance team three other marshals formed an observation post on the ridge north of the cabin.

At one point, one of the marshals threw two rocks at the Weaver cabin to test the reaction of the dogs. The dogs alerted and Harris and Sam Weaver left the cabin and followed the dogs to investigate. Weaver later told investigators that Sam had said he believed the dogs had sensed either a large animal or a man in the woods.

Once the dog alerted to them, the reconnaissance team retreated through the woods and took up hidden defensive positions at a "Y" intersection in the trails 500 yards west of the Weaver's cabin. Harris and Sam Weaver followed the dog, Striker, through the woods. Randy Harris took a separate trail and encountered the marshals at the "Y". The marshals yelled "Stop. U.S. Marshals," at Randy Weaver and Randy retreated from the marshals. About a minute later the dog and Harris and Sam came out of the woods. A firefight erupted between the marshals and Harris and Sam Weaver.

Accounts differ as to who fired first, but when the shooting ended, U.S. Marshal William Degan, 42, was dead. Sam Weaver was also dead and Kevin Harris was injured.

Ed Strickfaden, who was a major at the time of the incident, was sent to Ruby Ridge to be in charge of state police operations.

> We didn't know Federal Marshals had gone into the area. When we were called in, we were told the marshals had gone in on a surveillance mission and ended up in a fire fight in which one of the marshals was killed. From the beginning, the main mission of the Idaho State Police was to provide security at the site. We also provided support to the Boundary County Sheriff's Office and the Bonner's Ferry Police Department.

Strickfaden said as the area filled up with protesters, he assigned Captain Lonnie Richardson, who was a sergeant at the time of the incident, and four troopers to the Boundary County Sheriff's Office and Bonners Ferry City Police.

> Richardson's mission was to make himself and those four men look like twenty men and he accomplished that mission extremely well. Those men were a huge asset to local law enforcement and did the job I asked them to do in an absolutely dedicated and professional manner.

Dave Neal said the first he knew of Marshal Degan's shooting was when the CRT was called in to remove Degan's body and other marshals pinned down in the area. Neal said although the shootout was the first time the Idaho State Police learned of the incident, he and Major Tom Thompson were made aware of Weaver's alleged activities several months prior.

> Major Thompson and I were called a few months prior to the shoot out between the marshal's and the Weaver family. We were asked by the marshals to serve warrants on Randy Weaver. Both of us looked at the information and said, "absolutely not." We recommended that Weaver be picked up on one of the occasions

> he came to town. We felt that we could get Weaver but didn't want to have to defend ourselves fighting against his kids.

Within hours of the shooting, over 100 local, state, and federal law enforcement officers were at the scene. Idaho State Police District 1 received a call from the U.S. Marshals requesting CRT assistance. Dave Neal said the CRT arrived the evening of the shoot out, and the same evening, the Idaho State Police CRT made the recovery of the surviving members of the U.S. Marshal's team and the remains of Marshal Degan.

> We were flown into Coeur d' Alene and took Idaho Transportation Department vehicles out to the site. We were briefed that three U.S. Marshals were pinned down and that a fourth, Degan, had been shot and killed. Our job was to get them out. The CRT trained extensively in working in the woods, and in working a situation where not everyone had night vision goggles (NVG). Because of our training, we were able to do the job with only three NVGs for twelve of us. It was a very tense hike into the area where the Marshals were. We went hand to shoulder in and out, and were able to recover everyone safely. It was an excellent team effort; but then, I would put the Idaho State Police CRT up against anyone. These guys were truly the very best I ever worked with, and I was completely confident in our training.

The morning after the shoot-out, law enforcement entities had set up several tents and command posts in a meadow near the bridge. Along with the large number of law enforcement officers at the site, there was also a large number of protesters, including Aryan Nation skinheads.

Sergeant Dale Hughes, retired, ISP 438, was sent with four other troopers from District 2 to Ruby Ridge to guard the bridge over Ruby Creek, which was on the main road leading up to the Weaver's cabin.

> We spent eight days on the bridge and while we were there we had a chance to work with the FBI, ATF, and other law enforcement officers. It was a very interesting time. James Culpepper and I—everyone called us the long and short team because of our height difference… he was the tall one—were able to talk to the protesters at the site, and we basically told the protesters we could talk about hunting, fishing, whatever, but no

politics or religion. For the most part, the protesters were well behaved. They were really only active when the camera was on them. The state police were able to establish a good rapport with the protesters. We did see some arrogance on the part of officers from other agencies, but Idaho State Police officers made it a priority to approach the protesters with respect and professionalism. It paid off for us. The Idaho State Police was one of the only law enforcement organizations at the site that didn't end up with a black eye over the incident.

Larry Lehtola was among the troopers sent from District 2.

There was a lot of opportunity for the situation to get out of hand, especially when it was announced on about the seventh day of the standoff, that Vicki Weaver had been shot and killed. But by that time we had established a good rapport with the protesters, and they knew that although we weren't looking for trouble, we weren't going to back down either. We were there to do a job and I think everyone, including the Aryan Nation skinheads, respected that.

Steve Cazier was sent to Ruby Ridge with the MCSAP motor home.

When I got the call to go to Bonners Ferry, I was told to take the motor home up there so the state police would have its own command center. The motor home was equipped with radios. I stayed at Ruby Ridge for about two weeks. Taking the motor home to the site meant the state police could direct its own troopers without interference, which was very important to our command staff and our troopers.

Sean Daly said while the situation with the protesters had the potential to erupt, part of the reason it didn't was because the state police had a long history of treating Aryan Nation members fairly.

The local law enforcement at Ruby Ridge really didn't have a problem with the protesters because they didn't despise us. We (the state police) had a long history of treating everyone equally. They did despise the federal agencies, so we also acted as a buffer, which really helped keep the tension down. There were a few instances when the tension was pretty high, but we (troopers) maintained our professionalism and it showed in the respect we received from the protesters.

Glen Schwartz was the District 1 Commander during Ruby Ridge stand-off.

When I was the commander in District 1, it seemed like there was always something going on with the Aryan Nations. I actually got to know Richard Butler, the Aryan Nation leader, fairly well because we had coffee together a few times, and we'd gotten into a few conversations. When it was announced Vicky Weaver had been killed the protesters got pretty upset. Butler was in the crowd and I slipped across the line to talk to him and he did keep things pretty well under control. I truly think the coffee sessions I'd had with him, made him more willing to help the state police keep things under control.

The Ruby Ridge stand-off lasted for twelve days. Weaver was finally convinced to surrender by James "Bo" Gritz, a former Special Forces lieutenant colonel who acted as a mediator between the feds and the Weavers. Gritz persuaded Weaver and Harris, who was severely injured in the shooting that killed Vicki, to surrender.

Weaver was charged with multiple crimes, including firearms charges and murder. He was acquitted on all charges except for the original charge of failure to appear. Kevin Harris was charged with the murder of Marshal Degan, but was also acquitted on all criminal charges.

In 1995, the Weavers were awarded over three million dollars and Harris was awarded nearly $400,000 in settlements from the government. Schwartz said in the months of investigations that followed the incident: "...between the FBI investigators, the Department of Justice investigators, and the Senate Subcommittee hearings, I was read my Miranda rights more times than I ever Mirandized anyone else in my career."

The Ruby Ridge Incident did not end the way that the U.S. Marshal Service, FBI, and other federal agencies would have liked. Fortunately, the conduct of the Idaho State Police was commended by everyone involved in the incident including the news media, and the protesters. In a letter to Neal, Colonel Moore expressed his gratitude to the CRT for their work during the incident.

> As you know, I have expressed concerns from the management perspective as to whether or not the Idaho State Police could continue to financially justify the CRT. You and I have discussed at length the issue that one incident could easily justify the team's existence. This happened to be the incident. I have received many excellent comments regarding the team's professional and well trained approach during this incident. All of you can stand tall and be counted with the very best. You have said that all along; and you can rest assured that others of us now have the same appreciation for you and your team's capability.

Schwartz also commended the CRT for its outstanding performance in recovering Marshal Degan and other U.S. Marshals. In a letter to Neal, Schwartz stated:

> As District Commander, I felt much more comfortable when I knew that you and the CRT were en route. I had a great deal of confidence that whatever the situation called for your team would be able to handle it and bring the mission to a successful conclusion. As I watched you and the team start up the ridge the first night I gained additional respect for the courage necessary to embark on such a mission. You and your team deserve the highest award for that heroic action. One of the reasons I believe the U.S. Marshals were able to be convinced to wait for your arrival to mount a rescue attempt was the sincere faith that not only I, but Sheriffs Whittaker and Roos had in you and the CRT. I can tell you that even though I hope a similar situation does not occur in this area, I will have even more confidence in you, your leadership ability and your team. Thank you for a job well done.

After the Ruby Ridge incident, Lieutenant Mark Peterson, retired, ISP 566, and others in the state police recognized that while the protesters at Ruby Ridge did not riot, the majority of the troopers who responded to

Ruby Ridge did not have proper training in crowd control had a riot occurred.

> After Ruby Ridge, I started talking to headquarters about starting a Crowd Intervention Team Special Operations Group, because although a few of us in the state police had riot control training, the majority of troopers at the incident did not. Major Nickerson and Captain Schwartz really got behind me on the idea and headquarters finally allowed it. One of the main reasons I wanted to start CIT/SOG was because there was a lot of potential, especially in northern Idaho, for rioting. The Aryan Nation marches were always a tense time, and Coeur d' Alene also has a massive influx of people over the 4th of July holiday.

With approval from state police leadership, Peterson wrote an operations manual, and began the selection process for troopers interested in being on the team.

> We had our first training in March of 1993, and I had twenty-five troopers and three sergeants assigned to the unit. I think it was great for the state police to have that kind of force, the group of men I had were very well organized, and all of them had the right mind-set to do this type of work.

Peterson said the team trained twice a year, including once each year with the Idaho National Guard Red Platoon.

> The Red Platoon was a platoon of about fifty Idaho National Guardsmen, and their priority mission was to augment police entities in the event of a riot. When we first trained with them, I noticed they were using tactics that were basically from the 1950s. We trained them on updated tactics, like how to use riot batons, and we also trained with them on different scenarios.

Ron Kirtley, one of the team's sergeants, said it didn't take very long before the CIT/SOG proved its value.

> We were called in to assist law enforcement in the Coeur d' Alene area during the 4th of July celebrations. People in Coeur d' Alene were complaining that the park down by the waterfront was no longer safe because gangs had taken over. There were also a lot of problems with alcohol and fighting. We were brought in to supplement local officers. Basically, we were a foot patrol. We would pair up with local officers and walk around the area. The idea was to show a strong presence, and hopefully keep problems down.

Peterson said the CIT/SOG was very successful in its mission and by the second year of the team deploying to Coeur d' Alene, families were back to bringing their children to the park.

> We also went to Coeur d'Alene during the yearly Aryan Nation Congress. There was a lot of potential for problems during the Aryan Nations parade because the Jewish Defense League also showed up to the event. I think if we had not been there in force, there would definitely have been major violence between these two groups.

Peterson said in the late 1990s, the CIT/SOG was requested to assist the City of Lewiston during Hot August Nights.

> Hot August Nights was a show and shine for antique cars. In 1997, a group of people, mostly younger kids, got drunk and basically raised all kinds of trouble. Local law enforcement really had a rough time of it because they just didn't have the numbers to stop the rioting. I know a lot of District 2 cars were pulled in to help stop the riots. The next year, Lewiston Police Chief Baldwin requested the team. We did a lot of foot patrols and that really helped keep the potential for trouble down.

Sergeant Kent Oliver, retired, ISP 436, said CIT/SOG members were primarily trained on how to move crowds, control crowds, and how to take people in crowds into custody.

The CIT/SOG also trained in the component of community policing, such as arriving a few days before a scheduled event to show our presence. This idea went a long way in keeping violence down. I think we were an extremely effective unit. We trained the 116th in crowd control prior to its deployment to Bosnia, and there were a few times when we were called to the prison when during executions, because of the possibility of protesters.

Corporal Roger Rockwell, retired, ISP 452 was also one of the first members on the CIT/SOG.

Even before Ruby Ridge, the state police had a need for this kind of team. We were often called into situations where there was explosive potential. Along with what was happening up north with the Aryan Nations, we also had a lot of protest situations at the INL near Arco. The CIT/SOG did an excellent job both in training and in real situations. We had top of the line equipment, and training.

For the CRT team the end of the year would bring yet another major incident. On December 12, 1992, the Payette County Prosecuting Attorney, Bruce Birch, contacted the Idaho State Police and requested the assistance of the CRT in serving a felony arrest warrant on Bobbie Kessler. Neal said Kessler was a reserve deputy for the Payette County Sheriff's Office, and had been charged with three counts of lewd and lascivious conduct and with eight counts of rape, all involving his daughter.

Based on interviews with Kessler's daughter, son, and personnel from the Payette County Sheriff's Office, Birch believed Kessler could react violently to an arrest, and would probably be armed when approached. In meetings with Birch, the CRT was told that Kessler was a former Army Special Forces member, was trained in martial arts, and was proficient with a weapon. The CRT was also told Kessler was usually armed.

The CRT developed a plan for Kessler's arrest, deciding the warrant should be served on Kessler at the Payette County Sheriff's Office, where members of the public wouldn't be present in case of a confrontation. On December 14, 1992, Kessler was asked to come into the sheriff's department. When Kessler entered the building he came through a door which locked electronically behind him.

> As Kessler walked down the hall, CRT Trooper Jensen stepped into the hallway and identified himself as a state police officer. Jensen informed Kessler he was under arrest. When Kessler didn't submit to Jensen's commands, CRT Troopers Marsh and Case stepped forward and sprayed Kessler with Cap-Stun, a capsicum oil spray, in an attempt to incapacitate him. Kessler walked back toward the door that he entered through and then lunged at the door in an attempt to escape.

Neal said after discovering he could not open the door, Kessler crouched down and turned. As he turned, Kessler drew a handgun from a holster on his belt, and pointed it toward CRT Troopers Jones, and Nauman.

> In response, Jones, Nauman, and Marsh fired their weapons. After being shot, Kessler again pointed his weapon at the CRT members and conducted a defensive roll on the floor. The officers fired their weapons again and Kessler died of gunshot wounds received during the second discharge of weapons.

Despite the troubles in the northern part of the state having consumed a large number of man hours, the state police was still doing its best to curb drinking and driving, reduce fatality crashes, and provide safety instruction, especially to Idaho's children. One safety program in particular was recognized by the President of the United States for its success in teaching school children the importance of safety: The Idaho State Police (Crash) Safety Education Program.

In the late 1970s, when Rich Wills started his safety program in Idaho schools using ventriloquism and dummies to convey safety messages to children, it was considered a novel idea By mid-1992, state police leadership recognized the success of the program had grown to the point where more ventriloquist-trained troopers and dummies were needed to serve the demand for the duo in Idaho classrooms.

Using a grant from the National Highway Traffic Safety Administration, the state police cloned the dummy, Crash, increasing his number from one to six. The newly commissioned Crashes were dressed in state police uniforms, and six troopers from across the state were assigned to receive ventriloquism instruction from Wills.

Once the six troopers were trained, the goal of the state police to fan out across the state, taking Crash and his safety message to students, was realized. Troopers selected for the program were Corporal John Turnbull, Corporal Rick Field, Corporal Tom Wilson, Corporal Matt Phelan, Corporal Stan Wiggins, and Corporal Gayland Edwards. The Crash dummy program was extremely successful in imparting seat belt safety, bicycle safety, stranger danger, anti-drug, and other safety messages.

The success of the program won Wills and the Idaho State Police its first, and to date only, Presidential Citation of Honor and Wills said the honor was far beyond anything he ever expected.

> Never in my wildest dreams did I ever think I'd get to personally meet the President of the United States, who at the time was President Bill Clinton, let alone that I'd one day be standing on the lawn of the White House to receive an award from him. There were seventy-three officers there and I think all of them were moved by the experience. I know I was.

Wills said among the most memorable moments of the event, was when he showed up at the White House in uniform and wearing his side arm.

> We were told to wear our uniforms for the presentation, but no one said anything about not bringing our weapons so, I was one of several officers who wore my sidearm. The Secret Service didn't like it that we had our weapons. Finally, one of the Secret Service guys said, "Look, these are some of America's finest police officers. If we can't trust them, who can we trust?" So, I got to keep my sidearm which is pretty unheard of when you meet with the president and you're not one of his Secret Service agents.

The award was a crowning achievement for both Wills and the Idaho State Police, but unfortunately the Idaho Legislature did not see the program in the same light and despite its immense success, the "Crash"

Safety Education Program was dropped as a result of the "Legislative Intent" clause for the state police that came out of the 1994 session. Classroom presentations ceased at the end of the 1994 school year.

The positive side of programs like "Crash," may be tough to measure with statistical data—and therefore an easy target for law-makers looking to decrease budgetary spending—but to law enforcement officers the loss of school safety programs are all too quickly realized in the 'real world'. For the state police, the nearly twenty year successful run of "Crash" took away not only valuable safety education for children, but reduced the visibility of state troopers in Idaho schools.

The Crash Safety Education Program wasn't the only state police service that would soon be on the chopping-block of some of Idaho's legislators. In fact, a bill introduced into the 1994 legislature, proposed the idea of"...limiting state police jurisdiction." The proposed measure would have declared sheriffs and prosecutors as the sole law enforcement officials in each county.

The bill also proposed the state police could assert jurisdiction, outside of traffic, only if invited by local officials. The current provision allowing the governor to order state police into a county if it was felt the laws were not being carried out, would have been completely eliminated by the proposed bill. The bill was not passed, but the proposal reminded state police leadership that the tremendous amount of work being accomplished by state police troopers was not being either recognized or promoted.

Beginning in mid-1993, to promote better communication among employees, a briefing, dubbed the *ISP Daily Report,* was prepared by headquarters staff each day to inform employees of the numerous incidents and situations troopers faced on a continuing basis. While the reports were not shared with the general public, information, especially on critical incidents, was shared with state lawmakers.

A compilation of these reports over a three month period in 1994 further showed what the leadership of the state police and state troopers working across Idaho, had been claiming for a long time: Idaho's crime picture was changing more and more rapidly every year...and not for the better. From serious DUI-related accidents to murder, increased drug abuse and gang related activity, it was clear Idaho's citizens were facing a terrifying increase in serious crimes.

Law enforcement entities across the state were noticing another trend too: In a state where for many, many years a very few law enforcement officers had needed to pull their weapon, let alone use it, police officers were now facing a striking increase in threats to law enforcement officers.

One such incident involved the killing of Officer Ronald Wade Feldner of the New Plymouth Police Department, by a boy barely into his teens. On January 20, 1994, at about 2 a.m., Feldner was shot and killed while checking on a car that was parked in the New Plymouth High School parking lot. In the car were three teen-aged boys who had stolen the car. Feldner ran a check on the plates and when he returned to the car, the driver, who was then just fourteen years old, shot Feldner three times.

The three teenagers left Feldner lying on the ground as they drove off. The three youths were later caught. James Robert Lee Moore pleaded guilty to shooting Feldner, and was given a prison sentence of up to twenty-five years. He is eligible for parole in 2019. Feldner was twenty-nine years old at the time of his death and left behind a wife and four young sons.

With the increase in both crimes against citizens and critical incidents against law enforcement officers statewide, the Idaho State Police recognized a need to re-evaluate and enhance its own training program. By the end of 1994, the state police introduced the Idaho State Police Training Program, which basically consolidated the number of state police officers providing instruction across the state from eighty part-time instructors, to a core cadre of five full-time instructors. These five instructors were pulled from the ranks of patrol to serve at the Department of Law Enforcement Police Training Facility in Meridian.

Rob Storm was one of the five officers chosen to implement the new training program. Storm said among the reasons the program was instituted, was to provide continuity and control over what subjects were being taught.

> No one really knew what was being taught to troopers or other law enforcement agencies, because all of these instructors were coming up with their own training syllabuses. There was a lot of potential for problems, especially from a liability standpoint, in not having everyone teaching subjects to a specific standard. The idea that all lesson plans should be approved through a centralized training program was introduced and at first there was some opposition because the program permanently took five troopers off the road. There was also opposition because the centralized program took some informal power away from other instructors, but we conducted a refresher course at the Meridian facility and

almost everyone agreed this was a much better way to conduct and to control our training program.

Storm added although the state police had its stress academy, which trained troopers to a high-level, once troopers moved into their respective districts they didn't always have the opportunity to receive timely refresher courses or timely instruction on new techniques.

One of the problems with having so many instructors was that the state police couldn't afford to send all of them to training, so it was up to the instructors when they received updated training to get out to the different districts and pass on the information. There was a tremendous amount of time lost with these instructors having to travel all over Idaho. By centralizing the training, the state police was able to send the five of us all over the United States for training after which, we could bring troopers in for in-service training at Meridian.

Storm said the change in training philosophy meant state troopers and other Idaho law enforcement entities were quickly brought up to speed on a number of law enforcement tactics.

As an example, we introduced the PIT maneuver, which is a pursuit tactic for bringing car chases to a conclusion. We borrowed the PIT maneuver technique we use now from the California Highway Patrol. We worked with P.O.S.T to implement a skid car, which has absolutely helped officers learn vehicle handling skills, such as driving on slick roads. The skid car is a great training tool for officer safety. We also conducted a lot of training on firearms, DUI enforcement, arrest techniques, crash reconstruction, and introduced the DRE or Drug Recognition Expert program. I was the first DRE in the state. The DRE program offered troopers a way to determine if a person were driving under the influence of something other than alcohol. It's a very important part of our enforcement today.

Perhaps the most important aspect of centralized training for the Idaho State Police and allied law enforcement agencies is that it is continually updated with current law enforcement information and techniques.

> I truly believe the Idaho State Police training program is among the best in the nation. I'm very proud of what we do. Our program is designed to give officers the best possible training in officer safety and it's designed to hold up in court. The number one reason training is so important is because it prepares officers in worst case scenarios, and unfortunately those worst case scenarios do happen.

19 ★ Methamphetamine

The bad news is that as Idaho grows, crime is growing with it. The good news is that you, our officers, have risen to the challenge.

Colonel E. D. Strickfaden, Superintendent Idaho State Police, retired

In 1995, Phil Batt was elected Governor of Idaho and with the retirement of Director Dick Cade, Bob Sobba was named Director of Law Enforcement. Superintendent of the Idaho State Police Colonel Ronald Moore also retired and Ed Strickfaden was promoted to the position. The leadership of the state and of the state police changed, and to some degree, the mission of the Idaho State Police changed too as Idaho State Police troopers found themselves responding more and more to the state's growing methamphetamine problem.

In 1990, the Idaho State Police made 250 drug contacts. In 1995, the Idaho State Police made 1,990 drug contacts. There were all sorts of drugs available to Idahoans, but the one causing the most problems, not only for Idaho State Police troopers, but for Bureau of Narcotics agents and law enforcement entities statewide, was methamphetamine.

Detective Scott Ward said by the end of 1995 "... Meth wasn't just a problem, it was a plague."

> I can't even begin to count the number of drug cases I've worked since I hired on with the Bureau of Narcotics in 1990. When I started, marijuana and cocaine were the most common drugs we dealt with; but since the mid-90s, marijuana and meth are – in the majority of our cases – the drugs we deal with. We still work cocaine and occasionally heroin cases, but meth is by far the number one problem in Idaho.

Gary Kaufman said the reason meth quickly became a popular drug is because it's an extremely easy drug to obtain.

> Meth is a drug that's relatively easy to manufacture. Along with seeing an increase in methamphetamine use, we saw a massive increase in "mom and pop," clandestine labs manufacturing meth. Another reason meth became so popular so quickly, is because the "high" from meth lasts much longer than the high from cocaine or heroin. Meth really took off in this area in the 90s and we have busted literally hundreds upon hundreds of these labs across the state; it wasn't uncommon in the last half of the 90s decade to conduct two or more busts a week per district, on these labs.

Edwin Gygli said unquestionably the worst part about going after mom and pop labs was the amount of time these operations took away from other drug enforcement.

> Mom and pop operations took a tremendous amount of time to enforce, and because of them, we didn't have time to enforce other major traffickers. However, our enforcement efforts worked very well against these types of clandestine labs and we were able to bring a large number of them down very quickly.

Ward said that along with taking mom and pop labs out of business, narcotics agents were instrumental in enacting legislation to get the precursor chemicals used in meth production away from criminals.

> We helped to enact legislation to make a lot of the ingredients for meth, like ephedrine, red phosphorus, and white phosphorus, controlled substances. This legislation made it much more difficult for people to get these ingredients, which has made a huge, huge difference in the battle against meth.

Detective Beth Bradbury, retired, said meth labs were extremely dangerous, and detectives had to quickly learn the ins and outs of staying safe in the extremely toxic environment of a meth lab.

> Meth labs are extremely dangerous because the chemicals people used are volatile. We never knew exactly what we were

> walking into with one of these labs. They were dirty, nasty, disgusting things. We had to wear special suits if we went into one because they were so horrific.

Gygli added the epidemic of mom and pop labs unfortunately didn't just affect the adults in the homes where these labs existed.

> For me the worst part of the mom and pop labs was that so often they involved children. We would go into these homes and so often there were young children in the home exposed to all of those nasty, horrible chemicals. It was a terrible, terrible situation. Those kids usually ended up in the child welfare system. It was heartbreaking.

Wayne Longo said the methamphetamine epidemic spilled over into other areas of enforcement.

> The Bureau of Narcotics and Idaho State Police were still two separate entities in the 1990s, but it quickly became obvious we would have to work together to bring this epidemic under control. The simple truth is, drug pushers use the highway to move their product, and state troopers were finding drugs more and more frequently during traffic stops.

Bradbury added she especially enjoyed working as an undercover narcotics officer during the "bad meth years," because Idaho had so few female police officers, "…no one saw me coming."

> I worked meth lab after meth lab as an undercover agent and they never saw me coming because they just did not expect a female to be a cop. As horrible as these labs were, I have to say it was a lot of fun bringing them down. To be a successful law enforcement officer I believe you have to have a total type A personality and most people then didn't see a woman as capable of having that kind of personality. I will admit it was tough to unwind sometimes, the horrible things you see over the years

accumulate, but the most important thing for me always was getting the job done right and getting home to my kids.

Longo said north Idaho was by far the worst hit area of the state for clandestine labs, but added by the end of the 1990s, Idaho law enforcement entities had brought the epidemic of mom and pop labs across Idaho under control, however; "…the use of methamphetamine in Idaho is still a huge problem."

Ward agreed, saying the control of the mom and pop labs simply allowed detectives to get back to the business of bringing down "super labs."

Shutting down the mom and pop labs didn't stop the flow of meth. Now we deal with super labs, most of them in Mexico, smuggling meth into the area. A lot of the smuggling routes used during the heyday of the cocaine era became the routes for meth. It's a constant battle to identify these routes and most of the cases we work now aren't done in a few days. I've worked cases that take years to bring to a conclusion. The past seven or so years of my career I've worked a lot of mid- to large-scale operations and I'm very happy that every federal case I've worked has ended with a one hundred percent conviction rate. One case in particular that I'm very proud of, is one where I worked with FBI, ICE, ISP, and Blaine County Sheriff's Deputies. This case involved a family organization in the Blaine County area. It took about three years to work the case but we ended up with indictments against twelve people for human smuggling, drug running, money laundering, bank fraud, and several other charges. All of them were found guilty.

The increase in drug use across Idaho, wasn't the only major type of crime law enforcement officers found themselves dealing with on a rapidly increasing scale in the mid-90s. Murder rates were also rocketing upwards.

Jim Hopkins said in 1996, the District 4 area was slammed with several murders in a very short period of time.

It was simply unbelievable. In an area where murder was not that common, we were suddenly inundated with violent crime.

The worst one for me was when Jim Nice murdered his three children. The murder actually took place on December 22, 1995. He killed his two young sons and his baby daughter by feeding them rat poison. Nice was sentenced to life in prison without parole. The other two murders I helped investigate were the Schoolcraft/McCoy murders and the Hood/Hunter murders. In May of 1996, Corey Hood murdered his grandmother, Mae Hood, in Heyburn, and then raped and murdered seventeen-year-old Wendy Hunter. In June of 1996, Walt Schoolcraft murdered Denise McCoy, and her four children before killing himself. No motive was ever determined in the Schoolcraft/McCoy killings. It was truly a terrible time for the communities in which all of these murders took place, and for the law enforcement officers investigating them.

Hopkins said in all three of these murder cases, the cases came together fairly quickly, and, with the exception of Schoolcraft because he committed suicide, ended in convictions.

In the Hood case, everything came together very well through the cooperation of allied agencies. It was learned very early in the investigation that Hood's motivation for killing his grandmother was to get possession of her truck and her home. He knew Wendy because she had worked with him at a car wash in Burley. Unfortunately, Hood should never have gotten to know Wendy because he was a level three sex offender and was not supposed to be around anyone under the age of eighteen unsupervised. At any rate he was somehow able to get Wendy to come to his home where he raped and killed her. She put up a vicious fight. He then dumped her body in the desert. We ended up with a lot of good physical evidence in that case. Hood escaped the death penalty by making a deal with the prosecutor. I felt he should have gotten life without parole, but he will be up for parole in 2033.

Increased drug use, murder, and an escalating fatality rate certainly captured the attention of Idaho's citizens and law enforcement entities, but an incident in 1993 captured national attention.

On October 11, 1993, nine-year-old Stephanie Lynn Crane went bowling with friends in her hometown of Challis, after leaving the bowling alley, Stephanie disappeared. Detective Les Stimpson, (retired) was one of the officers who worked on the case.

> The last anyone saw of Stephanie, she was walking on U.S. Highway 93 toward the high school. We conducted an extensive search for her that covered several thousand square miles, but nothing was ever found. There's a lot of speculation about what happened to her, but we never found any conclusive evidence, and she is still missing.

Stimpson said the FBI initially took the case, and he was assigned to the case about four or five days later.

> When I got Stephanie's file, it was already massive, over the years it's grown even larger. Both her mother and father are now dead, but I've always half suspected her mother had something to do with Stephanie's disappearance. Stephanie fought with her mother quite a bit, and her mother had a very split personality. One of the things that really struck me about the family dynamics was that Stephanie's parents were divorced and when I went to her mother's home, there were no pictures of Stephanie. When I went to her father's home, he had pictures of Stephanie everywhere.

He said that regardless of what he felt might have happened, there was no crime scene to work, which made the case all the more difficult.

> Stephanie spent a lot of time running around town all by herself, and there were probably 150 to 200 convicted sex offenders in Challis because of the mines. U.S. Highway 93 is also a major roadway that goes clear into Canada. There are so many possible scenarios about Stephanie's disappearance, it is a horrific case and I don't know if it will ever be solved.

Stimpson said District 6 was also dealing with some brutal murders in the mid-1990s.

Probably one of the worst murders I worked was the Angie Dodge case. Angie was eighteen-years-old and she was brutally raped and murdered in her apartment in Idaho Falls on June 13, 1996. I attended Angie's autopsy and we were able to collect DNA and other evidence on her body.

In January of 1997, Christopher Tapp confessed to his involvement in the crime.

He implied at least two other people were involved, but he did not give us any names. To date, no one else has been implicated in the murder so even though we have a conviction, her case is unsolved. It was a terrible shock to the people of Idaho Falls and people were on edge for a very long time, even after Tapp was convicted.

For the Idaho State Police, the shooting of another of its troopers once again slammed home the dangerous business of protecting Idaho's citizens. In 1994, Lieutenant Ishmael Gonzales, ISP 497, was on patrol on Memorial Day, when he received a call of a reckless driver on east-bound US 20, near the small town of Chester. At the time of the incident, Gonzales was the Ashton resident trooper.

The call came in that a blue Jeep Cherokee was being driven erratically. I responded to the call and spotted the vehicle, at which time I initiated a traffic stop. As I approached the car, I leaned forward to talk to the driver, and he shot me twice in the chest.

Gonzales spun away and drawing his pistol, fired two rounds at the gunman, an escapee from a Florida prison. One round nearly struck the gunman, and the second round shattered the rear window of the Jeep. Gonzales attempted to fire again but his gun would not fire.

At first, I thought my pistol had jammed. I learned later that with the pistols we were using at that time, (the Smith and Wesson 4586 double-action), I was firing too fast and the trigger wasn't

> releasing. The term for this is called short-stroking. I cleared my pistol and fired another round into the ground to make sure it was working, but in the few seconds it took me to do that, the man and the woman with him, drove off. I got into my car and attempted to chase them, but they managed to turn down a back road and I lost track of the vehicle.

Gonzales said while he was in pursuit of the vehicle, his District Commander, Captain Pat McDonald, told him to end the pursuit and immediately get medical care. Gonzales was given first-aid by officers responding to the scene, while other officers continued the pursuit of the vehicle.

> That's when it hit me I had been shot! I stopped and checked myself and realized I was bleeding. I was taken to the hospital to be checked, but my bullet-proof vest saved my life. The impact had broken the skin where the bullets hit, but I wasn't seriously injured.

The Jeep was located on a side-road, where it had crashed into some rocks. The next morning, officers were able to capture the woman, but the man fled into a barn.

> The man who shot me holed-up in the barn and there was a stand-off for about an hour. The man ended up committing suicide. It turned out the Jeep they were in was stolen out of South Carolina, and the woman was his girlfriend. She had helped him escape from prison.

The suspects were later identified as Steven Bosserman, 23, and his girlfriend, Cynthia, 19. Cynthia was convicted of charges including helping Bosserman escape from prison.

Throughout the 1990s, for troopers, life on the front lines of highway safety had gone from the relatively straight forward mandate of enforcing Idaho's traffic laws and offering assistance to allied law enforcement agencies when requested, to working many unpredictable cases that even bordered on the bizarre. One such case was dubbed by the press as the Ligertown Incident.

Bob Laumann said the 1995 Ligertown Incident brought national and international media attention to the resort town of Lava Hot Springs.

> I think that was the most bizarre case I ever worked. I got a call from the Bannock County Sheriff and he asked me if I wanted to hunt lions, wolves, and lion-tiger mixed animals, known as ligers. So, I spent a night hunting cats. It was an interesting experience. No one living in Idaho would expect to ever have to deal with African animals in our own backyard, and honestly, I'm still not sure we got all of them.

Ligertown was the name of a compound near Lava Hot Springs, owned by Bob Fieber and Dotti Martin. The compound housed African lions, wolf hybrids and ligers. The animals were kept in cages on the Ligertown complex and Laumann recalled the night the animals escaped was one of the strangest times in his career.

> The people who owned the place had a bunch of these animals in old cages, and because they couldn't afford to feed the animals, the animals were starving and eventually broke out of their cages. The sheriff got a bunch of reports about animals being out of the compound. For example, a local rancher had called in and reported that he had killed one lion and wounded another. That's when it became apparent that there was a huge problem.

Laumann said the sheriff also received reports that Fieber and Martin were in the hospital for injuries they had sustained when the animals escaped.

> No one, including the owners of Ligertown, knew how many cats had escaped, so we spent the night hunting the animals and hoping we got all of them. I don't recall how many were shot, but it was quite a few. I think the total was somewhere around twenty cats.

At the time of the Ligertown Incident, there were no laws in place to protect exotic animals if law enforcement or others were suspicions of the animals being mistreated. The laws have since changed, and there are now several laws in place to protect the animals and to prosecute the owners of these compounds for animal neglect.

Following the incident, newspapers reported that Martine Collette, who ran an animal rescue facility called the Wildlife Waystation in California, offered to take the animals that had not escaped from Ligertown to his compound. News articles also reported that while numerous people had witnessed the animals on or near their property, no human injuries were reported.

While many law enforcement officers in the southeastern part of the state were hunting exotic animals, several law enforcement entities in District Two, were beginning a case that resulted in the largest cash seizure in Idaho history.

This investigation was also one of the Bureau of Narcotics' most successful drug cases. This nearly nine-year investigation involved marijuana trafficking, money laundering, and the discovery of a drug ring that went from Mexico to the Pacific Northwest, to the east coast of the United States. The case involved law enforcement officers from a number of entities including the Bureau of Narcotics, the FIND unit, the Idaho State Police, the Internal Revenue Service, the U.S. Attorney's Office, Winchester, Kentucky Police Department, Roseburg, Oregon Police Department, the Douglass Interagency Narcotics Task Force, (Oregon), and the Oregon Department of Justice. Because the case spanned many states and many years, the lead investigator on the case, Detective Vicki Carlock, said when it came to news coverage, the case, "...actually flew under the radar."

> The case really began in 1988, when Bureau of Narcotics Detective Ken White received information from a Confidential Informant that Leland Robert Lang had approached the informant about running loads of marijuana for him again. The informant had done so for Lang in the 1970s. In 1989, Detective White arrested Lang in a motel room with seven pounds of marijuana. Lang was charged and served local jail time then fell off law enforcement's radar. He came back on law enforcement's radar In July of 1995, when the Winchester, Kentucky Police Department seized 150 pounds of marijuana from a guy named James Rose. They contacted us because they suspected Leland Lang of being the source of the marijuana. Rose went to prison-camp and Lang, none-the-wiser that we had been tipped by Winchester Police

Department, went along his merry way. We opened a case on Lang and began the adventure.

Lang's base of operation was his seventy acre homesite in Stites. Carlock said Lang was exceptionally skilled at not drawing attention to himself and had for years, been smart enough to keep his trafficking activities away from, "…his own back yard."

We soon figured out that Lang was transporting marijuana to the east coast pretty much on a monthly basis. The problem was figuring out how to catch him. He also had business interests in coffin sales. We knew that he was picking up loads of marijuana grown in Mexico. The marijuana was coming up from Mexico to California where it would be stored in warehouses for distribution to Oregon and other states. We knew Lang was one of the distributors, but we didn't know if he was shipping the product in coffins or how he was transporting it.

Carlock said by the summer of 2002, detectives had been working the investigation for about six years.

We worked the case as a no-dope conspiracy, which meant we had a lot of incriminating evidence pointing to Lang, but we didn't have any drug busts. We eventually had enough information to arrest Lang and after his arrest we started getting information from other sources that Lang had buried a bunch of money on his property so we put together an affidavit for a search warrant on Lang's property. We executed the search warrant for the 'buried treasure' on July 30, 2002, and the search lasted five days.

Because the search area was so large, Carlock said geophysicists mapped the area with grids and used their equipment to locate anomalies in the ground.

We unearthed some of the money in the driveway on the second day, the amount of money totaled $615,510. We also found an ammo can containing $466,700 under a slash pile near the driveway. Lang had told us where some other money was located, but we learned one of his business partners, Ray Haddon, had stolen this money shortly after Lang's arrest. In all, we located $1,082,210, which did not include the $150,000-$175,000 Haddon took. With that money included, the total recovery was $1.2 million. Lang amassed this amount of money in just sixteen months of running loads of marijuana to Kentucky and other states.

Carlock said while this was the largest cash seizure ever in Idaho, it was the culmination of hard work by many, many dedicated law enforcement officers and support staff from a number of agencies outside of Idaho.

Lang was convicted and sent to prison, because all of the people involved in this case did such a fantastic job. No one agency could have conducted this case alone; it really required a massive cooperative effort of law enforcement agencies and working this case brought down some upper echelon drug traffickers as well. For example, the Roseburg, Oregon Police Department had been looking at a man named Kent Jones, who they suspected of running a large trafficking ring. This case showed Jones was Lang's source of supply. So, while dismantling Lang's organization had little impact on the local drug trade, it really hurt the upper echelon of drug traffickers. Jones was a "spin-off" case from Lang that we continued to work through 2005. It too resulted in over one-million dollars in seizures, most of which were hard assets such as real property.

With millions of dollars in cash and assets seized, the Idaho Bureau of Narcotics also received a large boon from asset sharing.

Asset sharing is a program that splits money made from cash seizures and asset sales, among the agencies involved in solving drug cases. The amount of money given to each agency is based on the involvement of the agency, and the man-hours put in by that agency's officers. The Idaho Bureau of Narcotics initially received a check for $745,094.08. We occasionally still receive money as other properties seized in the case are sold. Rules concerning how this money can be used are pretty defined, but generally, the money is used to purchase equipment and new technology for use in narcotics investigations.

With the significant increase of crime in Idaho, state troopers and other law enforcement officers also wondered if there would be a significant increase in fatality crashes when Idaho legislators in 1995, raised the speed-limit on most of Idaho's interstate system from 65 miles-per-hour to 75 miles-per-hour. Speed limits on many stretches of U.S. and state highways also increased from 55 miles-per-hour to 65 miles-per-hour.

Idaho was not alone in raising its speed limits; twelve other states increased limits to the 75 mile-per-hour mark, and eleven states increased their speed limits to 70 miles-per-hour, but Idaho State Police crash reconstruction experts were particularly concerned with whether or not motorists would understand the ten mile an hour increase in speed could dramatically decrease their ability to survive a crash.

Experts pointed out that traveling at 75 miles-per-hour it would take a typical passenger car about 250 feet to come to a complete stop. At 65 miles-per-hour it takes 187 feet, and at 80 miles-per-hour, that stopping distance increases to 284 feet. An article in the summer 1996 *Idaho State Police* magazine stated:

> These are stopping distances once brakes are fully applied and *not* including reaction time. Most accidents start with an inattentive motorist. Add the time it takes to recognize the danger ahead and transfer the foot from gas pedal to brake. If fatigue, alcohol, or drugs are involved, the reaction time will increase even more. When traveling at 75 miles-per-hour, a car is traveling at 110 feet per second. A delayed reaction of even a few seconds can make the difference between a near-miss and an accident.

The article reminded motorists that Newton's law of inertia: "Any object in a state of rest or of uniform linear motion tends to remain in such a state unless acted upon by an external force," is the law of motion that accounts for the injury or death of a vehicle's occupants.

> In a head-on or other high-impact crash the vehicle may decelerate from 75 to zero miles-per-hour in less than a second.

> However, the vehicle occupants will continue to travel forward at 75 miles-per-hour until stopped by another force. Often, this is the dashboard, steering wheel, windshield, or the roadway itself. It usually isn't the initial crash, but the secondary impact that injures and kills. Roadways and vehicles may be engineered to handle higher speeds, but the human body is not.

Troopers and other law enforcement officers were quick to remind motorists the first line of defense was to wear their seatbelts, and make sure their children were in child safety seats, in an attempt to debunk the myth that being thrown from the vehicle saved lives.

As the article pointed out, too many state police fatality reports carried the chilling phrase, "...ejected from the vehicle." Law enforcement officers also encouraged law makers to increase fines against motorists who refused to buckle up. The increase in fines, it was hoped, would convince motorists if not for their safety but for their pocketbooks, to use their seatbelts.

> Motorists must consider the driving habits of other motorists as well as their own. It won't matter if you are a careful driver, obeying the speed limit, and driving safe and sober, if the motorist coming from the other direction crosses the center line or runs a stop light. The laws of physics make no exceptions for who was in the right. If you don't have a seatbelt on, you've given up the only chance you may have at survival.

Despite irrefutable proof that seatbelts save lives, however, over thirty percent of the fatalities on Idaho's highways then, and now, are the direct result of victims being ejected from their vehicles.

James Culpepper said it was difficult for him when he responded to fatality crashes involving children, especially when the child would most likely have survived if a car seat or seatbelt had been used.

> I investigated numerous fatal crashes during my career, but the ones involving children were always the most difficult. It was especially hard when you have a sense that there wouldn't have been a fatality if the victims had been buckled up. My most difficult crash involved an eight year old boy who died in my

arms. Those are the kinds of things that stay with you the rest of your life.

Don Hiatt recalled an accident in which the victim also might well have survived had he been in a seatbelt. In this incident, Hiatt attempted to rescue the victim form the frigid waters of Lake Coeur d' Alene.

I had stopped a car for speeding and while I was on the stop a woman pulled up behind me and told me she had just witnessed a car hit a tree and then plunge into Lake Coeur d' Alene. I gave the driver I'd stopped back his paperwork and followed the woman to where the accident happened. I could see the car in the lake and a little ways beyond the car I could see the body of a man floating in the water. I took off my gun belt and went on into the water to see if the man was still alive. Unfortunately, he was not. From my experience, I figured he had broken his neck when he was ejected from the vehicle. I got him back to shore and the woman told me she thought there might be more people in the car, so I went back into the lake to search the car. Fortunately, there weren't any more victims. By the time I got out of the water other officers were at the scene so I was released to go home and get dried off and warmed up.

Phil Broesch who responded to the accident, said while there certainly weren't any guarantees the victim would have lived had he been wearing a seatbelt: "…his chances certainly would have been much better."

Corporal Marshall Thorp, retired, ISP 505, remembered one of his worst fatalities in which seatbelts may have made a difference.

I think the hardest part of being a trooper is dealing with the fatality crashes. Sometimes they are just so senseless. In one accident I investigated, three and one-half people died. I say one-half because one of the women was about five months along in her pregnancy. I believe they all would have survived if they had been wearing seatbelts. Unfortunately, they weren't and the result was carnage.

Rich Wills said he investigated more accidents than he cared to count in which he was certain there would have been many more survivors had people just buckled up. From 1956, when fatality records were first kept officially in Idaho, to 1996, 11,507 people died on Idaho's roadways. If it is true thirty percent of those fatalities could have been avoided by the simple use of a seatbelt, 3,452 lives may have been spared.

As Wayne Scoggins pointed out, when one considers in most multiple-fatality crashes those lost are family members, the difference a seatbelt can make, "...is staggering."

Seatbelt use has certainly increased in Idaho in recent years, but troopers say until everyone learns to fasten their seatbelt, the number of lives lost because victims are ejected from vehicles, will remain a major factor in fatality statistics.

In the spring of 1997, the Idaho State Police faced off again with one of its most prolific adversaries, Mother Nature. The winter of 1996-97 and the spring of 1997 were among the wettest in Idaho's history. Troopers in the northern part of the state battled raging floods, and were particularly concerned when a large ice dam formed in the Coeur d' Alene River above Enaville and threatened towns downstream.

Law enforcement officers and disaster coordinators soon discovered ice-dams were only one of the problems they faced especially in Kootenai and Shoshone counties as the melting, heavy snowpack was supplemented by heavy rains that assailed the area.

Thousands were displaced as flood waters devastated St. Maries, put Cataldo under water, and left Orofino, "...cut in half by a river of water."

In the southeastern part of the state, the Snake River swelled well above flood stage and thousands of acres of Idaho farmland was also soon under water. Several hundred homes were damaged or destroyed, and a section of Interstate 84 was closed when an overpass collapsed onto the roadway. Homes close to the Snake River or other streams and canals in the south central and western part of the state were also flooded, and in numerous areas the pavement was stripped from roadways.

While the state police and allied law enforcement agencies, and disaster coordinators certainly had a great deal of experience with flooding, this marked the first time eighteen Idaho counties were simultaneously declared disaster areas because of flooding. And along with the devastation to homes and farmland, officials faced the daunting task of securing homes from looting, routing traffic through devastated areas, and providing welfare checks and evacuation to residents who found themselves trapped by flood waters.

Hazmat Specialist Steve Cazier said among the biggest worries faced by officials, was the wide variety of hazardous materials swept up by the flood.

> As Hazmat specialists, we received excellent training and a lot of it. In incidents like this flood, where so much hazardous material was floating around, it was our duty to assume incident command and take care of the situation. I was sent to Ririe and Roberts when the flood came through. It washed a tremendous amount of farm chemicals and other hazardous debris into the river.

Cazier spent two weeks in the area assisting with clean-up and with the classification of hazardous materials.

> We went out in boats and pulled containers out of the water. Our job was to gather them and then classify them as to what type of chemicals they contained and what type of dangers the chemicals presented. We were at Level A, which meant we wore full rubber suits. We had to dip each canister we retrieved with a glass rod and then put the rod in test tubes to determine if the material was flammable, corrosive, poisonous, etc. We found a lot of pesticide and herbicide type chemicals. It was a little nerve racking when we saw barrels floating in the water with warning signs of "Dangerous When Wet!" We also encountered a lot of propane tanks floating around which made our mission extremely dangerous.

Cazier said the hazardous materials taken from the flooded areas were sent for disposal south of Mountain Home.

> Only the Hazmat team and the Coast Guard were allowed to retrieve containers. We flew over the flooded areas on several occasions so we could spot debris we may have missed. It was a lengthy operation, but I think we did an excellent job of securing the hazardous materials and disposing of them.

As the flood water receded across Idaho, officials estimated the damages at well over 100 million dollars.

Throughout the 1990s, Idaho experienced a 25.1 percent population growth and while the state's economy may have benefitted from the increase, law enforcement entities from across the state found their resources stretched even thinner toward the end of the decade. Once again the National Highway Safety Administration reported the Idaho State Police was seriously undermanned.

Although legislators did not authorize a massive increase in the number of troopers to the Idaho State Police ranks, or pass the requested two percent pay increase, a few new troopers were authorized and other laws passed in 1997 were beneficial to the state police and other law enforcement entities across Idaho.

Among the new laws was the passage of the .08 percent alcohol limit. Idaho and Illinois were the first states to comply with the federal government's 1996 mandate of lowering the blood alcohol limit required to arrest a driver for drinking from .10 to .08.

Colonel Strickfaden reminded legislators that while the state police was, "...continuing to do its best with available resources," it was still simply impossible to provide 24-hour coverage on Idaho's highways.

> In order to adequately cover Idaho's roadways at all times, we would need to almost double the manpower we currently have available. At minimum, to be able to provide adequate 24-hour coverage we would need ninety more officers. A few years ago, the state police was able to do quite a lot of accident prevention activities. Now, we struggle to have time to clean up the accidents as they happen.

Strickfaden further noted with the increase in traffic on Idaho's roadways, along with the increased maximum speed limits, troopers were facing increased dangers from other vehicles during routine traffic stops and accident investigations.

Kent Oliver said in the late-1990s, the Idaho State Police recognized one area it could improve on was crash-scene safety.

> Crash-scene safety has always been a priority for the state police, but we did recognize it could be improved on, so in the late 1990s, Lieutenant Colonel Ked Wills, who was a District 4

Trooper at the time, was tasked with putting together a table-top exercise. The impetus behind the table-top exercise was to help all emergency responders at the scene of accidents know what their duties are, as well as what precautions they need to take in order to ensure their safety and the safety of others. When P.O.S.T. saw the effectiveness of the exercise, it was decided the program should include actual crash-scene classes and practice scenarios, instead of just a table-top exercise, and that's when the crash-scene safety program we teach now was developed.

Oliver said that since the crash-scene safety program was implemented it has been extremely effective in keeping officers and other emergency responders safer at crash scenes.

The program has helped establish a number of guidelines for emergency responders as well as helped solve some of the issues law enforcement officers were witnessing at crash scenes. For example, it gave law enforcement the opportunity to explain that law enforcement has incident command over a crash because a crash scene is a crime scene. I believe the most effective outcome of the crash-scene safety program, however, has been the better working relationships between emergency responders that have grown out of the classes.

Oliver said along with law enforcement officers, emergency responders at crash scenes usually involve EMTs, firefighters, tow-truck operators, and in larger crashes, personnel from the Idaho Department of Transportation.

The crash-scene safety classes give all responders the opportunity to share information, and through scenario training, emergency responders learn how to deploy traffic cones, eliminate secondary crashes, keep traffic moving, and of course, ensure they and other responders are safe.

While it was apparent the state police was not going to get the needed ninety troopers, Colonel Strickfaden said he appreciated what the legislators in the 1997 session were able to do for the state police. In a letter to legislators he stated:

> I extend my sincere appreciation to the governor and to the Joint Finance and Appropriations Committee for passing a favorable state police budget this year. During a year with little monetary resources, you showed that you truly support the efforts of the men and women on our front lines. It is heartwarming to know our concerns were heard at the legislature.

By the summer of 1997, the state police was back to work on its primary focus of highway safety and criminal interdiction. Colonel Strickfaden thanked his troopers for their extraordinary effort in accommodating the needs of Idaho's citizens during the heavy floods, and reminded them their work was not going unnoticed.

Sadly, the year would end for everyone in Idaho law enforcement on a heartbreaking note, when September 20, 1997, Boise City Police Officer Marc Stall was gunned down in a high-risk traffic stop in Boise. Stall was the first Boise Police Department officer killed in the line of duty.

Boise Police officers had stopped a car for a routine traffic violation but the two occupants of the vehicle refused to comply with officer's orders. The officers called for back-up and Stall was among the officers who responded.

Officers once again ordered the occupants to exit the vehicle with their hands visible, but instead the occupants exited the vehicle and immediately opened fire on officers. Stall was struck on the right side of his body, just above his vest. Other officers returned fire and both suspects, brothers Brad Broderick, 29, and Doug Broderick, 27, were killed. Another Boise officer was injured in the shootout, but survived.

Stall left behind a wife and two young daughters.

With Stall's death, Idaho law enforcement officers were once again reminded the state had no memorial to honor their fallen comrades. Since the 1991 dedication of the National Law Enforcement Memorial, however, many Idaho law enforcement officers and Idaho citizens had been working toward the goal of creating such a memorial.

In May of 1998, the Idaho State Police joined law enforcement officers across the state to honor Idaho's forty-nine law enforcement officers killed in the line-of-duty throughout the state's history.

The officers and hundreds of others gathered at the Department of Law Enforcement headquarters in Meridian, for the unveiling of the Idaho Peace Officers Memorial. The completion of the memorial meant Idaho was no longer one of a small number of states that did not have a memorial to its fallen officers.

The memorial was built with donations from citizens, businesses, and law enforcement associations, and was completed in time for the observance of National Peace Officers Day which is observed every May 15.

The five point star-badge shaped memorial is comprised of three stones. The middle stone is flanked by the other two, which have the names, agency affiliation, and end of watch of the fallen. These stones are also lighted at night. The memorial contains a waterfall and more than 10,000 bricks, many of which are engraved to honor and memorialize loved ones, and create a walkway to and amid the memorial.

At the time the memorial was dedicated, the Idaho State Police honored four of its fallen officers.

Within a few months, troopers across the state were devastated and horrified when they learned they would be adding one more name to the wall, when Idaho's first female law enforcement officer was gunned down in Coeur d' Alene.

20 ✯ Linda Huff

No person was ever honored for what he received. Honor has been the reward he gave.

Calvin Coolidge.

At approximately 11:00 p.m. on June 17, 1998, Trooper Linda Huff, 32, a two-year veteran of the Idaho State Police, was shot to death as she walked out of the District One office in Coeur d' Alene.

Across the state newspapers and media outlets echoed the disbelief felt by many Idaho citizens and Idaho law enforcement officers that Huff had actually been ambushed and although she was able to return fire and injure her assailant, he assassinated her while she lay helpless on the ground.

State troopers, allied law enforcement officers, citizens, lawmakers, and Idaho Governor Phil Batt were shocked and outraged at Huff's murder. In a statement on June 18, Governor Batt expressed his grief over the death of Huff and also the death of two Department of Labor employees who were killed in a car accident near Orofino the same day as Huff's murder. In his statement Batt said:

> Idaho has been hit by two tragedies of unspeakable proportions. Linda Huff, an Idaho State Trooper, was murdered in Coeur d' Alene by a merciless assassin. This dedicated law enforcement officer, mother of three, and wife to another of our state's finest, Trooper Chad Huff, was waylaid without a chance for survival. According to reports, she bravely fought back wounding her assailant, but then was dispatched by a bullet to the head as she lay helpless on the ground. Two of our dedicated state employees from the Department of Labor were also killed yesterday, and three more were seriously injured in a car accident in the Orofino area. They were hit head-on by another car in which two other occupants died. We are in a state of shock and disbelief that these events have taken place. It is an odious fact of

life that vicious so-called human beings can deliberately murder law enforcement people who daily give of themselves so that we can enjoy freedom. Our hearts go out to all the victims of these terrible events and to their survivors (Batt).

Scott Yager, 34, of Rathdrum was arrested near the scene of the shooting and as investigators pieced together the evidence of the scene, it soon became obvious that the motive for Huff's murder was simply Yager's desire to kill a law enforcement officer.

Trooper Huff suffered injuries from at least eleven of seventeen rounds fired by Yager. Yager was hit by at least one of the rounds fired by Huff. The fatal wound to Trooper Huff was from a round fired by Yager at point blank range at Trooper Huff's head. Idaho State Police Troopers were on the scene within moments of the shooting and immediately made a security check of the area. Yager appeared from the trees, walking in the direction of deputies who were searching the area.

Ballistics evidence established that Yager's gun was the same one used to murder Huff and slugs removed from Yager's body were fired from Huff's gun. DNA evidence established that blood found inside the barrel of Yager's gun was from Huff. There is no evidence that Yager ever had any prior contact with Trooper Linda Huff, or with her husband Trooper Chad Huff (ISP).

Troopers who knew and served with Huff said the agony and horror they felt when they learned of her murder, "…was unbearable."

Willis Brownlee was the District One Commander when Huff was murdered.

I don't even know how to quantify the pain every one of us felt when Linda was murdered. I can't begin to express the pain I felt when someone in my command was murdered. Linda's death changed everything; it changed the whole organization. I think as an organization we lost all of our innocence that night. We have always trained our troopers that there are people out there willing to do us harm. That truth became devastatingly evident that night when Linda was literally murdered for absolutely no reason other than she was a law enforcement officer.

Sean Daly who was stationed in District One with both Linda and her husband, Chad and considered them close friends, said her death, "... shook me to the core."

It was just a terrible and difficult time for everyone. It was hard to believe that someone could commit such a crime for no reason at all, except Yager had decided to kill a police officer and she ended up being that officer. Linda was such a nice human being and to this day when I think of her I tear up. She touched my heart with her smile and my soul with her gentle spirit.

Lieutenant Vern Hancock, ISP 505, went through P.O.S.T. with both of the Huffs, who were the first husband and wife team to successfully make it through the academy.

Linda was very passionate about law enforcement. She was a down-to-earth, fun-loving person but she was also very serious about her job, and very good at it. What always struck me about Linda was she didn't want to be considered a "female" trooper she just wanted to be a trooper like everyone else. One of the things that made her so successful at the job was that she never had a problem talking to people.

Corporal Kathy Parsells, retired, ISP 445, was one of the troopers who interviewed Huff when she applied to the state police.

When Linda was shot it really upgraded my consciousness about the dangers of the job. I tried to step out of the box and look at the situation from the perspective of it could happen to any of us at any time. After she was killed, every time I put on my uniform, I promised myself I would try my best to get home.

Ed Strickfaden said Huff set the example as a trooper and her death rendered every citizen of Idaho and every Idaho law enforcement officer, "…as victims of a very grievous crime." He added the circumstances of her death were made even worse by the fact that Huff was ambushed in an unsecured parking area used by all District One troopers to access the District One office. Strickfaden ensured a trooper remained with Huff's body until her burial.

> When Linda was killed, the state police was housed in facilities that were never intended for law enforcement. She exited a building that had absolutely no security around it and became a target. No officer should meet their fate outside the back door of an unguarded and unprotected facility. After her death, we were able to get three new state police buildings approved to house our law enforcement officers in a secure environment, but sadly that came after her death.

Strickfaden said one of the shortfalls in state law enforcement throughout its history has been, "…our lack of adequate housing for our regional offices." Strickfaden retired from the state police in December of 2002, and in a letter to Governor Kempthorne, who was sworn in as Idaho's thirtieth governor in 2000, Strickfaden wrote:

> Among our accomplishments is a six-year building plan to construct state police facilities where services will be housed together in one location, in a secure environment to assure the safety of our employees. Standing near (Linda's) body for hours after her senseless death caused this effort to be one of my most sought after missions. Among all of our efforts together these past years, it will be with great pride and respect for our employees, that we open that first district office in the Magic Valley region in February of 2003. It is my sincere hope that this project will be completed during the second term of your administration.

Strickfaden added the support of all Idaho Legislators, and particularly the tireless efforts of Senator Denton Darrington (R), District 27, Senator Evan Frasure (R), District 34, Senator Atwell Parry (R), District 11, Representative Bob Geddes (R), District 32, and

Representative Maxine Bell (R), District 25, ensured the completion of these projects.

Wayne Longo said prior to getting approval for a new, secure facility for District One troopers, the community came together and raised money to build a fence around the parking lot where Huff was murdered.

Trooper Huff was posthumously awarded the Medal of Valor. Yager was convicted of first degree murder and sentenced to life in prison.

ISP honor guard. Front to back in the line: Fritz Zweigart, Aaron Bingham, Chris Elverud, Craig Boll, Ken Beckner, Darren Gilbertson, Holly Branch. The commander with the sword is Vern Hancock.

In the wake of Huff's murder, the Idaho State Police formed an honor guard, because when Huff was killed, no such unit existed and honor guard members from the Washington State Patrol were requested to assist with the honor guard duties during Huff's funeral.

At the time of Huff's death, Colonel Powell was the District Three commander and was tasked with making the funeral arrangements at the Nampa Idaho Center.

The task of coordinating the funeral for a fallen officer seemed monumental, especially when it was one of our own. The traditional planning element soon became eclipsed by the fact that an "Honor Guard" is an absolute necessity under these circumstances. We owe a great deal of gratitude to our colleagues from Washington, and other surrounding state police agencies, that helped the Idaho State Police through this very difficult event.

Immediately following the funeral, Powell formulated a request that developed and documented the need for an Idaho State Police Honor Guard unit. Powell presented the plan to Colonel Strickfaden, and was successful in his request to build the team.

Lieutenant Colonel Kedrick Wills, ISP 550, is a prior commander of the Idaho State Police Honor Guard, and said over the years since its creation, the honor guard has participated in many assignments.

Those assignments have ranged from performing honor guard duties at the funerals of fallen Idaho officers and retired state police employees, to posting the colors at local and national events. Each May, some members of the Idaho State Police are also sent to Washington D.C. by the Idaho State Police Association, to represent Idaho during ceremonies for the National Police Officer's Memorial.

Wills said the honor guard receives training as family liaisons to assist grieving families of fallen officers, and training on how to plan details for funeral services in which the honor guard participates.

The honor guard spends the bulk of its time training and preparing for funeral services for fallen officers because the sad reality is, it isn't if but when, Idaho will lose another law enforcement officer. The honor guard also trains to ensure it is prepared to perform every function with the ultimate goal of honoring one of our fallen heroes, whether it is an Idaho State Police trooper or an officer from an allied agency. For me personally, being a member of the Idaho State Police honor guard was one of the most rewarding assignments I have had.

Following Trooper Huff's shooting, the Idaho State Police also began the chaplain program. In a summer 2003 *Idaho State Police* Magazine, article, Editor Marjorie Lusk, who also serves as the District Six Patrol Administrative Assistant, said a decision was made to initiate an official program in 1999.

> The Idaho State Police Chaplain Program, through a statewide system of trained volunteers, strives to support and encourage law enforcement personnel and their families in times of need. These special volunteers also seek to meet the emotional and spiritual needs of victims and their families in a crisis. There are chaplains serving in all regions of the state police and they cover all areas of the state of Idaho. They've had many opportunities to assist state troopers in their jobs, especially in assisting with fatal crashes.

Lusk said although chaplains are not Idaho State Police employees, they work closely with the state police in providing service to the public.

> Those chosen to be Idaho State Police Chaplain volunteers must meet certain requirements and specifically be able to assist all people regardless of faith. Chaplains in the program have to have an unprejudiced understanding of all faiths. Each chaplain must be ecclesiastically certified and in good standing with a recognized religious organization. The chaplains all receive training in law enforcement ethics, state police history, chaplain appearance, law enforcement personality, legal liability and confidentiality, death notifications, chaplain safety, police procedures, and on scene procedures.

Lusk added since the program's origination, chaplains have played a vital role in assisting both Idaho State Police employees and Idaho citizens during and after critical incidents.

In 1999, the Idaho State Police celebrated its sixtieth birthday. Colonel Strickfaden was promoted from Superintendent Idaho State Police, to Director of the Department Law Enforcement. He would be the last director to hold this position. Mike Fosbury was promoted to Superintendent Idaho State Police, and would be the last to hold this position.

The Idaho State Police Reorganization Team: Ron Kirtley, Kathy Ruffalo, unidentified, Shawn Klitch, Margaret White, Tim O'Leary, Glen Schwartz, Glen Ford, Governor Dirk Kempthorne, Tom Thompson, Colonel Ed Strickfaden, Dave Rich, Ralph Powell, Ann Thompson, Kevin Johnson, Robert Lockett, Dan Charboneau, Gary Smith.

While the year started out mostly routine for state law enforcement officers in the Department of Law Enforcement, huge changes were on the horizon. By the end of the year, the Department of Law Enforcement was reorganized into the Idaho State Police, with the position of Director, Idaho State Police becoming a governor-appointed position. Fosbury retired from the state police and Strickfaden was named Director of the Idaho State Police.

In a statement to the employees now under his command, Strickfaden said:

> This unification of purpose for Idaho's state police agency brought vision, purpose, and mission into focus, creating one set of goals within the department. It allowed for benefits to our employees, enhancing morale, combining investigative resources, focusing on a single-minded philosophy; and it brought cost efficiencies in the process.

Strickfaden appointed Saundra DeKlotz to the position of assistant director. To date, DeKlotz is the only woman to serve in this capacity. In a letter to Idaho State Police employees, Strickfaden said DeKlotz would be heading the agency's support services programs.

Idaho State Police services include the state's three forensic laboratories, statewide training functions, statewide Criminal

Justice Information Services, and a number of criminal history record and identification services. As Law Enforcement Safety Program Manager, DeKlotz administered Idaho's commercial vehicle and hazardous materials safety programs. Under her management, the safety program reduced commercial vehicle crashes by half, while commercial vehicle miles traveled in the state more than doubled. She has designed and implemented a number of wide-ranging special projects dealing with highway safety in Idaho and nationally, including the program to assure safety of radioactive waste shipments to the Waste Isolation Pilot Plant in Carlsbad, New Mexico. In 1999, DeKlotz received the Distinguished Service Award for her work as a champion of employee civil rights and the development and delivery of values-based sexual-harassment and non-discrimination training for the entire Idaho State Police.

The reorganization while welcomed by many in the state police was met with resistance by others, especially those in the Bureau of Narcotics.

Wayne Longo was among the Bureau of Narcotics agents who now wore the Idaho State Police badge.

I know there were a number of detectives who did not support the reorganization, but I absolutely did. Ed and I had many conversations about it when he became the superintendent of the state police. He created a reorganization team and he invited me to be on it. I consider it an honor to have been part of the reorganization team because it finally gave all of us the opportunity to be part of one solid police organization instead of fractured units. It was absolutely the right thing to do.

Beth Bradbury said the consolidation helped everyone in the Department of Law Enforcement.

I loved it when we reorganized into the Idaho State Police because for the first time, we weren't basically slotted into one area. With the reorganization we had the opportunity to cross train and also to move laterally to other positions. Before the reorganization the different entities with the Department of Law Enforcement had become quite fractured from each other. There was a mentality of "us versus them," and the reorganization went a long way toward stopping that.

Glen Schwartz said in his opinion the reorganization was long overdue.

It seemed like the different departments within the Department of Law Enforcement were constantly butting heads. There was a lot of acrimony between patrol officers and investigations officers. Sometimes it felt like we were part of two completely different countries. The situation within the Department of Law Enforcement wasn't good for the people of Idaho, and it wasn't good for state law enforcement officers.

District 5 Investigations Lieutenant John Ganske said he initially had mixed emotions about the reorganization.

I was a member of the CRT team, which was integrated with Bureau of Narcotics and Idaho State Police officers in 1994, so I was part of the first truly integrated units between the bureau and the state police. With the reorganization in 1999, there were some pay and other benefits we hadn't had before, but it really was a marriage of two completely different cultures and there was a lot of contention because of it. It was hard for those of us in the Bureau of Narcotics to lose our chain of command.

Merrill Kelley said the individual bureaus should never have been consolidated.

The Idaho State Police needs to stay as a highway patrol unit, and the Bureau of Narcotics needed to remain a separate entity. The jobs of both units are completely different and combining them didn't serve either organization. For the Bureau of Narcotics, we needed to have our own chain-of-command. Our job was completely different from what patrol does.

Strickfaden said although there was opposition to the reorganization, if it had not taken place, both the Bureau of Narcotics and the Idaho State Police probably would not exist today.

> This reorganization was what the governor wanted and what a number of people in Idaho law enforcement wanted as well. Governor Kempthorne was looking for a way to make state agencies more efficient. What really enabled me to do the reorganization was that I had worked in five of the six state police districts and I had a good rapport with the sheriffs and chiefs of police throughout most of the state. They didn't speak out against the reorganization which actually showed their support for it. I also formed a reorganization team that cut across the breadth of the entire organization and this team worked tirelessly to find the best way not only to reorganize the state police but to make sure the reorganization worked efficiently and smoothly and in the best interests of the citizens of Idaho.

In December of 2011, Strickfaden's efforts and hard work in bringing about the success of the reorganization of the Idaho State Police was recognized when Strickfaden received a tribute which became part of the Congressional Record of the Proceedings and Debates of the 112th Congress, First Session. The tribute was read in Washington D.C., on December 1, 2011. In part the tribute read:

> Today, the Idaho State Police will be naming a building after Ed Strickfaden who served as the director of the Idaho State Police and was a thirty-five year veteran of the department. Colonel Strickfaden undertook a major reorganization of the Idaho State Police, streamlining its functions and enhancing training throughout the department. He initiated the name change to Idaho State Police. With his years of service, rising through the ranks and serving in all parts of Idaho, Colonel Strickfaden understood more than most what was needed and how to do it. Today, the Idaho State Police and the people of Idaho honor this humble man by putting his name on the building at the Idaho State Police headquarters. It is a fitting tribute to a great leader and a wonderful human being.

The same day the tribute was read, a building dedication ceremony was held at the Meridian Headquarters Complex at which Strickfaden was honored with a plaque, which recognized Strickfaden's "...visionary and progressive leadership was instrumental in the reorganization of the Department of Law Enforcement in 1999."

With the reorganization, the Idaho State Police became a fully empowered police department encompassing patrol, investigations, the Criminal Justice Information Systems, Forensic Services, Bureau of Criminal Identification, P.O.S.T. Academy, the Racing Commission, and one of Idaho's oldest law enforcement entities, the Brands Department.

In a short history of the Bureau of Brands, W. C. Overton stated:

> Recording of brands in Idaho became a state responsibility in 1905, fifteen years after statehood. Prior to 1905, official recording was done at the county level. The state auditor was the first ex-officio State Recorder of Brands, having been given that responsibility by the legislature as recorded in the Session Laws of 1905. The Session Laws of 1911 indicated the State Veterinary Surgeon had assumed the ex-officio responsibility, until 1919, when the legislature placed those duties with the Department of Agriculture.

In 1939 the legislature established a State Brand Inspector and a Bureau of Brands and Marks within the Department of Agriculture, and later, in 1943, transferred those duties to the Department of Law Enforcement. In 1999, the Bureau of Brands became part of the Idaho State Police.

With Forensic Services also now under the Idaho State Police, Rick Groff said the unit was in the "...best overall position to service law enforcement and the citizens of Idaho." Groff added all three laboratories of the forensics unit, which became part of the Idaho State Police Forensic Services with the reorganization, had obtained accreditation with the American Society of Crime Laboratory Directors/Laboratory Accreditation Board in 1987.

> The ASCLD/LAB is a nationally recognized accrediting body for forensic laboratories. The laboratories were accredited labs

number 52, 53, and 54, out of the current 212 accredited laboratories. In 1996, a law was also passed that authorized the creation of a data base for the retention of DNA profiles of convicted offenders for specific crimes such as rape, first degree homicide, etc.

In the early 2000s, the Idaho State Police Forensic Services sought accreditation to the ASCLD/LAB ISO standard, and became the numbers 40, 41, and 42 labs to be accredited to this new, higher standard.

Groff added after the reorganization, the three Idaho State Police forensic laboratories continued their quest to meet national quality standards and many of the technical staff members took the General Knowledge Examination offered by the American Board of Criminalistics. This organization is the certifying body for forensic scientists, and every Idaho State Police Forensic Scientist is required to be certified. The Idaho State Police is one of the few labs nationwide that holds its scientists to such a high standard.

Despite opposition from some officers, the reorganization had an immediate unifying effect. Where some departments had maintained different procedures for the same action, Strickfaden and his command staff were now able to work toward one system that best served the citizens of Idaho.

The newly formed state police had plenty to keep it busy as the millennium came to an end, including rebuilding much of the District 2 building after an “unbelievable” accident.

In April of 2000, troopers and office staff in District 2 experienced first-hand the terrifying results of a runaway truck, when the District 2 clerical staff narrowly missed injury, and possibly death, as an out of control semi smashed in the District 2 office and the adjoining Idaho Transportation Department supply building.

The semi was loaded with grain and completely destroyed the office of secretary, Carlea Koornney. Koornney had taken a late lunch so was not at her desk when the accident happened. The truck was driven by Patrick Brann of Lethbridge, Alberta, Canada. He failed to control the speed of his truck while taking the downgrade of US 95's, Lewiston Hill, which is comprised of a seven percent grade.

Brann lost control of his semi at the bottom of the hill, jumped a grassy median, clipped a Dodge pick-up truck, which injured the driver and passenger although not seriously, before smashing through the concrete barrier and into the District 2 building.

Danny Bunderson said the semi hit with enough force that the rafters collapsed and the cinder block wall, "...crumpled like cookies which all ended up in Koornney's office." In the fall 2000 *Idaho State Police* magazine Bundeson wrote:

> I have experienced a host of critical incidents throughout my twenty-three years of law enforcement, but I never expected that the critical incident could be in our own back yard. Immediately after the crash Troopers Howard, Swearingen, and CVS specialist Youngren under the supervision of Sergeant Dale Hughes worked the investigation. They were assisted by state police Detective Dave Kane, the FBI, Lewiston Police Department, and the Idaho Transportation Department. Through their efforts, Brann was charged with reckless driving and two separate driver's log violations.

Bunderson said prior to losing control of his vehicle, Brann disregarded three of the seven run-away escape ramps constructed to prevent disasters such as this.

> We were all so fortunate and blessed that it turned out like it did because careening across four lanes of traffic during lunch hour could have been devastating, especially if he had hit a loaded school bus or a flammable tanker truck. Brann's (semi) left a trail of debris, crumbled concrete, turf and spilled diesel fuel...and no one was seriously injured.

In March of 2001, the Idaho State Police learned a twenty-eight percent increase in general tax support for the state police, meant the hiring of more troopers. The $20.7 million dollar general tax budget for the state police put two more troopers on the road in the heavily populated southwestern Idaho and four more in the rural areas of the state.

The budget also allowed for a two-man team to work Internet crime, and three officers in the war on methamphetamine. Full time evidence technicians were authorized for Districts 1 and 4, and the Alcohol Beverage Control Office got two more agents.

The addition of six troopers was the largest infusion of manpower for the Idaho State Police in over two decades and allowed for the formation of a motorcycle unit in District 3. Strickfaden said the motorcycle unit would be able to respond to accidents and other calls more quickly, as the motorcycles were more navigable in traffic jams caused by accidents.

The motorcycle unit was truly needed. Over the five years previous to the creation of the unit, Ada and Canyon counties experienced a sixty-five percent accident rate increase, and a lot of times troopers responding to these accidents in patrol vehicles got caught up in the traffic jams.

In 2003, Corporal Duane Prescott proved motorcycles weren't just effective at responding to accident scenes. They could also be used to chase down runaway trains. The following account was taken from the summer 2003 *Idaho State Police* Magazine.

An Idaho State Police motorcycle officer jumped aboard a runaway locomotive and brought it to a halt after a twenty-two mile chase. No one was hurt in the noon-hour incident, but officers raced from intersection to intersection in the Treasure Valley's western suburbs to block traffic. The Union Pacific locomotive was first reported loose and rolling downhill at about forty miles per hour in west Boise.

As the 400,000-pound engine rolled out of town, Prescott raced his motorcycle to a railroad crossing in Nampa and waited for it. Meanwhile, officers learned another engine was sitting on the tracks just a few minutes away. Railroad personnel were not able to get the train moving in time to get in out of the way of the runaway locomotive.

As it approached Prescott, the runaway engine had slowed but was still traveling at about twenty miles an hour. Prescott tried to climb aboard with a railroad employee, but it was going too fast and they missed it. That's when Prescott hopped back on his bike and motored down the tracks, passed it, then jumped again as the engine rolled past him and made it. Communicating on his police radio with an engineer, Prescott was able to bring it to a halt. The only damage was to Prescott's motorcycle, which was scuffed when Prescott jumped aboard the engine.

Master Corporal John Gibbs, ISP 657, worked as a motor officer for four years.

Motorcycles are especially effective in heavy traffic. The reason District 3 was chosen for the motorcycle unit is because it has the longest riding season and the most traffic. The challenging part of being a motor officer was the challenge of making a high risk stop. Motorcycles don't offer any cover or concealment, so although high risk stops aren't recommended, sometimes we didn't have a choice.

The Idaho State Police had plenty to celebrate in the first few months of 2001, but on the morning of September 11, any sense of celebration came to an abrupt halt as Idahoans joined the rest of the nation in stunned disbelief, when terrorists turned civilian airplanes into instruments of destruction.

21 ★ Terrorism and Trafficking

We look forward to a world founded upon four essential human freedoms. The first is freedom of speech and expression—everywhere in the world. The second is freedom of every person to worship God in his own way—everywhere in the world. The third is freedom from want—everywhere in the world. The fourth is freedom from fear—anywhere in the world.

Franklin D. Roosevelt

On September 11, 2001, a series of four coordinated terrorist attacks killed nearly 3000 people in New York City and Washington D. C. The attacks were launched by the Islamic terrorist group al-Qaeda. Four passenger airlines were hijacked by nineteen terrorists. Two of the airplanes crashed one after the other into the north and south towers of the World Trade Center complex in New York City, and one crashed into the Pentagon in Washington D.C. The fourth airplane, intended for the White House, crashed into a field in Shanksville, Pennsylvania.

Despite the attacks being thousands of miles away, law enforcement officers across Idaho were aware that more attacks could be imminent, and Idaho, home to the INL, Dworshak Dam – the third tallest dam in the United States – five other dams between 300 and 500 feet tall, and a capitol building that bore a striking resemblance to the White House, offered terrorists a number of lucrative targets.

Director Strickfaden said the attacks of September 2001 focused the need to prepare the Idaho State Police's response to security threats.

> One of the first priorities of the state police after the terrorist attacks was to make sure the Idaho capitol was protected. We were receiving a lot of information from the feds about possible attacks against Idaho. One of the things that caused concern is that our capitol rotunda is very similar to the National Capitol. A picture of an attack on Idaho's rotunda could be convincingly photographed as an attack on the National Capitol.

In response to the attacks, Strickfaden placed the Idaho State Police on alert status.

> This required off-duty patrol officers to remain within twenty-five miles of their residence and be reachable by telephone. This was not in response to any specific threat, but was an appropriate stance of readiness to assist in maintaining normal operations and provide reassurance to Idaho's citizens.

Kathy Parsells was sent to Boise on four separate occasions to assist with capitol security.

> They had put concrete barriers around the capitol, and for several months we ran 24-hour patrols. The Idaho National Guard was also there. For awhile, there was a big concern for all of the state capitols because we just didn't know what else was coming after the 9/11 attacks.

Strickfaden said many Idahoans immediately expressed opposition to the idea of adding or increasing security at the capitol building.

> It was a controversial issue. People were upset because we closed some roads around the capital complex and we stationed troopers and Idaho National Guard troops around the capitol. A lot of people felt access to the capitol would be completely restricted, which was never the intent. The security at the capitol was in part about protecting the governor and legislators, but it was mostly about protecting the employees at the capitol and visitors to the capitol.

In a letter to Governor Kempthorne, Strickfaden thanked him for his trust in the Idaho State Police after the attacks, and for implementing many of the security measures recommended by law enforcement and military experts. Strickfaden added a survey had been conducted to determine the level of security at Idaho's capitol, and it was discovered the security was woefully inadequate.

> You are to be greatly admired for your courage in making decisions based on the knowledge available to you, and assuring the safety of state employees and Idaho citizens, all the while knowing that politically those decisions could be used against you. I firmly believe that we have done the preparation and training necessary for us to secure our critical assets and to respond to abnormal behavior near potential targets. This challenge will face America for years to come, and we must continue to build our capabilities for response, protection, and intervention.

Strickfaden added in the face of the September 11 attacks, it was also clear law enforcement entities across Idaho needed to meld together.

> Law enforcement in Idaho to be ultimately successful in our rural and diverse state must become mutually engaged and respected by all agencies in order to encourage a force multiplier for combating crime. The Idaho State Police enjoys a strong working relationship with the chiefs of police, sheriffs, and federal law enforcement agencies whose objective together is to provide protection for Idaho's residents and visitors.

Idaho did not become the target of any terrorist attacks, and by the summer of 2002, Strickfaden said he was, "comfortable," about Idaho hosting the National Governor's Association annual meeting.

In the fall 2002 *Idaho State Police* Magazine, Idaho State Police Public Information Officer Rick Ohnsman wrote:

> The state police had the opportunity to test and evaluate its capabilities during the summer of 2001 when the Western Governors Association held its annual meeting in Coeur d' Alene. The lessons learned there helped to some degree, but the National Governor's Meeting in Boise was far bigger and more comprehensive.

After all, it was after the September 11, 2001 terrorist attacks.

Due to the nature, size, and location of the event, Governor Kempthorne tasked the Idaho State Police as the lead security agency. Major Kevin Johnson was appointed to be the lead coordinator for the security detail. It was a daunting task, working out details with not only state police personnel, but coordinating with the leaders of numerous other law enforcement agencies as well as the staff of the National Governor's Conference.

The state police was tasked with ensuring security at indoor and outdoor events as well as providing security for the visiting dignitaries to and from each location. Twenty-nine governors and nine dignitaries attended the annual meeting. In a letter of appreciation, Governor Kempthorne thanked the Idaho State Police for its work

As Governor of Idaho, I express my gratitude and deep appreciation for all of the men and women who serve the state of Idaho in law enforcement. Particularly I am extremely proud of the Idaho State Police who have served and performed your duties with distinction over the past year. Twice in recent years you have been called to special duty as Idaho welcomed the Nation's Governors. I was proud as so many of the attendees, including many governors, commented on the professionalism and outstanding service of our Idaho State Police officers. I recognize the long hours that were required and the high expectations that were before each of you. But in every instance, you met or exceeded those expectations. In challenging times and with limited resources, the seamless effort of the Idaho State Police set a new standard.

Strickfaden said the success of the National Governor's Conference showcased the newly-formed Idaho State Police and further proved the reorganization maximized results for the state police and law enforcement across Idaho.

By the end of 2002, our records indicated we had seized over 700 methamphetamine labs since 1998; and these efforts led to a decrease in the manufacturing of this drug in Idaho, particularly north Idaho, the main focus of our enforcement. Major among drug investigations in recent years, was the arrest, conviction, and incarceration of over 100 individuals who participated in a major drug distribution organization directly connected to the Felix Cartel out of Mexico. This cartel distributed hundreds of pounds of drugs nationally through its southwest Idaho location. Our drug enforcement investigators were recognized by the Federal Organized Crime Drug Enforcement Task Force as having one of the four largest successful drug investigations in the nation.

Strickfaden added the newly-formed cyber-crime unit had been involved in major child pornography and child exploitation cases, enhancing the protection of children throughout Idaho.

The capability of technological enforcement and computer forensics, especially with our cyber-crime unit, is the future for police agencies. We must continue to enhance these capabilities. The first line of defense for our citizens is a trooper. Their daily work is diversified and brings immeasurable challenges. From public assists to engaging the criminal behavior of a felon, their response mechanism is fundamentally grounded in the fact that they bring value to the quality of life for every person living in Idaho. This attitude is fundamental to just and even-handed policing. The quality of the individual who passes the testing and training of an Idaho State Police trooper is one which would be welcomed by the public and private sector.

In a letter to Governor Kempthorne, Strickfaden said he believed the overall mission of the Idaho State Police was well served by its employees.

As a state police officer, and particularly with the privilege of the leadership duties assigned to me, I made a concentrated effort to expand and enhance officer training and in so doing to make certain that our Idaho State Police employees make a concerted and conscientious decision, with each determination of action, to treat all people with dignity and respect and to do the right thing, regardless of the circumstances they find themselves in. We've made a concentrated effort to exceed the expectation of those we

> serve, and I firmly believe this mission is foremost in the minds of all state police employees and will be accomplished.

In December of 2002, Strickfaden retired from the Idaho State Police and Dan Charboneau was appointed as Director of the Idaho State Police. Among his first duties as director, Charboneau formally dedicated the Idaho State Police's first facility to house both its patrol and investigation functions, the District 4 building in Jerome.

The dedication was held on April 16, 2003, and presided over by the Jerome Chamber of Commerce. The building has approximately 13,000 square feet, and provides space for forty troopers, investigators and support staff. Dave Neal said prior to the completion of the District 4 building, patrol and investigations were housed in separate, rented facilities. Neal was the District 4 Commander when the building was opened.

> The ability to house all functions in one location greatly improved coordination between our people, increased security, and allowed us to realize some cost savings through combined equipment and staff resources. The Jerome location also housed us much closer to the Interstate, where about seventy percent of our patrol calls originate so our response time was improved as well.

During the dedication ceremony, which was attended by Governor Kempthorne, Colonel Ed Strickfaden, retired, and many other dignitaries, Charboneau said, "We are most appreciative to all of those who made the funding of this facility a reality as well as to the community of Jerome who so warmly welcomed us." In September of 2014, the building was dedicated as the Fontaine Cooper building.

By mid-2003, the Idaho State Police recognized its worst nemesis, fatality crashes, were rising at an alarming rate. With 278 fatalities reported on Idaho's roadways in 2002, the state had witnessed its highest death toll in seventeen years. Among the reasons cited for the alarming increase in fatal crashes was aggressive driving, which in 2002 and 2003 accounted for nearly sixty percent of all crashes in Idaho.

Using a $50,000 federal grant, the state police ordered seventeen "slick-top" patrol cars to help in the fight against aggressive driving, which includes speeding, following too closely, running red lights, and failing to yield. The seventeen patrol cars had regular police markings but no external light bars and were distributed among the districts. The Idaho State Police cannot use unmarked patrol cars for regular patrol enforcement duties, but the slick tops offer troopers the ability to blend in better with traffic.

The persistent battle against fatality crashes accounted for a great many of the citations issued by troopers in 2003, but troopers were also issuing an increasing number of citations and affecting more arrests in the war on drugs.

Kent Oliver recalled one case in which an early morning traffic stop on a vehicle driving erratically on Interstate 84 near Twin Falls, ended in his arresting the driver on drug trafficking charges.

> The man was transporting two pounds of heroin and a small amount of methamphetamine. The heroin had an estimated street value of over $300,000. Criminals use the highways to get around just like everyone else. Criminal interdiction has always been one of the main focuses of our duties. As troopers we have to use our training to look beyond the obvious to detect criminal activities.

State troopers and detectives were called in on more and more agency assists as well, when many rural law enforcement agencies found themselves battling drug enforcement and other issues with extremely limited manpower.

In the summer 2003 *Idaho State Police* Magazine, the Washington County Sheriff's Office and Weiser Police Department were recognized as being "model organizations," for intra-agency cooperation in the delivery of law enforcement services to the public.

> One of the major reasons for the cooperation and teamwork between the city, county, state and federal law enforcement agencies and these two departments, is the leadership styles of Washington County Sheriff Marvin Williams, and Weiser Chief of Police Don Hughes. Each agency has limited patrol and investigative resources and depends on the assistance of many divisions of the Idaho State Police. Sheriff Williams sees the positive impact of multi-agency investigations. His style of leadership focuses on getting the job done with the best quality and professionalism.

The article related both William's and Hughes' had major concerns with drug enforcement. In small communities in particular, the effects of drug abuse are vivid. Many property and other crimes, including Idaho's increased child abuse cases, are directly related to illicit drug use.

Intra-agency cooperation also played a key role in solving a double homicide in Bellevue. The victims were Alan and Diane Johnson. Their sixteen year old daughter, Sarah, was convicted of shooting both of them. According to court documents, Sarah shot her mother in the head while her mother was sleeping, and then shot her father in the chest as he stepped out of the shower.

Scott Ward was among the Idaho State Police investigators who worked the case.

> This particular murder scene was one of the most gruesome I've ever seen. Diane Johnson was shot in the head at near contact range, and Alan Johnson was shot from about three feet away. Both of them were shot with a Winchester rifle. Early on in the investigation, we began to suspect Sarah of the killings. Her motive was that her parents were prohibiting her from seeing her boyfriend, who was nineteen years-old. Alan Johnson had threatened to go to the police when he found out Sarah had spent the night at her boyfriend's house.

Sarah told the police a number of different stories about what she witnessed the morning of the murders, but the evidence against her was overwhelming. One key piece of evidence in the case was preserved because of the quick thinking of Blaine County Resident Trooper Ross Kirtley. Kirtley was on a traffic stop a short distance away from the murder scene was able to immediately respond to the Johnson home when the shooting was called in.

When he arrived at the scene Kirtley noticed a garbage truck emptying trash cans in the area. He realized the Johnson's trash cans had been placed on the curb for emptying and moved them away from the curb. In doing so, Kirtley preserved several pieces of evidence that was later located in the trash cans.

Crime scene officers found a pink robe in the trash, inside of which they found a leather glove and a latex glove. Tests of the robe revealed biological material from the defendant and her parents. Testing of the leather glove revealed gunshot residue, and Sarah Johnson's DNA was found inside the latex glove.

The matching leather glove was found in Sarah's bedroom, and rifle was found in the master bedroom. The rifle was usually stored in the family's guest house, where Sarah had spent the weekend after being grounded by her father. Prosecutors in the case said Johnson committed the murders because her father was going to turn her boyfriend, a Mexican national, in for statutory rape and have him deported. There was additional evidence Sarah killed her parents to get their money so that she and her boyfriend could go away together. Ward said the Idaho State Police assisted the Blaine County Sheriff's Office and the Bellevue City Police in working the case.

> All of us worked on different aspects of the investigation and we each came up with various pieces of evidence that were key components to solving the case. One thing I remember in particular was that Sarah had bruises on her shoulder. We measured the bruises and they were the exact height of the rifle butt. Those measurements really came into play in the investigation and her conviction.

Sarah Johnson was sentenced to life in prison with no possibility of parole.

By the end of 2003, the War on Terrorism, which had been declared following the September 11, 2001 terrorist attacks, began to affect law enforcement entities across the nation as reserve and National Guard units were mobilized

Idaho was no exception. Soldiers with the 116th Cavalry Brigade were mobilized for an eighteen-month tour of duty. The largest call-up of Idaho National Guard soldiers in the state's history. The call-up left several of Idaho's smaller law enforcement entities in desperate straits as their deputies were called to duty.

The Idaho State Police lost twelve of its employees statewide, and the majority of those deployed were either troopers or detectives. For the state police, the loss of manpower meant a diminished presence on Idaho's roadways. The state police, like other Idaho law enforcement entities, could ill-afford to lose any of its officers as the fatality accident rates were once again on the rise. To add to the worry, the 2004 Crime in Idaho report showed a thirty-five percent increase in assaults against officers with 259 incidents.

In more than one case, these incidents led to officers being placed on light-duty or medical leave, often for several weeks, as they recovered from their injuries.

In July of 2004, Sergeant Sam Ketchum suffered a broken leg and dislocated ankle during an altercation with a truck driver at the East Boise Port of Entry. Ketchum was field training Trooper Jonathan Vance, and Vance and another truck driver were able to subdue and arrest forty-five year old independent trucker Issa Alwardiani, who was charged after the incident with battery on an officer.

Trooper Lee Edgley discovered this marijuana during a "routine" traffic stop.

By September of 2004, the state police was also back on the front lines of the war on drugs when more than 2,000 high-quality marijuana plants were discovered near Banks. Acting on an anonymous tip, the state police spotted the plants when officers flew over the area by helicopter. In a news release, Idaho State Police Captain Don Van Cleave said the plants were growing in an area about the size of two football fields. A spring was dammed to water the plants, and each growth area had its own irrigation system.

The street value of the plants was estimated to be around six million dollars. It was estimated each plant could produce a half-pound to a pound of "bud" which could have been sold for two to three thousand dollars a pound.

By the end of 2004, the Idaho State Police and lawmakers recognized another growing problem in Idaho's law enforcement capabilities, liquor control. Idaho employed a single liquor-control officer to enforce Idaho laws on the sale of alcohol, and one wasn't enough.

Top law enforcement leadership called the situation, "a public safety hazard." State law charges a division of the state police with overseeing liquor licenses and enforcing liquor laws. Unfortunately, the Idaho State Police was forced to acknowledge the majority of the sole liquor-enforcement officer's time was spent processing applications for new liquor licenses.

That meant, the state's liquor-control division rarely undertook life-saving prevention projects to keep people from driving drunk and to keep alcohol out of the hands of minors. The issue was highlighted in a special sting operation that was conducted to catch people selling alcohol to minors. Almost half of the establishments tested in southern Idaho sold liquor to minors and in one Boise check, seventy percent of the bars, restaurants, and stores sold alcohol to undercover minors.

After the sting, Alcohol Beverage Control Lieutenant Bob Clements said: "We aren't doing justice for the people of the state. This is an emergency situation. In my eyes, the bottom line is if we save one life by hiring more officers, isn't it worth it?"

According to state police archives, in 1997 ten officers handled enforcement duties, but limited budgets and other priorities—especially the shift in personnel to fight methamphetamine—forced cuts in ABC's staffing and services. Despite the cutbacks in personnel however, in 2004 ABC generated more than one million in state revenues through license fees. State liquor stores made about twenty-five million in profits annually. And of that, about twelve million went to substance-abuse treatment. Among other recipients were community colleges, public schools, and the state, with the lion's share going to cities and counties to spend where they deemed necessary.

As of 2013, the Alcohol Beverage Control Bureau's mission is to ensure all establishments selling and/or producing alcoholic beverages, including liquor, beer, and wine, are properly licensed and conform to the laws, rules, and regulations pursuant to Title 23, Idaho Code, and also to provide assistance to local law enforcement agencies in the enforcement of Title 23, Idaho Code. Along with a headquarters staff, each of the six Idaho State Police districts has an Alcohol Beverage Control Officer.

22 ✯ Challenges and Changes

Courage: the most important of all virtues because without courage, you can't practice any other virtue consistently.

Maya Angelou

In May of 2005, the Idaho State Police and allied law enforcement agencies in northern Idaho put intra-agency cooperation to the ultimate test in one of the most horrific and shocking cases in Idaho history. Wayne Longo said throughout the investigation of this case: "There was an absolute blurring of badges. Every police organization involved in this crime, desperately wanted to solve this crime."

The case involved a triple murder and the kidnapping of two young children. On May 16, 2005, Brenda Groene, 40, Slade Groene, 13, and Brenda Groene's fiancé, Mark McKenzie, 37, were bludgeoned to death at Brenda's home in Coeur d' Alene. Brenda's youngest children, nine year-old Dylan and eight year-old Shasta were abducted.

For over six weeks, law enforcement searched for any clues that led to the recovery of the missing children and the person or persons responsible for the triple murders and disappearance of Dylan and Shasta.

On July 2, 2005, employees at Denny's Restaurant in Coeur d' Alene called police and reported Shasta was in the restaurant with a man. Within minutes, law enforcement converged on the restaurant and arrested Joseph Edward Duncan III, 42, of Fargo, North Dakota.

As details about the murders and abductions became available, people across the state were staggered by both the ferocity of the attack on the family and the depravities inflicted on Shasta and Dylan.

Wayne Longo was the District 1 Commander at the time of the incident.

The Idaho State Police was on the ground with that case from the very beginning. We worked the case hand-in-hand with the

Kootenai County Sheriff's Office and the Federal Bureau of Investigations. It was the most horrific case I have ever worked in my career. It was without a doubt one of the very worst crimes ever committed in Idaho.

Longo said there were three unified commanders for the entire case. He was the commander for the Idaho State Police. Travis Cheney was the commander for the Kootenai County Sheriff's Office, and Donald Robinson was the commander for the FBI.

At one point we had about 130 people working the case. Our state police investigations unit was in charge of the evidence and they did all of the evidence work at the murder scene. From the patrol side, we supplied man-power at the command post. It really was a first class effort in cooperation.

When the bodies of Brenda and Slade Groene and Mark McKenzie were first discovered, Longo said investigators initially thought the crimes had been committed by someone who knew the family.

We had three people bludgeoned to death in their own home with what we learned later, was a hammer. The crime was so violent and seemed very personal, so there was speculation that it could have been some type of retaliation killing. There were questions about whether it could have been drug related or gang related. What didn't fit into those scenarios was why were the two youngest children missing? We spent days looking for the kids, and trying to figure out, were they dead? Were they alive? We talked about several scenarios, but we really didn't have a lot to go on.

Longo said Shasta and Dylan's father, Steve, and two older brothers, Jesse and Vance, were questioned, but soon cleared of having any involvement.

We knew that Brenda and her ex-husband Steve Groene had a very rocky relationship but he was cleared as a suspect as were

Brenda's two older sons. We also knew the day of the murders, Brenda and Mark had a party at their house. Among the friends at the party there was one person in particular we looked at because we found his fingerprints on the door to the house, but he also was cleared. There were a few other leads that were looked into, but all of them came to nothing.

With their most likely suspects ruled out, investigators found themselves back to square one with few leads and no suspects. It wasn't until Shasta was recovered that the police learned just how vile and evil the crime really was.

When we recovered Shasta, we had no idea where Dylan was or even if he was still alive. We tried to get information out of Duncan but it was ultimately Shasta who told us everything that had happened to her and her brother. Considering what she had been through, she was a very brave and excellent witness. We also found a video log that Duncan had kept of himself and the kids. I hope the public never has to see what we had to see. The jury in Duncan's trial saw some of it but they didn't see all of it. You can't imagine no matter how great of an imagination you have, you can't even come close to what he put those kids through the several weeks he had them out in the woods.

Shasta told investigators Duncan had murdered her brother, Dylan, and using the GPS tracker and other evidence found in Duncan's vehicle, a campsite in the Lolo National Forest was located. There, officers found remains that were later identified as being Dylan's through DNA testing.

Very, very minimal remains of Dylan were found because after killing Dylan, Duncan had burned the body. Discovering Dylan's remains brought up another issue for us. We now had another crime scene to guard and this crime scene was in another state. Our first question was how do we secure it? The campsite was in Mineral County, Montana and when we contacted the sheriff there, we realized he simply didn't have the manpower to do it. Thankfully, the Idaho State Police has long had Memorandums of Understanding, or MOUs with our surrounding states, so we asked the sheriff if we could provide the guards and he was very agreeable to that.

Along with being the District 1 Commander, Longo was also the CIT/SOG commander. As it happened, the CIT/SOG team was in Coeur d' Alene to assist the city with the annual 4th of July celebrations when Shasta was found.

I was able to use members of the CIT/SOG team to secure the campsites in Montana and to help guard Shasta at the hospital. I don't know how long those MOUs have been in force but I hope they are always there because it saved us a lot of problems in figuring out how to guard not only the campsite where Dylan was found, but also to search the other two campsites where he had kept the kids.

As the case unfolded, Longo said investigators learned the crime had not been drug related, gang related, or in any way retaliatory.

I still get chills when I think of how random this case was. That was what shocked us the most, the total randomness of how Duncan connected with this family. Basically, he was driving westbound on Interstate 90 and as he came off of 4th of July Pass, the first thing he saw was their house. Dylan and Shasta were playing in a field, and it clicked in his mind, "there's my target." He pulled into the next exit and for two days he conducted surveillance on the house using night vision goggles and also sneaking up to the house to peek in the windows. It's chilling, absolutely chilling when you stop and think about just how random his choice was. It could have been anyone. There was no rhyme or reason to his choice except in his own mind.

Longo said as Shasta told her story of both the murders and the subsequent weeks of torture she endured as Duncan's captive, he got a glimpse at "…what absolute evil is."

Shasta said her ordeal began when she was called into the living room of her home late at night by her mother. Duncan was holding her mother, her brother, and McKenzie at gunpoint and had tied them up with flexi-cuffs and duct tape.

Duncan also tied up Shasta and Dylan and took them outside, laying them in the grass, while he returned to the house to kill the rest of the family. Shasta recalled at one point seeing her brother, Slade, stagger to the door and she was hopeful he would help her and Dylan. But Slade was unable to help. Shasta also remembered Duncan bragging to her later about how he had killed her family.

Duncan eventually pleaded guilty to several charges including murder and kidnapping. He was sentenced to death, but his case is currently under appeal.

While Idahoans were still trying to process the "evil that invaded the northern part of the state," another crime in south-eastern Idaho led at least one citizen to wonder "...has the world indeed gone mad?" (This question was taken from a blog site about the murder, and the author was not named.)

The case that spurred this question was the murder of sixteen year-old Pocatello High School junior, Cassie Jo Stoddart. On September 22, 2006, Stoddart was found stabbed to death in the home of a relative. She had been house-sitting while her relatives were out of town.

John Ganske was one of the lead investigators on the case.

> This was a particularly brutal case. Cassie was stabbed twenty-nine times and a number of the wounds were found to be fatal wounds. Initially, the evidence didn't point in any direction so at first we just retraced the hours prior to her murder to see if we could figure out who our suspects might be.

Ganske said the investigation revealed that Cassie's boyfriend had been with her at the house for a time, the night she was murdered. He was initially a suspect, but he volunteered to take a polygraph test, and "...passed with flying colors."

> On one hand we were very glad that he was not responsible for Cassie's murder, but it basically sent us back to square one. We later learned there were two other boys who had been at the house that night, Brian Draper and Torey Adamcik, both of whom were classmates with Cassie. We called them in for questioning and at

> first I had a really hard time dealing with my belief that these two could be involved with such a brutal murder.

Despite how difficult it was to think two teenage boys could be responsible for such a heinous crime, Ganske said it didn't take long before it was obvious Draper and Adamcik were the most likely suspects.

> We called each one of them in for questioning. We questioned Draper first and he told us at the time Cassie was murdered he and Adamcik were at the movies. When we questioned him about what movie they had gone to see, he couldn't remember anything about it. We figured he was probably not being truthful about going to the movies, but my initial thought was he was lying to us because he had told his parents he was going to a movie and was worried if they found out he hadn't done that he might be in trouble.

When Adamcik was questioned by detectives, he too tried to claim he and Draper had gone to the movies. When investigators told Adamcik they knew that to be a lie, he changed his story and said the two of them had actually spent the time they were supposed to be at the movies breaking into cars in an attempt to steal money for gas.

Ganske said while investigators were convinced Draper and Adamcik had something to do with Cassie's murder they did not have evidence linking the boys to the scene. The day after the interview with Adamcik, however; this changed when Draper voluntarily came to an interview and told investigators that he and Adamcik had gone back to Cassie's house but that he, Draper, had not been in on the killing. It was Adamcik who killed Cassie and Draper said until he heard Cassie screaming, he thought the attack on Cassie was a joke Cassie and Adamcik had come up with to scare him.

Draper told investigators where he and Adamcik hid the items used in the attack, including knives, masks, and some clothing. When investigators found the items, they were surprised to find a video tape among the items.

Ganske said what was discovered on the video tape was, "… absolutely horrific." While the tape did not show the actual murder, it did show the boys talking about their plans to murder Cassie and after the murder was committed, their reaction to it. The following is an exact transcript of Draper and Adamcik discussing their plan to murder Cassie.

> Cassie in the house. Our plan is supposed to happen tonight so hopefully nothing will go wrong and go smoothly so we can get our first kill done and started and we can keep going. Hopefully we won't have eight or nine failures like we have. Yea, we've probably tried about ten times but they've never been home alone so…when they have, their parents show up. So as long as we're patient you know…we were patient and everything paid off because our victim's home alone so we've got our plan all worked out now. So…I'm sorry to Cassie's family but she had to be the one. We have to stick with the plan and she's perfect so she is going to die.

Adamcik and Draper, both seventeen years old, were tried as adults in the case. Both were convicted for murder and conspiracy to commit murder, and both received life sentences without the possibility of parole.

Heinous murders, it appeared, were becoming more and more commonplace in Idaho.

On June 16, 2006, Alofa Time, fifty, of Boise, intentionally crashed his Dodge Ram pick-up into another vehicle, killing thirty-six year old Samantha Murphy and her four year old daughter, Jae Lynne Grimes. As horrible as this crime was, however; law enforcement officers, including state troopers, responding to the crash were shocked to discover the severed head of woman that had been thrown from Time's vehicle during the crash.

Time was not injured in the crash and admitted the severed head belonged to his wife, forty-seven year old Theresa Time. Time pleaded with officers to kill him when his wife's head was discovered. Time had a history of violence and in the spring of 2006 had been charged with domestic battery against Theresa. Theresa's body was later found in her Nampa home.

Time pleaded guilty to first degree murder, admitting he had also tortured his wife before he killed her. He was sentenced to life in prison without parole. Time was also sentenced to fifteen years on two counts of vehicular manslaughter and one count of aggravated driving under the influence.

On August 3, 2006, Idaho State Police detectives arrested a Horseshoe Bend man in connection with the shooting death of an acquaintance in rural Boise County, approximately six miles northwest of Gardena. An Idaho State Police news release stated:

> Killed in the confrontation was forty-six year old Wes Bennett of Horseshoe Bend. Charged with the shooting was his acquaintance forty-two year old David L. Wallace, also of Horseshoe Bend. Wallace was arrested at the scene of the shooting by responding state police troopers and deputies from the Boise County Sheriff's Office. Detectives said the initial information is that the men had some kind of argument which culminated in the shooting.

Wallace was later charged and convicted of voluntary manslaughter in the shooting.

If Idahoans and law enforcement officers thought these horrific incidents were an anomaly, they thought wrong. On December 20, 2006, Idaho State Police employees and law enforcement officers across the state waited in apprehension and despair wondering if yet another Idaho State Police officer would give his life in an attempt to keep the citizens of the state he served safe.

Idaho State Police District 4 Corporal Chris Glenn was shot in the neck and critically wounded during a traffic stop south of Twin Falls. The incident began at around 7 a.m. on December 20, when Corporal Glenn heard an attempt-to-locate call over his police radio on a vehicle that had just robbed a Stinker Station. Glenn saw a vehicle matching the description of the one described in the attempt-to-locate. Glenn was on State Highway 74, just south of Twin Falls and stopped the car. As Glenn approached the vehicle and was giving the driver commands, the driver opened the driver's door and fired one shot from a 9mm handgun.

The bullet entered the front of Glenn's neck. Within moments of the shooting three Twin Falls police officers who were also looking for the suspect, arrived at the scene. Twin Falls City Police Sergeant Gardiner remained with the injured Glenn, and the other two officers pursued the vehicle.

The pursuit lasted almost fifty miles traveling southbound on U.S. 93, and finally ended when the vehicle crashed into the back of a commercial vehicle in Jackpot, Nevada. Twenty-four year old Adam Ted Mower had to be extricated from his vehicle after he lost control of his car and hit the back of a semi-tractor trailer.

Glenn was transported by ambulance to the Magic Valley Regional Medical Center and later taken by life flight to St. Alphonsus Medical Center in Boise, where it was determined he had sustained damage to his trachea, esophagus, and spine by the single shot, that hit him in the neck just above his bulletproof vest. Glenn was paralyzed from the chest down.

Mower was charged with aggravated battery on a law enforcement officer, armed robbery, and felony eluding. He was sentenced to thirty-six years in prison, with eligibility for parole in thirty years. He was also fined $5,000. On the charge of robbery, Mower received fifteen yearS with two years fixed to run consecutive to the battery charges.

On May 19, 2007, the Moscow Police Department, law enforcement officers across the state, and citizens were in mourning once again, this time at the loss of Moscow Police Officer Lee C. Newbill and three other citizens, including the shooter, in a rampage that made national news.

Jason K. Hamilton, 36, of Moscow murdered his wife, Crystal Hamilton, 30, a Presbyterian sexton, Paul Bauer, 62, and Officer Newbill, 49, before turning a gun on himself and committing suicide. During the rampage, Hamilton also wounded Moscow Police Officer Bill Shields, Latah County Deputy Sheriff Sergeant Brannon Jordan, and college student Peter Hussman.

In a narrative of the incident released by the Idaho State Police, Lieutenant Charlie Spencer said Hamilton taunted the fallen lawmen, yelling “officer down” after shooting Newbill. Newbill had served with the Moscow Police Department since 2001 and was the city’s first officer killed in the line of duty.

The narrative states:

> Hamilton went to Mingles Bar in Moscow at around 8:30 p.m. with a co-worker to drink beer. He returned home two hours later and had a confrontation with his wife that ended when she was killed by a gunshot wound to the head. Armed with two rifles, Hamilton went to the parking lot of the Latah County Sheriff’s Office and began firing rounds at the sheriff’s office. At about 11:22 p.m., Dispatcher Marci Williams reported the dispatch

center was under fire, with bullets striking inside the office. Hamilton fired over 100 rounds into the sheriff's office. At some point Hamilton went into the First Presbyterian Church, directly across the street from the sheriff's office and continued firing.

The report said that as sheriff's deputies and city police arrived, Hamilton opened fire on them as they were crossing the street. Newbill yelled, "Down" as he was hit in the chest by a round that penetrated his body armor. Shields was able to retreat to cover.

Hamilton then went back inside the church and a few minutes later opened fire on University of Idaho student Peter Husmann, who had heard the gunshots and rushed to the scene with a pistol. Hussman was hit four times and fell in the parking lot. As Hamilton continued firing a total of thirty-one times at him, Hussman was able to get out of harm's way and survived. Church sexton, Paul Bauer, who was sleeping in the building, got up to investigate the disturbance. At 11:41 p.m. Bauer called 911 from a room near where Hamilton was shooting at Husmann. Hamilton walked across the room and fired six shots at Bauer, killing him while he was on the phone.

When officers arrived to remove Newbill from the scene, Deputy Brannon Jordan fell out of the back of the rescue vehicle as it left the scene. Jordan was shot in the back and arm and took cover behind a tree.

About ninety minutes after Hamilton first opened fire, authorities heard one muffled shot from inside the church. Shortly before 6 a.m., SWAT teams entered the church and found Bauer dead. Hamilton was found sitting on a bench in the sanctuary with a rifle cradled between his legs. He had shot himself in the head. Four hours later, officers went to Hamilton's home and found the body of his wife. In the home, they found evidence indicating Hamilton was taking medication for depression, panic disorder, seizures, insomnia, anxiety, and paranoia. He had also been using a computer to research bomb-making techniques. No motive for the shooting was established.

Perhaps the world had indeed gone mad. But for the Idaho State Police and allied law enforcement, this “madness” made them even more determined to bring safety, and law and order back to the citizens of Idaho.

23 ★ Unsung Heroes

We are what we repeatedly do; excellence then in not an act but a habit.

Aristotle

In May of 2006, Governor Kempthorne accepted an appointment from President George W. Bush as the U.S. Secretary of the Interior. Lieutenant Governor Jim Risch became Idaho's thirty-first governor on May 30. Risch reappointed Dan Charboneau as the Director of the Idaho State Police.

In November of 2006, C. L. "Butch" Otter was elected as the thirty-second Governor of Idaho. Charboneau retired in January of 2007, and G. Jerry Russell was appointed Director of the Idaho State Police. In a news release, Otter stated:

> Of the many qualified individuals who I considered, Jerry Russell stood out because of the great working relationship he has developed in his current role with all forty-four sheriffs in every corner of Idaho. That kind of synergy, along with his understanding of the Idaho State Police's critical role in support of local law enforcement and his broad range of experience in public safety, makes him the best choice for this job.

Russell served twenty-six years with the Oregon State Police before becoming the chief security officer for Idaho's Fourth Judicial District in 2001. From 2004 to the time of his appointment to the Idaho State Police top spot, Russell was the deputy director for operations at the Idaho Bureau of Homeland Security. Much like his predecessors, Russell made it clear he expected those in his employ to continue with the exemplary service to the citizens of Idaho that had long been the hallmark of the Idaho State Police.

On July 11, 2007 the Idaho State Police and allied law enforcement agencies were back to business in the war on drugs, when law enforcement officials made the biggest drug bust in Idaho in over twenty-five years. Eight homes in Nampa were raided in a bust called "Operation Mountain Lion." The operation spanned many western states, but more than forty of the fifty arrests made, were in Idaho.

Along with the arrests, eleven pounds of crystal methamphetamine and over $100,000 in cash was seized. The operation had been in the works for over a year. Most of the crystal methamphetamine seized was smuggled from Mexico and then transported north for distribution. The bust left a major dent in the Idaho drug market.

In December of 2007, the Idaho State Police and allied law enforcement agencies made another significant dent in Idaho's methamphetamine problem when officers arrested two notorious gang members. Lucio Esparza was arrested in a Caldwell home and at the same time his father, Alfredo Esparza Sr. was arrested in Nampa. Both men were charged with distributing methamphetamine. In October of 2004, Lucio Esparza had been charged with first degree murder for a drive-by shooting in Caldwell that killed Sigmund Goode, 21, of Caldwell.

Information released by ATF officials said the Esparzas, "...have been known to say they were untouchable by law enforcement." The ATF, DEA, FBI, IRS, Caldwell Police Department, Canyon County Sheriff's Office, and the Metro Violent Crimes Task Force had been working together for nearly eight months on the investigation which led to federal charges against the Esparzas. The Idaho State Police and Nampa Police Department assisted in the arrests.

Liquor license violations were also topping the Idaho State Police agenda in 2007 and in January of 2008, seven bars in the Nampa-Caldwell and Boise area were punished for liquor license violations. The cases were opened in the spring of 2007 and after several months of investigation, each of the bars was cited on a variety of offenses including nudity, simulated sex acts, and other related acts. Several of the bars were fined $10,000 to $15,000 and were given fifteen to twenty-one day suspensions on their liquor licenses.

In February of 2008 the Idaho State Police received a spot of good news when its sex offender registry was named one of the best in the nation by the TopTenReviews.com, a technology review site. Idaho ranked sixth, just behind Florida, Arizona, Washington, Texas, and Indiana.

The reviewers praised the Idaho site for, "…clearly identified sexual predators, an exceptional mapping function, and flexible searches." The reviewers also pointed to clearly labeled profiles, large photos of the offenders, and complete information about the physical description and offense information. Colonel Russell said the state police was, "…gratified to learn of the honor."

> We are gratified, especially as the improvements pointed to are the result of a recent major revamping of our website. It is our objective to make our sexual offender registry website a location where concerned citizens can easily access information about the registered offenders in their neighborhoods. In doing so we better equip parents to be informed and to take those steps necessary to safeguard their children.

The Idaho sex offender registry is the most heavily visited location on the state police website, receiving between 100,000 to 300,000 searches per month. Governor Otter added his praise saying, "Colonel Russell and the folks at the Idaho State Police are doing great work informing our citizens. Our goal is always to give individual Idahoans the tools they need to protect their families and keep our communities safe."

Unfortunately despite its long string of successful crime-stopping efforts, it was clear by mid-2008, the Idaho State Police and indeed the entire state of Idaho was headed for rough economic times. The Idaho State Police, along with every other state agency and law enforcement entity in the state, would have to, "…tighten their belts," because of fast rising gas prices.

By June of 2008, gas prices across the state topped the four dollar per-gallon mark and many feared prices would hit five dollars by the end of summer. Subsequently, the Idaho State Police was forced to make cuts to its budget. Colonel Russell said the funding for gasoline was based on gas prices between the $2-$3 range and anything higher severely impacted the state police's ability to function. Russell said the state police would cut everything it could from training and other areas before it cut measures to protect the public.

Colonel Russell praised those under his command for their continued efforts despite a tight budget. He was especially pleased with the, "…strong emphasis on interdiction efforts," of his officers.

> All officers, all the time, should be looking closely at persons, vehicles, and circumstances when carrying out otherwise "routine" enforcement activities. Fully ninety-five percent of people engaged in criminal activities are on our highways and the interstate at some time; it is our mission to identify them and disrupt their criminal activities with every contact.

As it was in previous years, however, for state troopers and other law enforcement officers, these contacts occasionally resulted in injury to the officer. A nearly fatal incident on August 12, 2006, left Trooper Shane Langton with significant road rash and other injuries when he crashed his motorcycle while joining in the chase of a hit and run suspect.

Langton was pursuing a possible DUI suspect when he entered an intersection, hit a patch of sand and swerved to avoid another vehicle. Langton managed to avoid the car, but was not able to avoid crashing his motorcycle. The driver of the vehicle Langton was pursuing, was arrested by Ada County deputies a short time later, and charged with DUI.

On August 16, 2008, District 4 Sergeant Michael Wendler, ISP 562, was involved in a fatal shooting following a traffic stop in which he arrested Cody Hanks, 29, of Burley for DUI.

> I was following a vehicle on westbound U.S. 30 near Kimberly and I noticed the vehicle drift across the center line. I stopped the driver for failure to maintain his traffic lane. As I was talking to him, I noticed he had indications of being impaired so I conducted Field Sobriety Tests (FSTs), and subsequently arrested Hanks for DUI. I searched Hanks before I put him in my patrol car, and during the search I also discovered some methamphetamine.

Wendler said during the arrest, Hanks was cooperative and offered no resistance as Wendler placed Hanks in the rear of the patrol car.

> Hanks was very cooperative and complied with everything I asked him to do. At the time I arrested him, my only concern was that I didn't have my hand-cuff key to double lock his handcuffs. I knew there was a possibility the cuffs might tighten so I wasn't surprised when Hanks complained his handcuffs were too tight. I

got him out of the backseat and I was going to loosen his cuffs but as soon as I loosened one of them he became instantly combative.

Hanks pulled away from Wendler and ran toward his pickup.

I couldn't contain him and when we got to his pickup, I struggled with him for a few moments. I used my O.C. spray and also extended my ASP (extendable baton) in hopes of getting him to exit his vehicle. He didn't show any signs of stopping the struggle with either my use of O.C. or my use of the ASP. All of the sudden, I felt his vehicle lurch forward. I didn't know why at the time, but for some reason I couldn't disengage from his vehicle and he was starting to pick up speed.

Wendler later learned Hanks had grabbed his duty belt and was holding Wendler in the door of the pickup as he, Hanks, attempted to drive off.

As the pickup speed increased, I knew I was in a very serious situation. That was when I realized I was either going to be drug to death or I was going to have to shoot Hanks. When I started working for the state police, I really thought I would go my whole career without having to use my weapon.

Wendler said after he shot Hanks, the pickup crashed into a canal.

Hanks was still alive and I knew I had to take care of him so I called an ambulance and took Hanks up to the road. By that time, I also had back-up from other officers and because I was wet and covered with mud, they put me in a patrol car and after that I was taken in for debriefing.

Wendler credits the training he received through the Idaho State Police Advanced Training Class for saving his life.

> The training absolutely made the difference for me. Everything happened so quickly I had to rely on the instincts that were drilled into us at the academy. We are taught to treat people well, and I absolutely agree with that, but we are also taught to be ready to react when we need to. This incident just goes to show how quickly a situation can go downhill.

Wendler said he especially appreciates the treatment he received from the state police following the incident.

> I was amazed at how supportive the state police was and that support went a long way toward helping me with the healing process. I had to be cleared with a physical before I could come back to work, and I also had to go through counseling which was very helpful to me and to my family. The state police has very high standards in place not only for how it expects troopers to act, but also for how it responds to these types of incidents.

Hanks died from his injuries received in the incident.

Increased threats to law enforcement officers weren't the only worries the Idaho State Police was forced to deal with in the mid-2000s. Economists nationwide feared the recession that began rearing its ugly head after the 2001 terrorist attacks was not getting better, but worse.

Throughout 2008 the state's economic picture became more and more bleak. Colonel Russell announced in a letter to all employees the Idaho State Police would soon be feeling the impact of the nationwide economic downturn.

> While all of you are aware of the tough economic times that now face our country, we as an agency have also been impacted. You are aware of the holdbacks that we along with all state agencies have had to make for fiscal year 2009 and what those holdbacks have amounted to. One of the major funding sources for the Idaho State Police comes from the Highway Distribution account, which includes a portion of the state's gasoline tax and provides the state police with over $16 million in operating funds. Earlier this year, we were informed by the Idaho Transportation Department that the revenue being generated for the Highway Distribution account was substantially less money than projected.

Colonel Russell and his command staff were able to soften the impact of the economic situation on the Idaho State Police through fiscal year 2008, by making spending adjustments that allowed the state police to continue to operate at fairly normal levels, with minimum impact on employees. By fiscal year 2009, the economic situation worsened.

> We have been provided with the latest fiscal projections for the Highway Distribution Account, and those projections continue to show a downward trend, which means that the Idaho State Police will receive another $400,000 less in revenue than our 2009 budget authorized. This $400,000 budget shortfall is very serious and requires that we as an agency take immediate steps to ensure that our 2009 budget balances on June 30, 2009, as required by law.

While many state police troopers and civilian employees wondered if layoffs, similar to those witnessed in 1980 and 1981, were imminent, Colonel Russell and his command staff worked diligently to ensure that didn't happen. In the letter, Russell outlined some of the measures the state police would implement to offset the financial shortfalls.

> Effective immediately, all overtime payouts to patrol troopers are suspended. This step will save us over $100,000. We will also continue to reduce operating expenses by every possible means, including implementing a hiring freeze. While these actions will assist us in retiring the current $400,000 shortfall, there are numerous other options that the command staff will be taking that will help us deal with our financial conditions. We will continue to develop contingency plans to deal with the economic issues we are faced with; and while we will work hard to keep from negatively affecting our employees, you need to know that we will consider a course of action that could result in some lay-offs, multiple-day furloughs agency wide, and other cost saving measures.

Through Colonel Russell's leadership, the Idaho State Police weathered the economic shortfalls without having to lay-off or enforce but a very few furloughs on Idaho State Police employees.

There were other changes Russell felt were necessary however, to enhance the overall efficiency and effectiveness of the state police. One of these changes was the closing of the communications center in Pocatello.

On December 9, 2008, Russell announced in a continuing effort to increase agency efficiency and effectiveness the state police would be closing the Regional Communications Center in Pocatello, and restructuring to conduct statewide operations from the existing dispatch facilities in Coeur d' Alene and Meridian. The change-over was fully completed by July 1, 2009. The change was announced in a state police news release:

> Prior to 1997, the Idaho State Police operated dispatch facilities in each of its six district locations. It was determined that improved technology and enhanced management practices would allow consolidation to three centers. The centers in Lewiston, Twin Falls, and Idaho Falls were closed and operations were enhanced in Coeur d' Alene (RCC-North), Meridian, (RCC-West), and Pocatello, (RCC-East). The Idaho State Police has determined that just two centers are completely capable of providing quality public safety dispatch service for the state as well as bringing some significant effectiveness improvements.

The release stated reduced equipment maintenance needs and command staff efficiencies as well as the opportunity to enhance consistency in operations, management, use of technology, and more focused management and supervision were seen as positive outcomes from the move. Russell said:

> We are also sensitive to the needs of our employees. Currently there are eleven people working in RCC-East. We will be working to re-locate them in the Meridian or Coeur d'Alene centers or where necessary, assist them in finding work elsewhere. I am beginning this transition now to allow a full six months for the changeover.

Russell stressed the planned closure of the communication center was not part of the budget cutbacks the state police was requested to make by Governor Otter.

> We are always looking for ways we can become more efficient and while we would anticipate long-term cost savings as a result of this restructuring, that was not the catalyst for this decision and no immediate savings will be realized to contribute to this fiscal year's holdback. My continued charge as the Director of the Idaho State Police is to provide the people of Idaho with the best public safety service possible, while doing so in the most effective, efficient, and beneficial way possible. I believe this change is in line with those objectives and will further allow us to achieve our mission.

Economic issues aside, the Idaho State Police continued its mission of enforcing traffic laws, conducting interdiction patrols, assisting other agencies, and working special assignments. Among the special assignments troopers enjoyed the most, was the 2008 Special Olympics Invitational Winter Games hosted by Idaho.

The Special Olympics Invitational Winter Games were held in Boise and surrounding areas. The state police provided security at a number of venues including the opening and closing ceremonies. The security and safety of the games was a joint effort with a number of city, county, state, and federal law enforcement agencies involved. The 2008 games helped the state police and allied agencies prepare for the much larger venue of the February 2009, World Special Olympics which were also held in Boise and surrounding areas.

In the Spring 2009 *Idaho State Police* Magazine, Trooper Neil Stevens said the Idaho State Police was tasked with ensuring everyone attending the Olympics had a safe and enjoyable time.

> The job description quickly changed for the uniformed troopers. We quickly became icons for the athletes and their families. We were asked to be in hundreds of pictures and our arms were sore from shaking so many hands, giving high fives, and signing autographs. All of the athletes brought pins from their respective countries and this led to a huge pin trading event. We passed out Idaho State Police Junior Trooper stickers and an Idaho potato pin. The athletes also gave us their pins. We were able to participate in the award ceremonies by being escorts or placing the medal on the athletes. It was a great feeling seeing the joy in

the athletes' faces during the proud moment when they received their awards.

As enjoyable as the Special Olympics were to troopers who worked it, fatality crashes and criminal interdiction patrols were keeping troopers on their toes elsewhere. In October 2009, District 5 troopers recognized the heroic actions band teacher Heather Christensen, who tried to save a bus load of high school students who were on their way to a band competition when the bus they were riding in crashed. Unfortunately Christensen died in the crash.

District 5 Commander Captain Eric Dayley was among the troopers who responded to the crash.

> The crash involved a bus that was transporting fifty-one members of the American Fork High School Marching Band that had been in a marching band competition at Idaho State University. The driver apparently blacked out and Christensen attempted to steer the bus to safety. The bus overturned and Christensen was pinned underneath. About thirteen other passengers were injured, which taxed the mass casualty abilities of the local hospital and emergency responders. It was a very chaotic scene because along with dealing with the injured we were understandably inundated with information requests not only from parents of the children involved and school administrators, but also from local media, media from the Wasatch Front.

Two state troopers were also injured in an intentionally caused crash by David Paul Turnovec of Buhl. Sergeant Chris Duggan and Corporal Jon Vance were both struck and injured when Turnovec drove his Chevrolet Colorado pickup off the road and hit the troopers and their motorcycles. The incident occurred while the troopers were performing stationary patrol in the median near Micron in Boise.

Corporal Vance was treated and released but Sergeant Duggan was not as lucky. His injuries included a broken leg. Turnovec was not injured and was charged with two counts of aggravated battery on a law enforcement officer and one count of use of a deadly weapon during the commission of a felony.

More and more reports of drug seizures were also being reported on the state police's news and information blog. On September 25, 2009

Master Corporal Sellers stopped a vehicle for speeding and upon smelling a strong odor of marijuana coming from the vehicle began an investigation.

> Subsequent to the investigation, Sellers recovered about 5.4 pounds of marijuana and 27.1 grams of cocaine. These items have a street value of approximately $66,000. The driver was arrested for trafficking marijuana and possession of cocaine with intent to deliver.

On September 29, 2009, Corporal Noyes stopped a vehicle for a traffic violation near Pocatello and after arresting the driver for driving without privileges Noyes searched the vehicle and recovered two pounds of marijuana. The driver and passenger were arrested and convicted of trafficking marijuana.

Numerous other seizures of the same and sometimes larger scope were occurring across the state. One particular case in 2011 became a multi-state and federal investigation when Corporal Cox stopped a vehicle on a traffic violation and discovered evidence of several crimes including drug crimes.

> A subsequent search and inventory of the vehicle revealed several US passports that did not belong to the occupants of the vehicle, a stolen checkbook, numerous electronics, two-way radios, binoculars, bolt cutters and various instruments and tools commonly used during burglaries. In the days following the arrest, Cox discovered one of the suspects was wanted in San Rafael, California for a string of burglaries to residences, businesses, and churches in the area. The FBI, US Marshals, and Homeland Security assisted in the case with the FBI heading the investigation into the stolen passports.

The scope and severity of these types of crimes underscored not only the purpose of the Idaho State Police and its mission of keeping Idahoans safe, but also the need for more troopers if there is any hope of winning the battle against Idaho's escalating crime rate.

Colonel Russell put the issues faced by the state police into sharp focus for legislators when he told them in reality the Idaho State Police was doing its duty with 1977 staffing levels.

> There are the same number of Idaho State Police troopers patrolling the state's roads now as there were in 1977, even though the state's population has grown nearly seventy-five percent. We currently have thirty-three vacancies in the state police. Nine positions are being held vacant due to budget cuts, seven troopers are on military deployment, and I am hopeful of filling eleven positions this year. The cost to fill one of these positions is about $55,000 a year, which does not include the cost of training and equipping a trooper.

Russell added there were several detective positions also being held vacant because the state police had seen a nearly forty-five percent reduction in its state funding since fiscal year 2009.

Advances in technology, however, did bring a boon to state troopers, the electronic ticketing system. The state police began using electronic ticketing on July 1, 2010. In a news release, District 5 Commander, Captain Eric Dayley said the system was purchased with a $900,000 Federal Recovery Act grant which was awarded to the state police in 2008.

> The system will allow for quicker, more accurate citations which will be transmitted electronically to the courts and the Idaho State Police computer data base. "E-Ticketing," as it's been dubbed, will bring vast improvements to a process that hasn't had many changes in over fifty years.

Dayley explained the E-Ticketing system process:

> If a trooper issues a citation, the driver's license information and the vehicle's registration information is scanned into the E-Ticketing software using handheld barcode scanners. Troopers are then able to select from dropdown lists, violation codes and location identifiers. The citations are printed out on a four-inch printer, similar to printers used in department stores. The entire process of completing citations went from a five or more minute process to one that takes less than a minute. This will result in reduced time on the side of the highway for troopers and the public, which is safer for both.

Dayley said a major benefit to the system is the accuracy of the data collected.

> The court clerks will no longer have to decipher a trooper's handwriting or citations where the copy did not come through clearly. The accuracy of citation data is estimated to increase by at least ten percent. Another change in the ticket issuing process that will start with E-Ticketing is that people who receive tickets will no longer have to sign the ticket. The trooper will just print it out, hand it to the person and then they can be on their way. The entire citation serving process will be streamlined and more efficient.

The efficiency of the E-Ticketing system wasn't only appreciated by troopers, but by state police administrative personnel as well. Office Specialist Lorrie Oliver said the E-Ticket system increased administrative availability to troopers.

> Prior to the E-Ticketing system, we entered every trooper's citation by hand, and that is a very time-consuming process. Now that we no longer have to enter citations, we have more time to focus on other ways to support our troopers. It's imperative our troopers get support for whatever they need, whenever they need it because the less time they spend doing administrative work, the more time they have out on patrol.

With staffing levels still near those of the 1970s, anything to free-up time for troopers and detectives, was a welcome relief, and as the first decade of the 21st Century came to a close, the state police, as it had been for seven decades, remained on the front lines of traffic control, criminal interdiction, natural disasters, and agency support.

24 ★ The Mission Continues

We acquire the strength we have overcome.

Ralph Waldo Emerson

"Hotel Standoff Ends In Capture," read the headlines in the Saturday, July 16, 2011 *Times News,* but for the state police the story went far deeper, because yet another trooper was injured in an attempt to keep Idaho citizens safe.

The incident began when District 4 Trooper Joseph Chandler ISP 421, attempted a traffic stop of a vehicle on U.S. Highway 93. The suspect stopped and while speaking to and observing the driver, Chandler suspected impairment. Chandler asked the driver to step out of the vehicle for sobriety testing at which point the driver sped off, nearly striking Chandler with as the vehicle fish-tailed onto the roadway. Chandler initiated a pursuit but as the vehicle sped toward Twin Falls, the pursuit was discontinued to decrease the possibility of injury to other motorists or pedestrians. Despite the pursuit being discontinued however, the suspect vehicle continued to careen through Twin Falls, and ended up crashing into a recreational vehicle near the Hampton Inn on Fillmore Street.

There were two occupants in the vehicle. The passenger fled the vehicle but was apprehended by a citizen until law enforcement could take him into custody. The driver of the vehicle fled into the Hampton Inn and within a short time there were reports of shots fired. The suspect, later identified as Clark J. Cleveland of Spring Creek, Nevada, shot a hotel guest, and also shot District 4 Trooper, Nicholas Walker ISP 595. Walker's injury was not life-threatening and he survived the encounter. The hotel guest did not.

Following the shootings, Cleveland held another hotel guest hostage in a hotel stairwell for nearly four hours before surrendering to police.

This incident was among the reasons Colonel G. Jerry Russell directed the establishment of two-man interdiction teams within each district in the fall of 2011. These teams were directed to conduct a minimum of forty hours per month of planned interdiction operations focusing enforcement on all aspects of criminal activity.

In District 3, Corporal Christopher Cottrell, ISP 633 and Trooper Blake Higley, ISP 632, were selected as interdiction team members. They were supervised by Sergeant Jason Cagle, ISP 590, and for this team success came quickly. Cagle said:

Six drug seizures were reported in the last few weeks of 2011. As training increased, so did the drug seizures. More and more interdiction operations were scheduled and the excitement of criminal interdiction spread to all of the agencies in the Treasure Valley. Partnerships with area canine teams proved to be invaluable to the team's success. The year 2012 showed the true need for the work of criminal interdiction throughout the state. The District 3 team was able to increase the number of its drug seizures to forty-three. The success continued to grow today as the Idaho State Police develops and supports the aggressive detection and apprehension of all individuals involved in criminal activity.

In District Three, Senior Trooper Justin Klitch, ISP 405 also proved that enforcement and interdiction patrols were a proven way to fight crime in Idaho. After questioning, "…a person who was acting suspiciously," Klitch uncovered a human trafficking case.

> On March 8, 2012, I was on a traffic stop in the eastbound rest area on I-84 near milepost two. When I cleared the traffic stop, I got a call from Payette County Deputy Webber, who told me a suspicious vehicle had just pulled into the rest area. Webber and I were conducting a criminal interdiction patrol, which consists of detecting behaviors and driving patterns associated with criminal activity. Webber told me the driver of the suspicious vehicle immediately pulled into the rest area when he saw Webber.

Klitch said he observed the suspect vehicle park at the far end of the rest area parking lot, which he felt wasn't consistent with the normal behavior of motorists stopping at a rest area.

> Deputy Webber and I watched an adult male exit the driver's side, and a young female exit the passenger side. Both of them entered the restroom area and after about ten minutes, they both

exited the restroom building through the rear exit, which I've never seen anyone else do. This behavior heightened my suspicion of possible illegal activity.

Klitch parked his patrol vehicle several feet from the suspect's car, giving the suspect plenty of opportunity to leave if he chose.

I exited my patrol vehicle and approached both subjects, without my campaign cover on, and made consensual contact. I introduced myself and asked them if I could talk to them. They both indicated I could. I asked them where they were from and where they were going. The male said they had come from Ontario, Oregon and were going to Boise for the weekend. I found it suspicious they had just left Ontario and had already stopped at a rest area. The male subject told me they originally came from Tacoma, Washington. I asked the male subject for his license and he said he didn't have it. After more questioning, the male subject told me he was suspended.

Klitch said the male identified himself as Dyrell Swinson. After more questioning, Swinson said he had no illegal drugs in his vehicle, which a K9 search confirmed. Klitch then asked for the female subject's identification, and was told she also didn't have any. The female identified herself as Layline Nichole Daniels. Daniels said she was nineteen years old, but Klitch said he suspected she wasn't telling the truth because she couldn't spell her name.

While Daniels was telling me her identity she acted as if she had memorized the information, and that didn't seem natural for a person identifying themselves. I conducted a check through dispatch, which revealed no record for Daniels. I believed she was being untruthful about both her identity and her age. I informed her I believed she was being dishonest and she said she was being truthful. I told her I was going to take her to the jail and fingerprint her to get her true identity as I didn't believe her. The age she gave me was very inconsistent with her appearance.

Questioning the suspects further, and searching the vehicle, Klitch said he found items consistent with prostitution. Klitch arrested Swinson for driving without privileges, and also took Daniels to jail because she refused to identify herself or give a social security number.

> A deputy at the jail questioned Daniels about her age and learned she was actually fifteen years old and she gave her real name. After running her name through dispatch I discovered she was a missing person out of Olympia, Washington. She was listed as a runaway and had been missing since November of 2011. I looked through Swinson's cell phone, which I confiscated from him when he was arrested, and found a picture of a sign saying, "Warning Trespassers Will Be Prostituted." There were also several photos with Swinson in possession of large amounts of cash and what appeared to be ledgers.

Through further investigation, Klitch discovered the young girl was being used for prostitution. He also discovered Swinson had attempted to have friends erase his email and other online accounts, but Klitch was able to access one of the accounts and found photographs of the girl and advertisements for prostitution. Swinson was charged with several counts including felony kidnapping without intent to ransom.

For troopers in District 5 interdiction efforts were put on hold for several days in June of 2012 when troopers geared up to fight a nemesis most Idahoans are very familiar with, fire.

It's often been said depending on whom one may ask – and under what circumstances the question is phrased – fire is either man's best friend or man's worst enemy. When it comes to wildfires, the first word that comes to the minds of most Idahoans is devastating. On June 28, the citizens of Pocatello faced off against a human-caused wildfire that destroyed ninety-five structures, and as it had through numerous natural disasters, the Idaho State Police was on-scene to assist residents in the afflicted area.

Dubbed the Charlotte Fire, this fire devastated sixty-six homes as well as numerous other structures. While the fire was human-caused, authorities did not believe it was intentionally set. District 5 Commander, Captain Eric Dayley was the on-scene commander for the Idaho State Police.

In the days following the initial outbreak of the fire, while some areas where still closed to residents, District 5 troopers conducted special patrols to thwart looters and to care for people's homes while they were away. I had one especially touching story that was related to me by a citizen in the closed area. The citizen told me although he was not supposed to be in the area, he had gone to his home. At about midnight, he heard his dogs barking at something so he went to his window and saw a trooper talking to his dogs. He then realized the trooper was ensuring his dogs had water.

The Charlotte Fire destroyed ninety-five structures in the Pocatello area.

Dayley said there were many more instances of his troopers and detectives being lauded for their efforts during the Charlotte Fire. In a letter to those under his command, Dayley wrote:

During the fire I observed many of you working diligently in dangerous conditions to evacuate citizens to safety. I have since heard accounts of how some of you drove through areas where Juniper trees and propane tanks were exploding; where thick smoke and steep, narrow, windy roads had to be driven through to reach stranded citizens. Truly heroic efforts were performed by many of you and because of those efforts, and the efforts of other rescuers involved, no human lives were lost during the fire.

Dayley added the patience and compassion of his troopers was also noticed by himself and citizens.

I witnessed many of you patiently and compassionately escorting homeowners back into the areas devastated by the fire so they could check on their homes, or what was left of their home, their belongings, and their animals. These escorts were emotional situations for the homeowners but were very important to them. I know it was hot and tedious work but your service to the people in this instance did not go unnoticed by them. I received many words of praise and appreciation for your acts of service and kindness. Your acts of bravery during the Charlotte Fire were unparalleled in recent local history. Your acts of compassion in the days following will not be forgotten by those you served.

Dust storms are a perpetual problem for state troopers..

While wildfires and floods consume most of the time troopers spend on natural disasters, dust storms also cause havoc for motorists and law enforcement officers. In recent years, the state police has investigated numerous multi-car pileups caused by dust storms. In 2012, District Five troopers investigated a fifteen-car pileup while troopers in District Four investigated a seventeen car pileup.

Rob Storm said every state police trooper is aware of this, "... menace." Adding, "In the southern and south-eastern part of the state they are one of the phenomena troopers dread the most."

While state troopers place their lives on the line and are responsible for responding to, and investigating, the numerous and varied incidents that occur on a daily basis throughout Idaho, they are not without an equally talented and professional support system.

Justin Klitch said without the dispatchers that provide a life-line to every trooper, and the administrative support staff that, "...takes such great care of us." Troopers would have a great deal more difficulty in doing their duties.

> Our dispatchers and support staff are critical to our success. Personally I contribute every success I've had as a trooper to them. Their support to troopers and their professionalism in dealing with the public makes all the difference in how we as troopers and the state police as a whole is perceived.

Colonel Ralph Powell said of dispatchers in particular:

> They are the unsung heroes of public safety and serve on the very front lines. Every one of us (troopers) know this personally from being on patrol and relying on the voice on the end of the radio to ensure our well-being. We also know this from the countless stories we have heard over the years from other law enforcement officers, firefighters, and emergency medical service personnel. Those officers, firefighters, and medics find comfort in knowing that there are highly trained personnel answering the calls of the public during a crisis and making sure they arrive quickly and are aware of what they are walking into on scene. You are the reassuring voice on the line when a child calls for help when their mother won't wake up. You provide guidance to the

hiker lost on a mountain or a lost soul contemplating suicide. You are the reason that field personnel make it home each night.

As one of the first civilian dispatchers hired to serve in the Idaho State Police, when dispatch became a civilian function in 1980, Lorrie Oliver said the appreciation of the troopers for the work of dispatchers and support staff is deeply appreciated.

When I hired on there were four dispatchers hired to each district and we were under the supervision of the district commander. We worked eight-hour shifts which meant there was always one dispatcher on duty even though the state police was not running 24-hours shifts. We would change shifts every week, which was a huge challenge. It was a great job, but being a dispatcher is extremely challenging. We had to learn the area we served in, which for example in District Four is eight counties, and we had to support our troopers, most of which we rarely saw, but we definitely knew their voices on the radio.

Oliver has served with the state police for over thirty years – currently as an office specialist – and she credits the dedication of state police employees, and the advances in technology for making the state police the premier organization it is today.

I'm the only one left of the original dispatchers hired in 1980. There have been so many changes it's hard to remember what it was like back then! But I do remember the hardest part of being a dispatcher for me was sending my troopers into the unknown. It was very emotional for all of us in dispatch when there was a critical incident. We were the life-line for our troopers and in many cases we were the only call they could get in before everything blew up in his face, as was the case with Steve Hobbs.

Gina Webster hired on as a dispatcher in 1984. Like Oliver, she eventually became a dispatch supervisor, which she said was, "…an extremely rewarding experience." Webster described her experiences as a partnership with troopers.

Our priority was always officer safety. Anything to do with tracking and assisting the troopers took precedence over walk in or phone traffic. Dispatchers like any person who works for the Idaho State Police, have to have some version of a "Type A" personality. They have to be perfectionists, methodical, adaptable, and personable. To be a successful dispatcher, a person has to have extra in the "adaptable" department. Most other jobs, including patrol for example, can usually decide how busy they want to be. Dispatchers never dictate their own work load. Our work load is dictated in large part by outside forces ranging from weather conditions to the mood our troopers are in. Anything and everything can and does happen, and it usually happens all at once!

Webster said of the many dispatch calls she dealt with over the years, one stands out in her memory.

This incident happened in the early 1980s when we still only had four dispatchers in each district. District Five, where I was a dispatcher, held an emphasis patrol where every trooper was on duty and looking for drunk drivers in the Blackfoot area. It was a Friday night and at that time we kept written logs. Troopers were stopping cars almost constantly, so often that I had to review three and sometimes four full pages to log them clear as they resumed patrolling. It was nearly impossible to carry on any phone conversation if a citizen called with a question or to report something. I was actually keeping up and feeling pretty good about how the night was going, when I got a call from a young lady who told me she had just swallowed a bottle of pills.

Webster said the call came from a payphone and between troopers calling in with requests for driver's checks, she managed to talk the young girl into letting an ambulance respond to the girls location.

She said she was going to start walking down the street because if she stayed where she was all the people in the restaurant near where she was, would be looking at her. I couldn't convince her to stay put, so I started trying to get her to describe herself and her clothing for the responding ambulance personnel.

> Right about then, a trooper who was on a traffic stop screamed across the radio that he was in need of help. I was so immersed in what was going on with the girl, it seemed to take an eternity for it to register in my mind that I had a trooper in trouble. Thankfully, I knew my troopers by voice and I was able to thumb quickly through my logs and determine where he was located. When it was all said and done I was able to get both my trooper and the young girl the help they needed, but if I'd had to ask the trooper who he was or where he was located, I would never have been able to forgive myself. When I look back now, it seems like the stress we had on us was unrealistic, but that's how we did our job.

Webster and Oliver both said they appreciate the support dispatchers now get from the state police organization, because there were times in the past when that support was less obvious.

> In the 1980s the dispatch supervisor was always a trooper whose main motivation was getting supervision experience to improve their chances for a promotion. We worked shifts, always alone, and rotated through swing shifts, day shifts, and night shifts. Although I have fond memories of my trooper supervisors, they weren't willing to change, "...how we've always done things." It changed for the better when the state police went to civilian dispatch supervisors. We were motivated to make the job better and attract qualified people who would stay for longer than the average two years. We were also motivated to make the job easier with whatever we could find to do it, whether it was equipment, streamlined protocols, office organization and work aids, and training. From my perspective the state police can still improve on training. Now that dispatch is located in two areas of the state, dispatchers are very unfamiliar with the outlying areas. I think our dispatchers would be even better if this training were mandatory and reoccurring.

Like Oliver, Webster became an office specialist when the dispatch unit she supervised, RCC-East, was closed down and all radio traffic was moved to the Boise dispatch center. Both say they miss being dispatchers, but consider their duties as office specialists every bit as important. Oliver says how one treats the public is the most important part of working in administration.

At the top of my mind always is that administrative support personnel should treat people the way they themselves want to be treated. It doesn't matter what a customer asks me for, whether it's a road report or a public records request in which the record actually belongs to another agency. It's my job to make sure they are getting exceptional customer service. I want people to go away from their experience in dealing with me with the best feeling they can have toward my district, and the Idaho State Police as a whole.

Marjorie Lusk, who started with dispatch, but has served over twenty years as a senior administrative assistant and support staff supervisor said:

The job of administrative personnel is to be part of the overall state police team, and provide exemplary service to all of our customers. As administrative support personnel, whatever we can do to make life easier on our troopers is a huge contribution to their success. Once a person contacts our office, it's our job to make sure they are getting whatever help they need to make sure that whatever their issue is, it's resolved. The most important attribute an administrative support person has is the knowledge and knowhow to answer questions asked by the public and by state police employees.

Lusk added, the administrative support people are the "heart" of the office.

Administrative support people make a huge difference not only in the success of their district's mission, but also in the success of the state police mission overall.

We have to be familiar with the laws and codes of the state, we have to deal with every type of personality, and often with every type of emotion imaginable, and because we are the central point of business for our district, we also help set the tone for the overall morale of our employees. Sometimes we're overlooked,

> but when the administrative support team does its job, everything in the district works better.

Dave Neal said the administrative support staff is imperative to the success of the state police.

> Administrative support personnel make all the difference in the success of the state police. Troopers might be the "face" of the state police, but the majority of people who deal with the state police will see a lot more of our administrative support people than they will anyone else. One thing troopers and detectives need to remember is after they are done dealing with a person on a traffic stop, or a family on a fatality crash, their administrative support staff will take over dealing with those people, and those dealings can last for weeks, even in some cases months.

No matter what position an Idaho State Police employee serves in, one constant remains for those who serve now, and those who went before—service to the citizens of the state of Idaho.

As Harvey Riffle once said, "…among the traits a state police officer should have is a healthy dose of humble, as police officers are generally not the most liked of people."

Still, one must always ask the question: as wary as the typical civilian may be of police officers, what would our personal lives, our communities, indeed our great nation be like without them?

Epilogue

Strength does not come from physical capacity. It comes from an indomitable will.

Mahatma Gandhi

Throughout its storied history the goal of the Idaho State Police has had little variation: Those who serve are required—not expected, required—to represent and serve the citizens of Idaho and the Idaho State Police to the highest professional standards. Although every employee of the state police can, and should, be commended for their service, there are those whose service has gone above and beyond even these highest of standards.

All give some; these gave all:

Fontaine Cooper

Benjamin Newman

Walter Cox

Douglas Dean

Linda Huff

The Idaho State Police recognizes these troopers with four different awards: the Life Saving Award, the Purple Heart Award, the Silver Star Award, and the highest award a trooper can receive, the Medal of Valor Award.

To receive the Medal of Valor, a trooper must display courageous action beyond the call of duty and in the highest ideals of professional law enforcement service. Those who receive the Medal of Valor knowingly expose themselves to extreme danger. In its seventy-five year history, the Idaho State Police has awarded the Medal of Valor to seven troopers. One trooper, Dave M. Cordova, is the only trooper to receive the Medal of Valor twice. Other awardees of this highest honor are:

John K. Ferris

Dale T. Hughes

Linda C. Huff

Wayne M. Longo

Fred L. Swanson

James A. Kilton

The Silver Star Award is given to troopers who knowingly expose themselves to potential danger, while assisting others whom are either innocently placed, or purposely place themselves, in danger. Awardees of this high honor are:

Ismael Gonzales Jr.

Dan C. Howard

Kedrick R. Wills

Jose A. Banda

Guy R. Schensky

Paul E. Berger

Dan C. Howard

Tim J. Harms

Gene E. Wunsch

Vance C. Cox

Chris L. Nelson

Dwayne C. Prescott

Ted J. Mcintyre

Jeffory B. Talbott

Jeremiah W. Sharp

Scott E. Tulleners

John Kempf

Tom R. Wright

Gerald A. Stemm

Allen B. Ashby

The Purple Heart Award is presented to troopers who are injured in the course of their law enforcement duties. These awardees are:

Allen Oswald

Steve Hobbs

Chad Goody

Sam Ketchum

Chris Glenn

Craig Boll

Jeffrery Talbot

Joe Lake

Chris Duggan

Nick Walker

The Life Saving Award is presented to troopers who have gone beyond their typical duties to save the life of another. Troopers who have received this award are:

Jeff Jayne

George Phillips

Dean Matlock

Dustin Kralik

Patrick Mooney

Shane Langton

Terry Morgan

Ed Westbrook

Sean Lind

Jeff Jayne

Paul Olsen

David Noyes

Brian Stradling

Author's note

Writing the history of the Idaho State Police in celebration of its 75th Anniversary has truly been a labor of love. It is with a humble spirit I acknowledge this opportunity as it was my honor and my privilege.

I owe a heartfelt and sincere thank you to the many troopers and support personnel—those who have retired and those who are still in service—who gave me the opportunity to complete this work by giving of their precious time, their individual perspectives, and their personal memories in numerous interviews with me. I thank you sincerely for your candid responses to my pointed and more often than not very personal questions. Without your willingness to share those thoughts, personal perspectives, and memories, this book would not have been possible

To Colonel G. Jerry Russell, (retired), Colonel Ralph Powell, Lieutenant Colonel Kedrick Wills, and Captain Robert Storm, your faith in me and your willingness to give me this wonderful and amazing opportunity is deeply and sincerely appreciated. I would also like to thank Lorrie Oliver for her unselfish support during this process. You worked many months in the District Four office by yourself, Lorrie, and without your willingness and ability to do my job and yours, this task would have been impossible.

Last but by no means least I would like to thank my husband, Dalen, and my children Malorie, HaLee, Ian, Jace, and Zackery. For the past two-plus years I've spent working on this book, you have supported my strange writing hours and the unbelievable mess of my research scattered all over our house. As has always been the case, you support me, you encourage me, and perhaps most importantly of all, you believe in me. Thank you. I would be remiss if I didn't also thank my mentor and one of my very closest friends, Mary Ann Hagen. You have left us, Mary Ann, but your mentoring and tutoring in the art of writing will always be of utmost importance to me. You will never be forgotten.

About the Author

Kelly Kast is a native Idahoan and life-long "amateur historian." Kast and her husband, Dalen, own and operate a 550-head cattle ranch near Bliss, Idaho. Currently, Kast is the patrol administrative assistant for District Four, Idaho State Police. She has published numerous articles with IDAHOMagazine and has published in other regional and national magazines. Prior to her service with the Idaho State Police, Kast was a staff writer for seven years, and the editor for three years, of the *Gooding County Leader.*

Kast's love of history and writing can be traced to her duties as an all-source intelligence analyst during her service in the United States Army.

Notes

All interviews were conducted by the author and all of the seventy plus interviews were conducted over the course of a two year period. Citations of these interviews are not dated. Interviewees are listed in alphabetical order:

Barnes, Harold
Becker, Fred
Bolon, Lyle
Bradbury, Beth
Broesch, Phil
Brownlee, Willis
Brumbaugh, Jack
Bunderson, Brent
Bunderson, Danny
Carlock, Vicki
Cazier, Steve
Culpepper, James
Daly, Sean
Dayley, Eric
Fehling, Jim
Ford, Terry
Furniss, Don
Ganske, John
Gibbs, John
Glenn, Chris
Gonzales, Ishmael
Goeckner, Larry
Groff, Rick
Gygli, Edwin
Hancock, Vern
Hiatt, Don
Hughes, Dale
Ikenberry, Don
Jones, Delon
Kastens, Kirt
Kaufman, Gary
Kelley, Merrill
Kirtley, Ron
Kirtley, Ross
Klitch, Justin
Kotrason, John
Lee, Harold
Lehtola, Larry
Longo, Wayne
Lusk, Marjorie
Miller, Marvin
Mills, Gordon
Neal, Dave
Oliver, Kent
Oliver, Lorrie
Owen, Duane
Parsells, Kathy
Peck, Dawn
Peterson, Mark
Platt, Larry
Powell, Ralph
Reese, Bill
Rice, Fred
Riffle, Harvey
Roberts, Cyril B.
Rockwell, Roger
Rollins, Clark
Scoggins, Wayne
Schwartz, Glen
Stimpson, Les
Storm, Robert
Strom, Brad
Strickfaden, Ed
Swainston, Dorothy Cooper
Thorp, Marshall
Tomlinson, Larry
Watkins, Cole
Webster, Gina
Wendler, Gina
Wills, Kedrick
Wills, Rich
Wright, Bob
Young, Arnie

References

Department of Law Enforcement, Bureau of Constabulary, Breshears, Frank, Superintendent: Biennial Report to the Governor covering period May 1919 to December 1920

Davis, D.W., Governor, papers courtesy of Idaho Historical Society

Oral Interview, Goeckner, Theodore, courtesy of Goeckner, Larry

Moore, Charles C. Governor, papers courtesy of Idaho Historical Society

Biennial Report of the Department of Law Enforcement of the State of Idaho, Pfost, Emmitt, Commissioner of Law Enforcement, 1931-1932; 1933-34; 1935-36

Ross, C. Ben, Governor, papers courtesy of Idaho Historical Society

Biennial Report of the Department of Law Enforcement of the State of Idaho, Balderston, J. L. Commissioner, 1937-1938, 1941-42

Clark, Chase A. Governor, papers courtesy of Idaho Historical Society

Eighteen Month's Report, January 1, 1943, to June 30, 1944 of the 1943-1944 Biennium of the Department of Law Enforcement of the State of Idaho, July 1, 1944 Chas. E. Spoor, Commissioner

Gossett, Charles C. Governor, papers courtesy of Idaho Historical Society

Robins, C. A. Governor, papers courtesy of Idaho Historical Society

Biennial Report July 1, 1946 to June 30, 1948 1947-1948 Biennium of the Department of Law Enforcement of the State of Idaho, July 1, 1948 Lewis, R. C. Commissioner

Jordan, Leonard B. Governor, papers courtesy of Idaho Historical Society

Biennial Report of the State of Idaho Department of Law Enforcement July 1, 1950-June 30, 1952, June 30, 1952 Summers, Wayne Commissioner, 1952-1954

Jordan, Leonard B. Governor, papers courtesy of Idaho Historical Society

Smylie, Robert E. Governor, papers courtesy of Idaho Historical Society

Biennial Report of the State of Idaho Department of Law Enforcement July 1, 1954-June 30, 1956, June 30, 1956 Koehler, Earle E. Commissioner

Biennial Report of the State of Idaho Department of Law Enforcement July 1, 1958-June 30, 1960, Hopper, E. R. Commissioner

Samuelson, Don Governor, papers courtesy of Idaho Historical Society

Andrus, Cecil D. Governor, letters courtesy of Idaho State Police

Batt, Phil Governor, letters courtesy of Idaho State Police

Kempthorne, Dirk Governor, letters courtesy of Idaho State Police

Law Enforcement Bulletin, Federal Bureau of Investigation, United States Department of Justice, J. Edgar Hoover, Director, October 1957

Biennial Report of the State of Idaho Department of Law Enforcement July 1 1970-June 30, 1972

Annual Report of the State of Idaho Department of Law Enforcement July 1, 1973-June 30, 1974

Annual Report of the State of Idaho Department of Law Enforcement July 1, 1974-June 30, 1975

Annual Report of the State of Idaho Department of Law Enforcement July 1, 1975-June 30, 1976

Annual Report of the State of Idaho Department of Law Enforcement July 1 1976-June 30, 1977

Historical papers, Idaho State Police Archives

ISP News Vol. 2 No. 1, publication of the Idaho State Police

Annual Report for 1981, Idaho State Police Patrol

Idaho State Police Annual Report-1982

Annual Report 1983, Idaho State Police

Idaho State Police 1985, Annual Report

Idaho State Police 1986, Annual Report

Idaho State Police 1987, Annual Report

Idaho State Police Annual Report-1988

Golden Anniversary 1939-1989, Idaho State Police, Annual Report-1989

Idaho State Police Annual Report-1990

Idaho State Police, Department of Law Enforcement, Annual Report 1992

Archival photographs, Idaho State Police, Department of Law Enforcement, Bureau of Narcotics

Brands in Idaho-A Little History by W. C. Overton

History of Forensics in Idaho, Groff, Rick

Idaho Department of Law Enforcement Interceptor, Volume 3, Number 5 September-December, 1975

A Message from the Deputy Director

Lt. Colonel Kedrick R. Wills

One of the earliest memories I have is watching my father, Corporal Richard Wills, ISP 550, (retired) polish his boots and brass to prepare for an Idaho State Police inspection. I recall him shining each individual bullet, because with the leather of the day, you could see the spare bullets he had for his pistol on his belt. I recall thinking my father was literally a superhero and that Idaho State Police was where the best of the best went to work every day. It was during those formative years, as I watched the pride and esprit de corps of the organization, I, like many others, decided to follow a father's example and become an Idaho State Police Trooper. It was with so much pride that I stood, together with my brother and ATC #15 classmate, Kipton, in the rotunda of our Capitol, and watched our father pin the five point Idaho State Police star on each of our chests, to become among the elite and wear the distinctive Idaho State Police campaign cover. Even today, I cannot think of that moment in time without sitting up a little taller and feeling a little more proud to be counted among the members of such an elite organization.

Idaho State Police has a proud history of providing quality service to our state. It is due to those who decided to make a career of service, that this history is so rich with personal sacrifice. It is the missed family events, the lost sleep, the long shifts and the tough duty assignments, handled with such professionalism that sets Idaho State Police apart from any other organization.

In short, it is the people that make the organization. Regardless of assignment, duty location, or job description, every part of Idaho State Police shares in its rich history, because of the caliber of people who work every day to make the Idaho State Police star shine brighter. To those of us who now carry this torch, it is up to each of us to make sure that when we leave, the Idaho State Police is better than it was when we joined. It is up to each of us to remember all those who sacrificed before us, so we can enjoy this great organization we are a part of today. It is our responsibility to ensure their sacrifices were not in vain. This is our turn to handle the watch. We cannot fail because those who have gone before us sacrificed too much and have placed in us the confidence to hold steadfast, the Idaho State Police during our watch. To those who will come after us, it is your responsibility to carry this organization into the future, so that the citizens of Idaho can look upon the next 75 years of Idaho State Police history with as much pride as we all have in the service and sacrifices of those who shaped the past 75 years.

I am profoundly thankful I have had the opportunity to be counted a member of the Idaho State Police and humbly appreciate those who have carried the torch before me. Thank you to Kelly Kast for her efforts in making this book to honor the history and the members of Idaho State Police and for her willingness to share her talents with us so we can all learn to more fully appreciate our rich Idaho State Police heritage.

Sincerely,

Lieutenant Colonel Kedrick Wills, ISP 550

Deputy Director, MTD

Idaho State Police

The Idaho State Police Association

WHAT:

The ISPA is an independent employee association and is not affiliated with any other state or local organization. The ISPA is administered by Idaho State Police Officers and support personnel, is registered by the State of Idaho, and is listed as a non-profit corporation.

Active membership includes Idaho State Police (ISP) sworn officers and civilian employees. The membership's governing body is a seven member Board of Directors; a state president and six chapter representatives from each of the State Police regions across Idaho. The vice chairman, treasurer and the secretary positions are filled from these presidents. The Board of Directors may also hire or appoint outside contract employees.

HOW:

IS THE ISPA CONNECTED WITH THE IDAHO STATE POLICE?

The ISPA is an independent employee association representing Idaho State Police employees. Its views, opinions, policies, and publications in no way reflect the viewpoint of the ISP.

OUR MISSION:

The ISPA was formed in 1982 and is a non-profit corporation under the laws of the State of Idaho. The mission of Idaho State Police Association is defined in Article 4 of the ISPA Restated Articles of Incorporation, which states:

The corporation is organized, and shall be operated exclusively for the following purposes:

a. To provide a continuing effort to better police services to the public.
b. To stimulate mutual cooperation among Idaho State Police Association chapters and other law enforcement agencies and corporations.
c. To establish and maintain a line of communication among all members of the Idaho State Police.
d. To evaluate the standards of Idaho State Police employees and to promote the professionalism of its members.
e. To assist in obtaining better equipment, salaries, pensions, fringe benefits, promotional opportunities and working conditions for ISP employees.
f. To provide a vehicle through which we may promulgate factual data for the purpose of collective bargaining and legislative lobbying.

Please visit the Idaho State Police Association online at www.ispaonline.org

Printed in Dunstable, United Kingdom

91224001R00199